British Settlers in Natal, 1824 - 1857
A Biographical Register

Volume 1

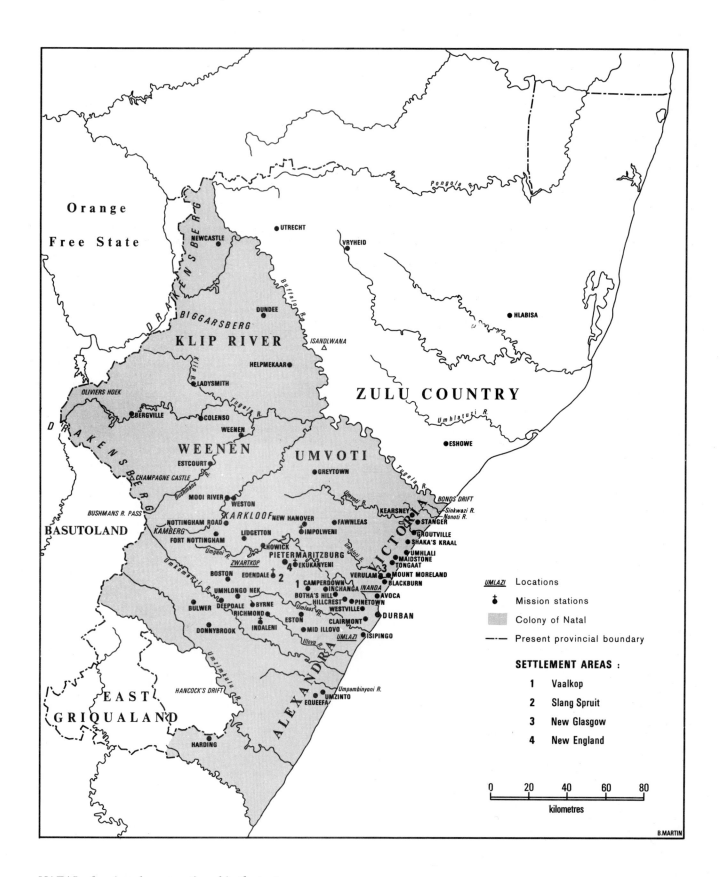

Orange
Free State

NEWCASTLE
UTRECHT
VRYHEID
DRAKENSBERG
BIGGARSBERG
DUNDEE
KLIP RIVER
ISANDLWANA
HLABISA
HELPMEKAAR
LADYSMITH
Klip R.
ZULU COUNTRY
OLIVIERS HOEK
BERGVILLE
COLENSO
Tugela R.
WEENEN
Umhlatuzi R.
DRAKENSBERG
WEENEN
UMVOTI
ESHOWE
ESTCOURT
GREYTOWN
Tugela R.
CHAMPAGNE CASTLE
Bushmans R.
BONDS DRIFT
MOOI RIVER
WESTON
Umvoti R.
KEARSNEY
Sinkwazi R.
BUSHMANS R. PASS
KARKLOOF
NEW HANOVER
Nonoti R.
STANGER
NOTTINGHAM ROAD
FAWNLEAS
VICTORIA
BASUTOLAND
KAMBERG
LIDGETTON
IMPOLWENI
GROUTVILLE
FORT NOTTINGHAM
Umgeni R.
HOWICK
SHAKA'S KRAAL
PIETERMARITZBURG
Tugela R.
UMHLALI
ZWARTKOP
4 EKUKANYENI
MAIDSTONE
BOSTON
EDENDALE
2
VERULAM
TONGAAT
Umkomaas R.
1 CAMPERDOWN
MOUNT MORELAND
UMHLONGO NEK
INCHANGA
INANDA
BLACKBURN
BOTHA'S HILL
AVOCA
BULWER
DEEPDALE
BYRNE
HILLCREST
PINETOWN
Umlaas R.
WESTVILLE
RICHMOND
ESTON
CLAIRMONT
DURBAN
INDALENI
MID ILLOVO
DONNYBROOK
UMLAZI
ISIPINGO
Illovo R.
Umzimkulu R.
ALEXANDRA
HANCOCK'S DRIFT
Umpambinyoni R.
EAST
UMZINTO
GRIQUALAND
EQUEEFA
HARDING

UMLAZI   Locations
✝   Mission stations
   Colony of Natal
–·–   Present provincial boundary

SETTLEMENT AREAS :
1   Vaalkop
2   Slang Spruit
3   New Glasgow
4   New England

0   20   40   60   80
kilometres

B.MARTIN

NATAL showing places mentioned in the text

SHELAGH O'BYRNE SPENCER

British Settlers in Natal 1824 - 1857

A Biographical Register

Volume 1

Abbott - Ayres

University of Natal Press
Pietermaritzburg

© 1981 University of Natal
Box 375, Pietermaritzburg, 3200
Natal, South Africa
2nd impression 1987

ISBN 0 86980 266 6 (Series)

ISBN 0 86980 267 4 (Vol.1)
      0 86980 351 4 (Vol.2)
      0 86980 430 8 (Vol.3)
      0 86980 543 6 (Vol.4)

Typeset in the University of Natal Press

Printed by
Multicopy Centre, University of Natal,
Durban, South Africa

Contents

Maps and Illustrations

Foreword

Natal historical studies have developed prodigiously within the last twenty years. The field which A. F. Hattersley cultivated almost single-handed from the 1930s to the 1950s is now crowded with workers producing a scholarly yield more varied than anything Hattersley contemplated. Within that throng, there is still a place — indeed a need — for workers in the Hattersley tradition. Shelagh Spencer has gone a long way towards meeting that need. By meticulous research, she has compiled a mass of data that vastly extends our knowledge of the British settlement of Natal. With few exceptions, all whose scholarly pursuits lead them back to the early days of the colony — be they family historians, agricultural historians, urban historians, social historians — will need her volumes within reach of their desks. So will scholars whose interests extend beyond the confines of Natal settler history; for the men and women who feature in this Biographical Register shackled Natal and its hinterland to the north Atlantic world of commercial and industrial capitalism, and initiated revolutionary social and economic change amongst the peoples of south-east Africa. The detailed information which Shelagh Spencer has assembled about the careers and the families of these men and women, and about source materials for further research, thus has wide scholarly relevance. Hers is the notable achievement of having compiled a reference work that will serve interests as diverse as those of genealogists tracing descent-lines and historians exploring the processes of European expansion and colonisation in southern Africa. Such a work scarcely needs to be commended to the public by the writer of a 'Foreword'. It commends itself by its manifest usefulness.

C. de B. Webb

Preface

This *Biographical Register* is an attempt to record details of those British men and women who settled in Natal between 1824, when the first party of hunter-traders arrived, and the end of 1857, when a new wave of immigration was about to begin under a government sponsored scheme.

When work on this project began in 1963 it was intended to include information about all the pre-1858 white settlers — British, German, French and Dutch, as well as the few Voortrekkers who remained in the territory despite the establishment of British rule in 1843. The decision to limit the project to persons of British stock, was in part, a response to initiatives taken by the 1820 Settlers National Monument Committee (now the 1820 Settlers National Monument Foundation) who contacted the University of Natal in 1968 in an effort to find someone to work on the Natal settlers for their projected *Roll of the British settlers in South Africa*, Part 2 (1827–1850), Part 1 by E. Morse Jones being then in the process of publication. The Late Professor K.H.C. McIntyre of the Department of History and Political Science heard that I was working in the field of Natal settler history and approached me to undertake the task. His success in securing funds from the University of Natal's Research Committee and from the Oppenheimer Trust gave the project a great fillip for these monies made possible the employment of student assistants. With their aid, from 1969 to 1973, research was completed in Durban and extended from Pietermaritzburg and the Midlands to certain country districts I had not had the opportunity to visit. Much new information was gathered in this way. Furthermore, the help of the students made it possible to consult the official records of births and deaths at the Department of the Interior in Durban and at the offices of various rural magistrates. These records have since been centralized in Pretoria.

Scope

What is envisaged is perhaps better categorized as a reference book than as a series of biographical sketches. It is estimated that the complete work will consist of about 2 600 entries of which nearly 1 250 have been completed. The present volume, comprising 93 entries, is limited to settlers whose surnames begin with the letter A. The appearance of this volume in advance of its companions will, hopefully, elicit criticism and comment that can be used for improved planning and presentation of later volumes.

Entries

Entries have been made under the names of heads of families or single men and women who arrived in Natal without their parents, and normally consist of three parts: a biography, a list of children and a source list.

1. BIOGRAPHIES

   These are of two types — a conventional biographical entry and what might be termed a *curriculum vitae* entry. The latter has been used for subjects who already appear in the *Dictionary of South African Biography*. To have excluded them altogether would have resulted in incomplete coverage, but to have written full biographies for these persons would have involved duplication of readily available information. The pre-Natal careers of these people have been dealt with only briefly in this work. It is known that three of the subjects of this volume, viz. Robert Acutt, Philip Allen and James Arbuthnot, are scheduled for inclusion in the *Dictionary of South African Biography*, but as vol. 4 of that work has not yet appeared, they have been given biographical entries here. The length of the ordinary biography varies according to the amount of information available. Further unevenness may be found within particular entries due to the fact that certain periods of a subject's life may be better documented than others. Whenever information is available as to the class of ship-board accommodation occupied by immigrants, this has been included in the entries, since it provides an indication of their financial circumstances.

2. LISTS OF CHILDREN

   The ideal here is to provide details of birth, marriage and death of each child, as well as the name, parentage and birth and death date of each child's spouse.

3. SOURCES

   For conciseness and to save repetition these have been numbered, the numbers referring to the Source List at the end of the volume.

Spelling

When evidence survives as to how the settlers themselves spelt their names, these spellings have been retained. An example to be found in this volume is Henery Arnold. Zulu names are given in the form commonly used in the colonial period. Also retained is the archaic 'emigrant' for someone arriving in the Colony, since this was the word in general use at the time. For this reason too, rivers, locations and mission stations have generally been given the names and spellings used on the 1855 map compiled by J. Alfred Watts 'from plans in the Office of the Surveyor General'. The main exceptions to this are the Pietermaritzburg's Little Bushman's river, which in this volume is usually referred to by the now well-established name Umsindusi, and the Itongati river which is here identified by its better known version Tongaat. Similarly the name Umlaas has been used for the Umlazi river. Also Durban is not spelt D'Urban.

Place names

Place names are not necessarily those that would be found on a present-day map of Natal. Two such that come to mind are Blackburn on the Little Umhlanga (tributary of the Umhlanga river), and Williamstown, the seat of the magistracy of Lower Tugela Division, Victoria County, before it moved to Stanger. Because of the paucity of well-identified landmarks in early colonial Natal, localities were often indicated in a general way by referring to rivers, eg. 'at the Illovo', which could be anywhere along the length of the river. Sometimes, however, more specific descriptions were given, eg. 'Upper Umkomanzi' for areas near the inland stretches of the river, and 'Lower Umkomanzi' for those near the coast.

Place of marriage

In many cases this is derived from the church register in which the marriage entry was found. Sometimes, however, the marriage may not in fact have taken place in the church itself but possibly on a farm in the area or in a church served by a larger centre; for example, in the case of York, baptisms, marriages and burials in the Anglican church were at first entered in the register of the Parish of the Karkloof with Howick as its hub. Similarly the Wesleyan community at York in the early days formed part of the Pietermaritzburg circuit, so the early baptisms and marriage entries will be found in those registers.

Pietermaritzburg erf identification

Another source of possible confusion is the naming of Pietermaritzburg's erfs. Each erf runs the whole depth of a block and takes the name of the street nearer the Umsindusi, eg. the erf opposite St Peter's Church in Church Street is erf 17 Church Street, while St Peter's itself is on erf 17 Longmarket Street. For Loop, Longmarket, Church, Pietermaritzburg, Berg, Boom and Greyling Streets the numbering runs from 1 west to 55 east. Burger Street is the exception in that the erfs on both sides bear the name of the street, and the numbering runs from 1–55 on the side furthest from the Umsindusi and from 56–110 on the Umsindusi side.

County identification

British and Irish county identifications following town or village names are either those given by the settlers themselves or those shown on Geographia Ltd.'s *County map of the British Isles* (scale 19 miles to 1 inch) and *Map or Ireland* (scale 10 miles to 1 inch).

Index

The material collected in this volume lends itself to very full indexing which would undoubtedly enhance the usefulness of the work, particularly for those researchers pursuing topics in economic or social history rather than personal biographies. The compilation of such an index would, however, also have added considerably to the complexity of the book and have delayed its publication. I have therefore decided that in the first instance the index should be limited to personal names. The need for a broad subject index is recognised and may be provided at a later date especially if a willing collaborator can be found.

Abbreviations

A.B.	able-bodied seaman
c.	*circa*
Co.	County or Company
C.T.	Cape Town
d.	daughter
D.S.A.B.	*Dictionary of South African Biography*
Dbn	Durban
Jhb.	Johannesburg
J.P.	Justice of the Peace

K.C.M.G.	Knight Commander of St Michael and St George
lb.	pound (weight)
L.R.C.P.	Licentiate of the Royal College of Physicians
M.Ch.	Master of Surgery
M.L.C.	Member of the Legislative Council
M.L.A.	Member of the Legislative Assembly
M.R.C.S.	Member of the Royal College of Surgeons
N.G.R.	Natal Government Railways
N.R.	North Riding (Yorkshire)
O.F.S.	Orange Free State
P.E.	Port Elizabeth
Pmb.	Pietermaritzburg
R.A.	Royal Artillery
R.E.	Royal Engineers
Tvl	Transvaal.

Devices used in the text

* after a personal name	indicates a separate entry in this or a future volume.
(unverified) after a place name	indicates that the name has not been found in the Great Britain Ordnance Survey's *Gazetteer of Great Britain*, or in Geographia Ltd.'s *Map of Ireland*.
? before a place of birth	signifies possible place of birth, and in the case of children usually derived from parents' place of residence.
? before place of marriage	indicates that the place name which follows is taken from the centre where the special licence was issued or from the residence of the bride or her parents.
? before place of death	indicates that the place name which follows is taken either from the deceased's place of residence or burial, or, in the case of children, from the parents' place of residence.
•	twins
/-	shilling
£	pound (sterling)
10/-	ten shillings
7/6d	seven shillings and sixpence

Acknowledgements

It was because of my interest in early Natal settler history that I met my husband, Brian. Through his understanding, encouragement and practical help this work is evolving from a mass of data on cards, in note-books and files, to a form acceptable to a publisher. My long-suffering daughter, Angela, deserves recognition for the fact that she has always had my 'old men' as a backdrop to her life, and a restricting influence they have been too, at times. The help and encouragement of my parents is also acknowledged. While still in the family circle I should like to record appreciation of Mrs Gladys Dumakude, without whose cheerful and efficient help over many years, the uninterrupted work periods at home and the hours of research in the Archives would not have been possible.

Work in the Archives and with the Master of the Supreme Court's records has been greatly aided by Mrs Jennifer Duckworth, who for some years has assisted me with the copying of records. I am particularly indebted to her for her accurate work and the numerous hours she has put into the project.

The late Professor A. F. Hattersley made a substantial contribution to the early stages of my work by lending me his passenger lists — comprising nearly 40 pages, they embodied the result of many years research in Natal, the Cape and London.

Another major contributor to the success of the project was the late Professor K. H. C. McIntyre who obtained funds for student research assistants from the Oppenheimer Trust and from the University of Natal, and who supervised their work. My debt to him, to the funding agencies, and to the students themselves is considerable.

Dr John Clark and Mr M. C. Martin helped me with constructive criticism, both of style and content when I first began writing. Dr Clark has also been most helpful in providing information and photographic material. Mrs Daphne Strutt of the Local History Museum also gave enthusiastic assistance in the tracking down of old photographs.

To Professor C. de B. Webb thanks are due for his encouragement and reassurances that what I was attempting was worthwhile.

Professor J. A. Benyon and Dr D. R. Edgecombe were most helpful in guiding me with the compilation of the source list.

The Natal University Press deserve special commendation for their patience with my inaccurate typing and the way in which on numerous occasions they willingly agreed to reset completed entries when new information came to light at an advanced stage.

I wish to record my gratitude to the staffs of the Natal Archives, the Natal Society Library, the University of Natal Library, Pietermaritzburg, the Killie Campbell Library, the Local History Museum in Durban and the Office of the Master of the Supreme Court in Pietermaritzburg for their willing assistance.

Furthermore I should like to place on record the generosity of Ms Sheila Meintjies who freely allowed me the use of material collected during research for her doctorate undertaken in the School of Oriental and African Studies in London for my entries on the Rev. James Allison and the Rev. James Archbell.

Finally may I thank all settler descendents who have helped me with information on their forebears, and to all clergy who allowed me and the students access to church records.

Sources of illustrations and maps

Photographs were supplied by the following institutions which are warmly thanked for their ready assistance.

Don Africana Library, Durban
Hilton College
Killie Campbell Africana Library, Durban
Local History Museum, Durban
Macrorie House Museum, Pietermaritzburg
Natal Museum, Pietermaritzburg

Thanks are also due to Mr Bruno Martin of the Cartographic Unit, University of Natal, Pietermaritzburg, who drew the map of Natal (frontispiece) and prepared for printing the maps of Pietermaritzburg and Durban and some of the photographs. Mr Walter Yerbury of the Local History Museum also gave skilled assistance with the preparation of photographs.

Shelagh Spencer

Cover Picture

The first auction of Natal-made sugar took place on 23 June 1855 on the Durban Market Square. The auctioneer was Robert Acutt and the sugar was from the *Springfield* estate. In the background can be seen the premises of Wirsing & Acutt on the corner of Smith and Gardiner Streets (which in the early days also housed the Post Office and the Court Room), Agar's Canteen, Acutt's auction mart and George Potter's saddler's shop.

This engraving was made from a sketch by James Lloyd (born *c.* 1827) and printed in the *Illustrated London News* of 16 February 1856. It is reproduced here by courtesy of the Killie Campbell Africana Library.

Introduction

The British population of Natal during this period was largely made up of the following:

Immigrants from the Cape (including 1820 Settlers and their descendents)

From 1824 Cape colonists had filtered into Natal for purposes of trade and/or settlement. A significant boost to their numbers occurred after Natal had been annexed to the Cape in 1845 and a civil service of almost entirely Cape men was structured for the new District.

Also in the mid-forties a small number of Cape colonists trekked to Natal from Buntingville in Pondoland. These, former residents of Butterworth, had abandoned their homes as a result of disturbances during the Seventh Frontier War. They came in two parties, in 1846 and 1847, the latter group being led by James Calverley*.

Soldiers discharged from British regiments serving in South Africa

The greatest number of these had served in the 45th Regiment, which was stationed in Natal from 1843 to 1859. Among other regiments whose members settled in Natal were the 27th (it was two companies of the 27th that marched to Natal with Capt. T.C. Smith in 1842), the 72nd, the 75th, the Royal Artillery and the Royal Engineers. A sprinkling of Royal Naval men also came to the Colony.

Immigrants from Britain and Ireland

Most of these settlers arrived between 1849 and 1851. Some emigrated independently, but many came under the aegis of one or other emigration scheme.

Before detailing the various groups it is necessary to sound a note of caution with regard to the occupations of the emigrants as they appear on the passenger lists. For an emigration promoter to receive a drawback on his deposits with Her Majesty's Land and Emigration Commissioners, each emigrant despatched had to be approved by the Commissioners, and then a certificate issued by the Natal Government attesting to the emigrant's good treatment on the voyage and his location on his allotment had to be obtained. The Emigration Commissioners stipulated for Natal that the approved occupations were those of labourer, mechanic, tradesman, farmer, or persons of small capital. To meet these requirements many an emigrant's calling was falsified on his emigration certificate. The emigrants ex *Haidee* were an exception. By and large they were what their emigration certificates stated — tradesmen, small farmers or farm labourers.

1 NATAL COTTON COMPANY

Among the earliest group of British immigrants to Natal were the 26 settlers imported by this Cape Town based company which had been allotted 22 750 acres on the Umhloti river. In lieu of part of the purchase price the company had undertaken to introduce immigrants to grow cotton, construct roads and buildings and generally develop their land. In 1848 the company arranged with the Cape immigration authorities to take over certain government immigrants to the Cape ex *Duke of Roxburgh*, and divert them to Natal. The Company was unable to carry out its undertakings and the land reverted to the Crown.

2 J.C. BYRNE & CO.'s NATAL EMIGRATION AND COLONIZATION COMPANY

This company handled the greatest number of immigrants. John Swales Moreland* was the agent in the Colony. Areas where the settlers were located included Plessis Laager, Little Bushman's River, New England and the farms *Slang Spruit, Uys Doorns* and *Vaalkop and Dadelfontein*, all in the vicinity of Pietermaritzburg, land on the Umhloti (viz. the land previously allotted to the now defunct Natal Cotton Co. and commonly known as the Cotton Lands), land on the Tongaat and Umhlanga rivers, and land on the river Illovo (including the estates *Dunbar, Beaulieu, Harmony* and *Little Harmony*). Villages laid out on these locations included Thornville to serve the *Uys Doorns* and *Vaalkop and Dadelfontein* settlers, Verulam, Mount Moreland and New Glasgow on the Cotton Lands, Byrne for the allotments near the sources of the Illovo including *Dunbar*, and Richmond as a centre for *Beaulieu, Harmony* and *Little Harmony*. Two of Byrne's ships, the *Ina* and the *Conquering Hero* sailed from Glasgow and Scotsmen were in the majority amongst the passengers. The *Unicorn* ex Liverpool also carried a number of Scottish people.

3 THE CHRISTIAN EMIGRATION AND COLONIZATION SOCIETY

This was a co-operative scheme initiated by William Josiah Irons*, and was at first under the patronage of the Earl of Verulam. About 400 settlers came to the Colony under this Wesleyan-orientated society. The bulk of these were shipped and provided with land under arrangement with Byrne & Co. They were located as a group on the Cotton Lands. 'Verulam' had been chosen by Irons as the name for the centre of population for his settlers, and the site for Verulam was chosen by a committee of these settlers in March 1850.

4 BUCCLEUCH SETTLERS

Another group to come out under arrangement with Byrne & Co. was some of the tenantry of the Duke of Buccleuch's Hampshire estate, *Beaulieu*. They joined the *Lady Bruce* at Portsmouth and were settled near Richmond on the *Beaulieu* estate.

5 RICHARD MERCHANT HACKETT

Hackett, a London shipowner, advertised a scheme offering better terms than Byrne & Co., viz. 30 acres for a £10 deposit, instead of Byrne's

20 acres. This scheme also aimed at attracting Wesleyans. These settlers came out on the *Hebrides* and were located on lots near the Karkloof, viz. 67, 68, 69 and 75. Hackett's agent in England was Thomas Bond* who himself took passage on the *Hebrides*, while Henry Milner* was his Natal agent. (Edwin Griffiths* later acted with power of substitution granted by Milner.) Hackett afterwards joined with John Lidgett in despatching emigrants on the *Nile, Choice* and *John Bright*.

6   JOHN LIDGETT

Another London shipowner and a prominent Wesleyan, Lidgett offered terms similar to those of Byrne & Co. Here again Wesleyans were to the fore. The first ship despatched was the *Herald*. Thereafter he co-operated with Hackett, sending further shiploads on the *Nile, Choice* and *John Bright*. The Natal agents were at various times, J. E. Methley*, Robert Anderson*, then James Archbell* and Richard Lawton*. By Oct. 1853 Edwin Parkinson* had the agency. These settlers were located on the farm *Riet Vallei*, the name given their village being Lidgettown (now Lidgetton). The nearby lots 70, 71 and 72 (3 281 acres) were also purchased by Lidgett.

7   THE HAIDEE SETTLERS

Many Yorkshiremen came to Natal in these years. One scheme that catered for them exclusively was the Wesleyan-orientated co-operative scheme conceived by Henry Boast*. The committee assisting him consisted of Samuel Cordukes*, Robert Smith (*c.* 1804–1881)*, Richard Brough*, Joseph Smith*, William Lund* and James Tutin*. The latter two preceded the main party on the *Herald* in order to find suitable land. Benjamin Lofthouse* was also involved, he travelled around Yorkshire interviewing would-be settlers. The ship chartered, the *Pallas*, was declared unseaworthy by the Emigration Commissioners on the eve of sailing with the result that the emigrants were detained at Hull pending the fitting out of another vessel, the *Haidee*. On some of the emigrants applying to the courts for redress it was found that Boast and not the shipowner, Joseph Rylands, was technically liable for paying them subsistence money. The strain of these difficulties resulted in Henry Boast succumbing to 'brain fever' before the *Haidee* sailed. His widow Mary kept the party together and they finally sailed in July 1850. Lund purchased the farm *Mielie Hoogte* about 20 miles from Pietermaritzburg for the immigrants. York was the name given to the village laid out for them.

8   THE MURDOCH/MOREWOOD SETTLERS

George Pavitt Murdoch, a clerk in the employ of Byrne & Co.'s solicitors, and Capt. Richard Wilson Pelly, R.N., modelled their Natal Company's scheme on that of Byrne, but offered 10 acres per child instead of five. The first batch of 95 immigrants arrived on the *Ballengeich*, and more followed on the *Justina*. E. Morewood* was the agent in Natal and also apparently supplied some capital. These settlers were located on Lots 69 to 71 on the coast between the Tongaat and Umhlali rivers.

9   THE GARROD/JOHNSTON SETTLERS

Dr Charles Johnston* and William Garrod* gathered a small party which came out on the *John Gibson*. Garrod acquired land on the Tongaat river, viz. Lot 86 (508 acres).

10 THE McCORKINDALE SETTLERS

In April 1856 another sizable party arrived on the *Portia*. This group, nearly 80 strong, was collected by Alexander McCorkindale* who in the sixties was to form a company to introduce immigrants into the Eastern Transvaal (New Scotland on the border of the Swazi country). Included in this party were members of both his and his wife's families, and 22 young boys from reformatories who had been apprenticed to him. These settlers were located on the Sinkwazi river near the Zululand border. The intention was for them to grow cotton.

11 COLENSO'S MISSION PARTY

Another cohesive group were the passengers on the *Jane Morice*, which arrived in May 1855. Bishop Colenso* had chartered this vessel to bring his missionary party to Natal, so few of those on board were immigrants as such, although a number were to end their days in the Colony. Besides the mission party there were also some of Colenso's friends, and a few ex-parishioners on board.

Immigrants from Mauritius

During the period under study there was a limited immigration from this island. A. Drummond*, George Williamson (1800–1881)* and family, the Rathbones* and the Shires* were among those of British stock to reach Natal in this way. J. R. Saunders* had also lived in Mauritius.

The Mauritius element, both French and English, with its experience in sugar cultivation and manufacture, gave an important fillip to this Natal industry which was then in its infancy.

* * * * *

Natal suffered a set-back starting in 1852 when the newly-discovered Australian goldfields drew off a number of her colonists. Four ships sailed direct for Melbourne, viz. the *Hannah* and the *Sarah Bell* in 1852, the *Wee Tottie* in 1853 and the *Golden Age* in 1854. In addition many others sailed for Australia via Mauritius or the Cape. Some had no intention of returning, but others had, leaving their families in Natal. Throughout the rest of the 1850s there was a trickle returning from the Antipodes. This was not confined to those whose families had remained in the Colony.

Biographical Register

ABBOTT, George

Born c. 1827.

He was a miller who emigrated to Natal on the *Edward* under arrangement with W. J. Irons's* Christian Emigration and Colonization Society.

He may have been the Abbott of Abbott & Co. of Verulam who were traders in Zululand c. Sep. 1850.

For a period of six months, which included Feb., Mar. and Apr. 1851, Abbott was employed by Moreland's* surveyor, Edmund Tatham*, to assist with surveys. It is likely that he left Tatham in about Apr. 1851, as in this month he applied for government employment. Writing from Durban on 7 April he asked the Secretary to Government for a position as a tide-waiter, there being two such vacancies. He was informed that the Collector of Customs, not the Secretary to Government, hired tide-waiters as required. A week later he applied for the post of Clerk to the Resident Magistrate of Durban but here again he was unsuccessful.

In Sep. 1851 he sold his 20 acre emigrant's allotment at the Umhloti to William Johnson* for £11.

It appears that he was still in Durban in Feb. 1852 for in July a George H. Abbott (presumably he) advertised that he had taken over the commodious premises at the end of Smith Street as a livery and bait stable.

A Mr Abbott was a passenger on the *Hannah* which left for Melbourne in Sep. 1852. This very likely was he. Francis Spring*, writing to his nephew from Melbourne in Apr. 1853, stated that he had seen Abbott, who had married Dr Brooking's* servant and was working in a mill at £4 per week plus house, wood and water and that he appeared 'comfortable and contented'.

An item appeared in the *D'Urban Observer* in Dec. 1853 giving news of various ex-Natalians in Australia. It reported that Abbott had married and was employed in a mill near Melbourne.

SOURCES

Private source material
   34 Box 2. Surveyors' and Immigrants' correspondence book — E. Tatham to Moreland, 24.2.1851, W. Osborne to Moreland 18.4.1851

Unpublished official papers
   125 51(3) nos. 227 and 228, 2241 no. C288; **126** 64, 73; **131** IV/7/16 nos. 264a and 266, IV/7/17 no. 368

Newspapers, periodicals, etc.
   177 15.12.1853; **184** 5.9.1850; **188** 23.1.1851, 9.7.1852; **189** 10.5.1850

ABBOTT, John Henry

Born c. 1828.

A carpenter and joiner who came on the *Henry Tanner*. By 1857 he had not claimed his 20 acre *Slang Spruit* allotment (Lot 5). This land, however, does not appear on the list of unclaimed Byrne allotments which was compiled by the office of the Registrar of Deeds in 1873.

Abbott was living in Durban c. 1851–1853. In Sep. 1851 he bought 20 acres of government land on the Umbilo river (Lot 5).

By Aug. 1856 Abbott was in the Orange Free State although he still owned property in Durban.

SOURCES

Private source material
   34 Box 4. *Henry Tanner* lists

Unpublished official papers
   125 56(2) no. 251, 2242 no. C332, 2263 no. H287; **157** *Henry Tanner* list

Official printed sources
168 15.8.1854

Newspapers, periodicals, etc.
185 8.8.1856, 13.8.1857; **188** 12.9.1851,
13.10.1851; **189** 11.1.1851, 9.5.1851

Miscellaneous unofficial contemporary printed sources
220

ABBOTT, Thomas

A builder, carpenter and joiner of Durban. In 1854 he was renting land on 'Cato's Farm' [sic, Cato Manor?].

Abbott was in partnership with James Putterill* from at least the beginning of 1853 until June 1855. Thereafter Abbott continued alone as a builder, cabinet-maker, etc. A letter dated Apr. 1853 from Francis Spring* in Melbourne to his nephew Arthur Spring* in Durban, reveals that Abbott had a boat which Spring had contemplated buying. Spring bemoans the fact that he had not done so as by taking it to Australia he could have made between 200% and 300% profit on it.

In Oct. 1855 Abbott presented a 'handsome' chair to the Verulam Wesleyan Chapel.

The name of his wife was Mary Ann.

CHILDREN

Susan Mary (born Oct. 1851, ?Dbn).
Mary Anne (born Dec. 1853, ?Dbn).

SOURCES

Private source material
44

Unpublished official papers
125 2242 no.C595; **131** IV/7/17 no.368

Official printed sources
168 15.8.1854

Newspapers, periodicals, etc.
180 1.6.1855; **187** 3.10.1855; **188** 4.6.1852,
16.7.1852

Later sources
234 p.153

ABLETT, William Henry

Born 26 Nov. 1793, Suffolk[‡]. Died 30 June 1876, Pietermaritzburg.

Farmer. Zulu name: Idumapezula n'Tabeni. Before emigrating Ablett had owned property in County Cavan, Ireland. He came to Natal on the *Amazon* with three of his sons, William, Arthur and James. Mrs Ablett and the other child, Charles, followed in Jan. 1854 on the *Lady of the Lake*. W.J. Irons*, the emigration promoter, to whom the Abletts were known, was of the opinion they would be 'a valuable addition to the Colony'.

To start with the Abletts tried farming near Pietermaritzburg. By Jan. 1852 Ablett was living at Camperdown. In April 1853 he took over J. Vanderplank's* Milton mill near Pietermaritzburg from A. Clarence* but after about two months he realised he could not make a profit, and told Vanderplank that if he remained he would be ruined.

In June 1854 an advertisement appeared in the *Natal Witness* in which Ablett offered all his implements and animals for sale as he was giving up farming and retiring. Three of his sons who had been farming with him, William, James and Arthur, had at this stage to find other employment. Details of Ablett's experience during the four years he farmed and ran Milton mill come to light in a memorial he addressed to Sir George Grey in Nov. 1855, during the latter's visit to Natal. Ablett petitioned for a grant. (None of the *Amazon* passengers had been allotted land.) He stated that while in Natal he had paid nearly £300 on land rentals, and despite being 'economical and industrious', had lost the greater part of his capital, by losses occasioned through the scarcity of labour, the lack of a good market for his produce, and 'other casualties incidental to a young colony'. When he submitted this memorial he was living in Pietermaritzburg, and here he remained for the next few years but not having been able to recover financially, in Mar. 1856 he surrendered his estate. Vanderplank submitted a claim for £564 for leases, but this was disallowed under a section of the Insolvency Law.

Early in 1857 Ablett was living in Pietermaritz Street, Pietermaritzburg, making a livelihood as an agriculturalist and wagon proprietor. Later in the year, he and his son Charles joined up with the Churchills (J.F. Churchill*) on a journey to Mooi River Dorp (Potchefstroom). At this time two sons, William and Arthur, were employed as clerks by the firm Evans & Churchill, one in Pietermaritzburg, and the other in Mooi River Dorp. The trip was

‡ Three sources give Ablett's birth place as Libton Hall, Suffolk. No Libton can be found in the *Gazetteer of Great Britain*, but there is a Sibton in Suffolk. The likelihood of this being the correct form of the name is strengthened by the fact that one of the grants making up the Ablett property was called *Sibton Hill*.

undertaken in three of Ablett's wagons that Churchill had hired. Unbeknownst to his family, Arthur, for two months had been seriously ill with bronchitis. As the party neared their destination the Abletts received letters per wagons travelling from Mooi River Dorp of Arthur's dangerous state. They hurried on ahead and reached the village the day before he died.

When in 1857 land grants were offered to colonists, Ablett and his four sons all applied. During 1858 he and his surviving sons each received lots on the Nonoti river, viz. Lots 19, 20, 21 and 22, in all 2 100 acres. The names given these lots were, *Holwood, Kirkly Vale, Woodgreen* and *Sibton Hill*. James immediately occupied the land and in Sep. 1858 he and his brother William went into partnership. By the end of 1859 Charles appears to have been living on the estate as well.

The Abletts had plans for cultivating sugar and other tropical products on an extensive scale. By 1862 they had three whites and about 40 Zulus working on the estate. By mid–1863 the fruits of the labour of these workers included 125 acres under cane (40 of which were due for crushing in the 1863 season), and a house worth about £700. Further improvements contemplated were sugar mill machinery and the buildings to house it.

Ablett's own sojourn at *Kirkly Vale*, as the estate was known, appears to have been of short duration. He was back in Pietermaritzburg by May 1863. However, it was in the plantations of *Kirkly Vale* that he earned his Zulu sobriquet – literally 'Thunderer of the hills'.

William also appears not to have remained long on the estate. He and his father continued the transport business together, and then *c*. Apr. 1862 William became the Pietermaritzburg manager of the Commercial and Agricultural Bank of Natal. Thereafter, as he himself put it, his only connexion with the carrying trade was in meeting his liabilities for as his father had no property, the losses fell on him. In May 1865 James had bought out William's interest in *Kirkly Vale* for £1 400 and this money went to relieve his most pressing liabilities. In about Nov. 1865 William went insolvent. It appears that he had losses in oxen totalling about £2 201.

James was also a victim of the depression of the mid–1860s. In May 1865 he had bonded his property for £4 000 to W.B. Lyle. Lyle had been acting as agent for the estate since Feb. 1864. In about Feb. 1867 James went bankrupt and Lyle was appointed one of the trustees of his estate. The reasons for the insolvency were said to be bad crops (owing to bad seasons and to the crops being planted in bad soil), and the heavy amount of interest being paid owing to insufficient capital. The creditors were advised to sell the estate as soon as possible. From *c*. 1868 to 1871 W.M. Ash was either the owner or manager of *Kirkly Vale*, while by the end of 1872 W.B. Lyle seems to have taken it over. In 1877 *Kirkly Vale* ceased to be a sugar estate and all the machinery was sold. By 1888 it had

become one of Natal's foremost tea estates, second only to J.L. Hulett's* *Kearsney*. At this stage it was owned by A.T. Reynolds (son of T. Reynolds*) and W.B. Lyle.

In the early 1870s James went on trading trips up the east coast from Durban. By 1878 he was in Kimberley, and in 1892 moved to Johannesburg where he became auditor for several gold-mining companies. He returned to Durban in 1916.

Ablett's wife was Sarah ?Potter (Oct. 1799, Kent – 4 Aug. 1880, Dbn). Before the family emigrated she had inherited money from James Potter of Clapham, London who presumably was her father.

CHILDREN
William Henry (Feb. 1829, London – 10 Oct. 1890, Dbn) unmarried. William in the 1860s was Pmb. manager of the Commercial & Agricultural Bank of Natal.

Charles Grey (*c*. 1832 – 3 Feb. 1874, Pmb) unmarried.

Arthur Willson (*c*. 1834 – 25 Nov. 1857, Potchefstroom) unmarried.

James Potter (31 Dec. 1835 – 19 May 1917, Dbn) m. 10 Mar. 1863, Verulam, Rosario Winn (*c*. 1839 – 17 May 1917, Dbn), d. of Dr James Mitchell Winn, M.D. of Hammersmith, London.

SOURCES
Private source material
　1; 9 Churchill, Marianne: Letters, 7.10.1857, 27.11.1857, 1.5.1858; **29** *Amazon* list;
　36 W.J. Irons to Theophilus Irons, July 1850; **84**; **92**; **102**

Unpublished official papers
　125 2244 no.D231, 2247 no.D788, 2248 no.E78, 2250 no.E253, 2253 no.F163, 2257 no.G194, 2259 no.G457, 2260 no.G603, 2261 no.H31, 2263 no.H419; **126** 73; **129** 7/230;
　130 1/30 no.1, 1/31 nos.27 and 33;
　132 III/5/19 no.646, III/5/26 nos.283–6, III/5/32 no.35; **136**; **137**; **147**; **156** 247/1875, 41/1880

Official printed sources
　165

Newspapers, periodicals, etc.
　181 9.4.1862; **184** 15.1.1852, 21.4.1853;
　185 31.12.1857, Mar.1863, 12.2.1874, 4.7.1876, 6.7.1876, 5.8.1880; **189** 30.6.1854, 4.7.1876;
　197 1863, 1865, 1872, 1873, 1876

Later sources
　231 p.246; **267** p.164; **273** p.12; **297** pp.186-7

Portraits, photographs, etc.
　358; **361** (William Henry and Sarah Ablett)

ACUTT, Julianna

Born 14 Feb. 1835, Ottery St Mary, Devon. Died 3 June 1909, Durban.

She was the daughter of Cotton Acutt (born 1805) and Lydia Brown (*c.* 1810–1876). Julianna came to Natal on the *Borneo* with her uncle Robert Acutt* and his family.

On 20 Oct. 1853 she and James Grundy* were married in Durban.

Two of Julianna's brothers and a sister, Lydia, followed her to Natal. The brothers, Harry and Cotton both married daughters of Hugh McDonald*. Lydia became the wife of Leonard Acutt, son of her uncle Richard Acutt.

SOURCES

Private source material
114 14.2.1869

Unpublished official papers
125 2282; 126 73; 137

Newspapers, periodicals, etc.
188 3.10.1851

Later sources
227

Personal communication
352

Portraits, photographs, etc.
293 p.53; 362

ACUTT, Robert

Born 9 Aug. 1814, Torquay, Devon. Died 8 May 1894, Durban.

Auctioneer. He was the son of Robert Acutt (1781–1849), Supervisor of Excise in Cornwall, Devon, Wales, etc., and Julianna Cotton (d.1855), and grandson of John Acutt and Joan Callaway, great-aunt of Henry Callaway*. Before emigrating Acutt had been a dealer in paintings in London.

Robert followed his brother W.H. Acutt* to Natal, arriving on the *Borneo*. He was accompanied by his family and his niece Julianna Acutt*. His sister Mary Jane Beater* also came to Natal before 1858.

Towards the end of 1851 Robert purchased G.C. Cato's* auctioneering and general agency business with premises in Gardiner Street, facing the Durban Market Square, on part of erf 16 G belonging to the firm Middleton & Wirsing (see W.H. Middleton and G.H. Wirsing), in which his brother William was a partner. Robert traded under his own name until 1872 and thereafter to 1907 the business was known as Robert Acutt & Sons. After this the name was changed to R. Acutt & Sons. Only in 1972 did it cease to exist.

To Acutt fell the distinction, in June 1855, of selling the first Natal-manufactured sugar, grown on H. Milner's* and J.B. Miller's* *Springfield* estate. The event, at which his services were rendered gratuitously, drew a large crowd, the eight tons of sugar offered being sold by the bag so as to effect a more widespread distribution. This auction, which took place on the Market Square, opposite his premises, has been kept on permanent record through the sketch of James Lloyd*, which later appeared in the *Illustrated London News*.

Acutt was one of Durban's prominent businessmen. In 1859 he became a director of the Natal Railway Company, an enterprise with which he was to be associated for many years, both as director and chairman of the board. In the same year he was appointed a director of the Commercial and Agricultural Bank of Natal. Other directorates he held included the Durban branch of the Natal Bank (1864–5), the Marine Insurance & Trust Co. (1864–5), the Natal Boating Co. (1864), and the Commercial and Agricultural Exchange (1868). From 1866 to 1872 he was on the committee of the Natal Chamber of Agriculture.

His interest in the latter sphere could possibly be traced to his sugar planting days. In about 1862 he had started the *Phoenix* sugar estate. In 1866 *Phoenix* was combined with William Wilson's* *Auchenglas*, and Henry Binns's *Sunderland*, and taken over by the Umhlanga Valley Sugar and Coffee Co., Ltd., a company initiated in London by Binns.

Acutt did not escape the depression of the 1860s. In 1868 and 1869 his estate was assigned, but he managed to escape insolvency. The extensive list of his immovable property which is filed with his assigned estate papers shows that *Trenance*, the sugar estate founded and managed by his brother Richard, was at this time actually owned by him.

Acutt was in the forefront of Durban's affairs, ecclesiastical, municipal and educational. In July 1852 he was elected a member of the committee for the building of St Paul's Anglican Church, and was the people's churchwarden in 1855–56, during the dispute between Bishop Colenso* and the congregation of St Paul's. He was one of the leaders in the conflict, and on more than one occasion presided over vestry meetings held by the dissident parishioners. At the Church of England Conference held in 1858, he and H. Gillespie* represented the laity of St Paul's. In Sep. 1858 he resigned as churchwarden, but was elected once more at the 1860 Easter Vestry meeting. He was also a committee member of the Evangelical Alliance, a Protestant body, founded in Feb. 1859.

Acutt was elected a Durban town councillor in 1856, 1858, and 1859. His cultural activities included a long-term trusteeship of the Durban Mechanics' Institute, and during the early 1860s, the vice-presidency of the Natal Agricultural and Horticultural Society. He was also a committee member of the Durban Club until about the end of 1871.

The Acutts first lived in central Durban, but were among the first families to move on to the Berea. Their home, *Montpelier*, was on what is now North Ridge Road.

Robert Acutt married Mary Louisa East on 27 Dec. 1842 at St Mary's, Lambeth, Surrey. She died in Durban on 18 June 1887, aged 66.

CHILDREN

Horace (28 Feb. 1845, London – 15 Mar. 1927, Dbn) m. 24 Oct. 1878, ?Dbn, Angenita Maria Behrens (1850, Pmb. – 26 July 1912, Dbn), d. of Carl Behrens (1818 – 1893).

Walter (15 Nov. 1846 – 3 Feb. 1849) died in childhood.

Florence (9 Aug. 1848, London – 15 Feb. 1905, Torquay, Devon) m. 1 May 1873, Dbn, Robert Noble Acutt (20 Mar. 1849, Lambeth – 20 Dec. 1935, Torquay), son of her uncle Henry Acutt (1816–1856).

Herbert (23 May 1850 – 13 Oct. 1854, ?Dbn) died in childhood.

Stanley (2 Aug. 1852, ?Dbn – 9 Oct. 1853, ?Dbn) died in childhood.

Evelyn (17 Mar. 1854, ?Dbn – 12 Jan. 1856, ?Dbn) died in childhood.

Ernest Leslie (26 Nov. 1855, Dbn – 9 Apr. 1927, Dbn) m. 17 Apr. 1890, Dbn, Madeleine Churchill Gillespie, d. of Hugh Gillespie. Ernest was Mayor of Durban 1901–2.

Harold Lindley (22 Aug. 1857, ?Dbn – 13 Jan. 1882, Pmb.) unmarried.

Constance Louisa (born 19 May 1860, Dbn) m. 31 May 1883, Edward Snell (born *c.* 1857, Monkhampton, Devon), son of William Snell, and nephew of Edward Snell*.

Horace and Ernest Leslie joined their father in the auctioneering business.

SOURCES
Private source material
15; 44; 45; 48; 90; 92; 113; **114** 16.4.1878, 20.10.1878, 24.10.1878

Unpublished official papers
125 2282, 2286, 2287; **126** 64, 73; **128** 2/1 nos.11 and 15; **129** 46/173; **131** IV/16/4 nos.103, 105, IV/16/5 no.51/1865, IV/16/6 nos. 3, 9, 42, IV/17/18 no.534, IV/19/36 no.94; **137**; **147**; **156** 44/1894, 122/1905

Official printed sources
168 15.8.1854

Newspapers, periodicals, etc.
177 20.12.1853; **178** 2.1.1852; **180** 21.10.1854; **185** 22.3.1854, 13.5.1858, 24.5.1860, 6.5.1873, 26.10.1878; **187** 28.11.1855; **188** 3.10.1851, 19.12.1851, 16.4.1852, 2.7.1852, 6.8.1852; **189** 18.1.1856, 29.10.1878, 14.1.1882, 19.4.1890, 9.5.1894; **194** Apr. 1858; **197** 1863–1879, 1881, 1882, 1884, 1888, 1895; **198** 1852

Journals, biographies, autobiographies, letters
212 p.11

Miscellaneous unofficial contemporary printed sources
220

Later sources
227; **234** pp.166, 179, 236, 240–3, 263–7, 274, 345, 394–5, 402, 433, 440, 441 450; **267** p.172; **278** pp.378–384; **293** pp.1–2, 41–2, 107–137; **297** pp.230–7; **329** pp.1, 4, 62

Personal communication
352

Portraits, photographs, etc.
293 p.139; **358**; **362** (Robert and Mary Louisa Acutt)

ACUTT, William Hayes

Born 14 Dec. 1821, Dartmouth, Devon. Died 29 Jan. 1896, Lidgetton.

Merchant and broker. Brother of Robert Acutt* and Mrs Mary Jane Beater*. For antecedents, see entry for Robert Acutt. William came to Natal for health reasons arriving as a Byrne settler on the *Edward*.

In Aug. 1850, a few months after landing in Natal, he joined the existing partnership of W.H. Middleton* and G.H. Wirsing*. Their general storekeeping business was situated on the Smith Street/Gardiner Street corner of the Durban Market Square in the town's first double storeyed building. During most of 1854, and maybe longer, Acutt was domiciled in Pietermaritzburg. 1854 also saw the withdrawal from the firm of Middleton, the partnership thereafter being known as Wirsing and Acutt.

By 1860 Acutt was associated with David Leslie, the son of Mrs E. Leslie*, under the style Acutt & Leslie but this firm did not survive the severe depression of the 1860s and the partnership was dissolved in Feb. 1866. Acutt and Leslie's estate was sequestrated on 26 Apr. 1866. His personal estate had been sequestrated a short time before.

For some years after, Acutt appears to have carried on business alone. By the end of 1875, however, he and his wife's nephew, George Blaine (see Benjamin Blaine), had established the firm of Acutt & Blaine, later Acutt, Blaine & Co., merchants and commission agents.

After his retirement William continued living in Durban for a time. By 1891 he was living at Lidgetton. His property there was named *Bilscroft*.

Like his brothers, Richard, John and Robert, William tried sugar cultivation. By 1860 he and the Pietermaritzburg mercantile firm of de Kock and Bresler owned the estate *Umlaas* (10 560 acres). Possibly this was the large sugar estate 'on the Umlazi' that by 1865 was owned by the firm Acutt & Leslie and J.D. Koch*. In 1868 Acutt purchased R.P. King's* sugar estate at Isipingo, but by 1870 this property had become part of the *Reunion* estate. Sometime before 1870 Acutt also owned the farm *Springvale* at Avoca. This was a coffee plantation in the 1870s.

Acutt held various directorates. From 1859 to 1864 he was on the board of the Commercial and Agricultural Bank of Natal, and during 1864 he was director of the Natal Railway Company. He was also on the Natal committee of the Natal Land and Colonization Co. from 1862 to 1865.

William was a town councillor of Durban during the years 1858, 1859 and 1862. During this latter term, he and Adolph Coqui donated land for a street from the Bay to the Market Square, i.e. Acutt Street. Until 1874 the Acutt home was at the Bay end of Acutt Street but in that year the family moved to Musgrave Road on the Berea.

He was a foundation member of both the first Durban Club (1854) and the second (1860).

William was the first of the children of Robert Acutt and Julianna Cotton to come to Natal. His brother Robert followed in 1851. Mary Jane Beater was the next to arrive. She accompanied William to the Colony in 1856, at the conclusion of his first visit to England after emigrating. John Acutt and his family came to Natal in 1858, and Richard and his family in 1859. Penelope, the widow of another brother, Henry, arrived with two of her children in 1866, her two elder boys having preceded her. Mrs Julianna Knight, a widowed sister, made Natal her home in 1870. Four children of yet another brother, Cotton Acutt, reached the Colony at various times between 1851 and 1872.

William Acutt married twice. His first wife was Agnes Mary Williams (*c.* 1832 – 5 Feb. 1878, Verulam), the daughter of the Rev. John Harries Williams, Rector of Llanelieu, Brecknockshire, and sister of the wife of Benjamin Blaine. They were married at Inanda on 5 Aug. 1853. Four years after Agnes's death, he married Mary Caroline Gower, the daughter of Dr Samuel Gower*. This marriage took place in Pietermaritzburg on 6 May 1882.

CHILDREN

Isabel Hope (22 May 1854, Pmb – 1932, ?England) m. 6 Jan. 1881, Dbn, Edward Arthur Robert Innes (19 Nov. 1852, Shevaroy Hills, near Salem, Madras, India – 16 Dec. 1887, Pmb), son of Lewis Charles and Matilda Innes of Leyton, Essex. Innes senior had been a judge in Madras. Edward Innes was the Resident Engineer of the Harbour Board from 1882 until his death. (See *D.S.A.B.* vol.3)

Harriet Jessie Jermyn (26 Oct. 1855 – 12 Jan. 1857, Dbn) died in childhood.

Henry Callaway (19 Apr. 1857 – 1 Feb. 1893, Barberton, Transvaal) unmarried.

Arthur Blaine (1861 – 25 Jan. 1865, ?Dbn) died in childhood.

Frederick William (14 July 1863 – 14 Nov. 1871, Dbn) died in childhood.

Agnes Maud Emily (13 Apr. 1865 – *c.* 1950, buried Dbn) m. Anson Jason Woodall.

Ethel Laura (28 Dec. 1866, Dbn – 8 Mar. 1940) m. 12 Aug. 1897, Dbn, Percy Binns (Mar. 1862 – 7 Jan. 1920, ?Dbn), later Chief Magistrate of Durban, son of Henry and Clara Binns (born Acutt), and her first cousin once removed.

Philip George (24 June 1869, Dbn – 1936, ?Witbank, Transvaal) m. 19 Aug. 1901, Pmb, Mary Frances (Dolly) Graham (died Feb. 1962), daughter of an Anglican minister at Funchal, Madeira. Philip worked in Johannesburg, Standerton and Witbank.

Ronald Conway (2 Dec. 1871, ?Dbn – 8 Dec. 1962, ?Dbn) unmarried.

Cecil (9 Aug. 1874, ?Dbn – 6 Dec. 1874, Dbn) died in infancy.

SOURCES
Private source material
2; 11 James Grundy to E.P. Lamport 18.2.1878;
15; 29 Acutt papers; 34 Box 4. *Edward* lists;
35 16.5.1891; 41; 44; 45; 71; 84; 90; 92; 113;
114 22.5.1854, 16.7.1855, 12.6.1861, 30.8.1861,
30.9.1865–2.10.1865, 25.10.1865, 24.3.1866,
24.10.1874, 29.10.1874, 7.12.1874, 23.12.1875,
24.7.1877, 16.4.1878, 9.10.1878; 122 pp.17, 28

Unpublished official papers
125 2282, 2287; 126 73, 74; 129 39/24, 50/238;
130 1/31 nos.28 and 30; 131 IV/2/66 no.279,
IV/7/17 nos.320 and 321; 137; 141; 156 17/1896,
21/1888; 161 1862

Official printed sources
168 8.8.1854

Newspapers, periodicals, etc.
185 11.8.1853, 9.8.1854, 2.11.1855, 5.8.1862,

July 1863, Jan. and Apr. 1865, Dec. 1866, June 1869, 8.2.1878, 8.6.1881, 15.3.1940; **187** 31.10.1855; **188** 29.8.1851; **189** 10.5.1850, 30.8.1850, 30.1.1857, 1.5.1857, 12.1.1878, 1.2.1896; **197** 1863–1879, 1881, 1882, 1884, 1888, 1895

Journals, biographies, autobiographies, memoirs
217 p.26

Miscellaneous unofficial contemporary printed sources
220; **224** p.74; **227**

Later sources
234 pp.153, 346, 356, 419, 433, 487; **259**; **267** p.172; **293** pp.167–182; **297** pp.283–4; **324** v.3, p.142

Portraits, photographs, etc.
358; **362**

ADAMS, Charles

Died 26 May 1842, Durban.

Adams was in Natal by Sept. 1834. He was present on the historic 23 June 1835 when a site for the town of Durban was chosen. In May 1837 he was named by A. Biggar* as one of the lieutenants in the short-lived Port Natal Volunteers, a force raised in expectation of an attack on Port Natal by King Dingane.

Adams met his death during the clash between the Boers and the British troops in 1842 when the Boers made a surprise attack on Fort Victoria at the Point and captured it. Adams apparently tried to escape by swimming out to the brig *Pilot*, which with the *Mazeppa* was then in port, but when a short distance from the shore he was observed and shot.

In May 1876, while excavations were being undertaken for the new Point Road, a skeleton was uncovered near the 'Addington boundary'. It was that of a white man and there was a hole in the skull as if made by a bullet. Early newspaper reports conjectured that it was the remains of a casualty of the 1842 conflict. J.N. Wheeler*, who remembered the circumstances of Adams's death, stated that it was his skeleton. Wheeler averred that the bullet had struck Adams in the back of the head and had passed through to the front. He said that the body had been washed out to sea and had finally landed up on the Back Beach, where it was found and buried in nearby bushes. Wheeler described Adams as a young man in the employ of Henry Ogle*. (For further details of Adams's career in Natal see Tabler, E.C.: *Pioneers of Natal*.)

SOURCES
Private source material
29 Hogg papers

Printed documents
175 p.307

Newspapers, periodicals, etc.
185 20.5.1876; **189** 16.5.1876, 23.5.1876

Later sources
209 p.236; **290** pp.183, 197, 275; **303** p.1

ADAMS, George

Born *c.* 1813, Scotland. Died 15 Oct. 1900, Verulam.

Land surveyor and farmer. He and his family emigrated to Natal on the *Emily* under arrangement with W.J. Irons's* Christian Emigration and Colonization Society. According to the *Natal Independent* they had formerly lived at Dyrnham Park (unverified), Hertfordshire.

Adams was anxious to get on to his land, but, a month after landing, much to his chagrin, he was still in Durban, 'living at heavy expense, and yet very uncomfortably'. Writing to Moreland* from 'Tent 51, Durban', he requested an early date for *Emily* passengers to select their lands. Later in November he again wrote to Moreland, asking him for a plan of the location. He said he had been up to the lands but had been unable to find the beacons and had been compelled to make a blind choice. His apprehension that this 'blind choice' may have led him into selecting the wrong land appears to have been well-founded, because J.F. Churchill*, in his diary in Oct. 1851, records visiting Adams, 'a hard-working settler', and observed that he had been placed on the wrong land, and consequently had had four months labour in vain.

In both Mar. and June 1851 Adams corresponded with Moreland from *Umhlanga Farm*. Presumably by then he was on his correct allotment. It would seem that initially Adams concentrated on farming his 110 acres, but by mid–1852, judging by a letter he wrote to the *Natal Times*, he was becoming disillusioned with farming conditions. He stated that if maize and potatoes, crops that did not pay, were to be the staple products of the Colony, he would abandon farming. He asked that information be disseminated about the cultivation of 'ginger, arrowroot, cassava, coffee, sugar, and a lot of other things *that will pay*'. Adams did, at a later stage, try his hand at sugar planting.

It appears that farming began to play a subordinate role for Adams from about the mid-fifties. By at least early 1856 he was working as a government surveyor, and it is as a surveyor that he is best known. Among his surveys were the Crown lands on the Nonoti river, that were granted to settlers under the Proclamation of 29th April, 1857. Also, early in 1858, he laid out the Fort Scott village at Umhlali.

By at least 1870 Adams was planting sugar. Osborn's *Valiant Harvest* records that in 1872 Adams had a 10 horse-power steam mill operating on his *Umhlanga Lodge* estate. By 1874 his son Thomas was in partnership with him. Besides their original 110 acres (lot 39 Umhlanga), they had Lot 40 Umhlanga (70 acres), Lot 21 Umhlanga (28 acres), and an unnumbered Umhlanga lot of 60 acres.

In Feb. 1874 George Adams & Son surrendered both their joint and their personal estates. The sale of their assets was set for 11 Apr. 1874. George was allowed by his creditors to retain his furniture and his survey instruments.

Henceforward he concentrated on land surveying. In the late 1880s he was still living at the Umhlanga, but by the end of 1894 had moved to Verulam.

He was a prominent resident of Victoria County. In Nov. 1859 he was made a J.P. for the County and in the same month was appointed to assist the Resident Magistrate, Inanda Division, in the trial and decision of criminal cases to be held in Ward 1 of the County. In Dec. 1862 he was gazetted Acting Resident Magistrate, Inanda Division, during the temporary absence of J.W. Shepstone*. Dr Blaine*, the Magistrate, was on leave and Shepstone was his replacement. He was one of the County's field cornets — the first reference found to him in this post dating to June 1856, and the last to 1872. He was elected Major of the Victoria Mounted Rifles from its formation in Sep. 1862, and remained so until he retired at the end of 1867.

Adams was an active Anglican, and represented the laity of Umhlali, Mount Moreland and Verulam at the 1858 Church Conference. He is reputed to have prepared the plans for the Anglican church at Mount Moreland, completed between 1857 and 1860.

He was married twice. His first wife Elizabeth (born Dunlop), died on 25 Apr. 1867 at their home *Umhlanga Lodge* aged 52. In Nov. 1868, in Verulam, he married Mary Ann Henderson, widow of John Henderson*.

CHILDREN

Sally Richards (*c.* 1840 – Oct. 1928, ?Dbn) m. Dec. 1863, Verulam, John Henry Harvey, son of Francis Harvey*.

Thomas (*c.* Sep. 1841, Durham – 5 May 1911, Kearsney) m. Sep. 1864, Verulam, Mary Logan, d. of Robert Logan*.

Martha (*c.* 1844 – 31 Jan. 1933, Ladysmith)
   m. (1) Dec. 1864, Verulam, Frederick Thomas Bagley (*c.* 1841 – 14 Dec. 1872, Blackburn)
   m. (2) Oct. 1876, Verulam, Henry Reynolds (*c.* 1846 – 10 Jan. 1895, Verulam).

John George (*c.* 1846 – 3 July 1879, Greytown) unmarried.

Maria (born May 1847)
   m. (1) 18 Aug. 1866, *Umhlanga Lodge*, John Wilcox, son of John Wilcox*
   m. (2) Oct. 1877, ?Verulam, Richard Stone (born *c.* 1819, Wilts.).

James (1849, Barnet, Herts. – 20 Sep. 1929, Verulam) m. Jan. 1881, Verulam, Margaret Thompson (*c.* 1854, Liverpool – 17 Nov. 1919, Verulam), d. of John and Margaret Thompson (born Williams) ex *Priscilla*, 1860.

Child born at sea, 1850.

Alice (died 29 Jan. 1856, Umhlanga) died in childhood.

Mary (died 29 Feb. 1856, Umhlanga) died in childhood.

Elizabeth (19 Jan. 1854, Umhlanga – 21 Apr. 1932, Maidstone) m. Oct. 1883, Verulam, Benjamin Everitt Field, son of E.M. Field*.

Anne Alice (born 28 Sep. 1857, ?Umhlanga) m. Nov. 1881, Verulam, John Hawksforth Foster Brimelow (*c.* 1851, China – Mar. 1927, Pmb.).

Charles Frederick (28 Aug. 1858, ?Umhlanga – 16 Feb. 1886, Verulam) unmarried.

SOURCES

Private source material
   9 Churchill, J.F.:Diary 7.10.1851; **29** Lister papers; **34** Box 2. Surveyors' and Immigrants' correspondence book — G. Adams to Moreland — 2 undated letters (both written Nov. 1850), 17.11.1850, 1.3.1851, 18.6.1851. Box 4. *Emily* lists; **48**; **72**; **81**; **82**; **84**; **85**; **113**

Unpublished official papers
   125 2287; **129** 5/103, 6/242, 8/381, 14/168, 29/242, 41/215; **130** 1/97 nos.18–20; **132** III/5/31 nos.35–6, III/5/32 no.122; **137**; **143**; **147**; **151**; **154**

Official printed sources
   166; **168** 11.7.1854, 29.8.1854, 22.11.1859, 16.12.1862

Newspapers, periodicals, etc.
   184 13.2.1851; **185** 28.1.1858, 4.11.1858, 1.12.1859, Aug. 1866, May 1867, 17.12.1872, 21.8.1879; **187** 11.12.1862; **189** 18.10.1850, 14.3.1856; **194** Apr. 1858 p.95; **197** 1864–1879, 1881, 1882, 1884, 1888, 1895

Journals, biographies, autobiographies, letters
   210 p.123; **214** p.77

Later sources
   232 pp.42, 46; **264** pp.13, 19; **285** p.29; **297** pp.34–5, 238

ADAMS, Henry

Born c. 1813.

He came on the *Emily* and is described on the passenger list as a labourer. His name is grouped with that of John Adams (John Corbett Adams*) and family. He did not claim the land allotted to him in the Richmond area, viz. 3 Block F within circle, Richmond and Lot 4, *Little Harmony* (20 acres). In Sep. 1873, under Law 4. 1872, this land became subject to forfeiture to the Government. A Henry Adams was in Durban as late as Dec. 1856.

SOURCES

Private source material
   34 Box 4. *Emily* lists

Unpublished official sources
   125 2263 no.H287

Newspapers, periodicals, etc.
   187 3.12.1856; **189** 18.10.1850

ADAMS, Isaac

Born c. 1797.

A brickmaker who came on the *Dreadnought*, together with his wife and two children. Within a month of landing, his 17 year old son, Isaac, wrote home in glowing terms about the Colony. He said they had 100 acres freehold near Pietermaritzburg [this was at *Vaalkop*] plus 4 acres given to his father by the Government to make bricks, and also an acre in the town of Durban. He added 'I have no wish to return to England to stay, I like Natal better. . .'

   By the end of 1852 Adams was living in Pine Terrace, Durban, and was described as a 'tile and pottery maker'. In Dec. 1852 his wife, whose name was either Eliza or Eleanor, died in Durban aged 44.

   Perhaps he was the Adams who left Natal with a child in May 1853 for Cape Town. They travelled steerage in the *Sir Robert Peel.*

CHILDREN

Isaac C.S. (born c. 1832).
Eleanor Letitia Isabel (born Sep. 1842).

SOURCES

Private source material
   34 Box 4. *Dreadnought* lists; **53**

Unpublished official papers
   157

Newspapers, periodicals, etc.
   185 6.1.1853; **188** 3.10.1851; **189** 14.1.1853;
   192 June 1850 p.47

Miscellaneous unofficial contemporary printed sources
   220

ADAMS, John

Born c. 1790, Dublin. Died 15 Oct. 1882, Durban.

Barrack sergeant and Messenger of the Court, Durban. By 1855 Adams had been in the Army for thirty years, which period included 'long service' in the 'East Indies'. In his pre-Natal days he had been a sergeant-major in the 3rd, or East Kent Regiment (the Buffs). He was stationed in Natal from about 1851 as barrack sergeant, and later Ordnance storekeeper, in Durban.

   With impending old age and his large family in mind, Adams, in Jan. 1855, petitioned the Lt.-Governor for a grant of land, or for permission to buy land at a nominal sum but he made no headway as the Lt.-Governor was not then empowered to give land grants. A few months later, in June, he purchased part of a Durban erf (viz. Lot 11, Block F). This, however, was not where he finally settled. His case had been sympathetically treated by the Board of Ordnance, and he was granted, for life, a pensioner's lease of about an acre of Ordnance land. This faced Gardiner Street, and here he built a solid brick cottage. George Russell in his *History of old Durban* tells us that when the Durban-Point railway was built in 1860, the Durban terminus was on Ordnance land, 'but out of consideration for the old veteran the terminus stopped at his boundary'.

   By the end of 1857 Sergeant Adams was still employed at the Camp in Durban. From 1863, until he was pensioned in Feb. 1874, he was the Messenger of the Durban Magistrate's court. His son, John Havering, took over from his father and remained Messenger until the end of 1878. Adams also served as a field cornet for Durban County, was involved in the volunteer movement and acted as drill instructor of the Durban Volunteer Guard (formed 1854).

   Adams was married to Katherine or Catherine Ann Harrison (c. 1820, Ireland – 30 Dec. 1899, Stamford Hill, Dbn).

CHILDREN

?L.C. (born c. 1842).
David (c. 1845 – 26 Nov. 1857, Dbn) died as a result of a kick from a horse.
Ann Louisa (born c. 1846).
William Havering

John Havering (5 Nov. 1850, at sea, between Isle of Wight and Portsmouth 16 Jan. 1880, Dbn) m. 15 Apr. 1875, Umgeni, Dbn, Mary Anne Brennan, d. of Thomas Brennan*.

Mary Ann (31 Dec. 1852, ?Dbn – 18 July 1915, Dbn) m. 25 Feb. 1884, ?Dbn, James Broomfield Surgeson (c. 1841, Lancaster – 29 Jan. 1897, London).

?David (born 2 Oct. 1854, ?Dbn).

Agnes (8 Dec. 1856, ?Dbn, died ?Australia) m. Aug. 1878, ?Dbn, John McDonnell (born c. 1851, died ?Australia).

Ellen (17 June 1858, ?Dbn – 30 Oct. 1926) unmarried, became a nun, Sr St John.

Daniel Jacob (born 23 May 1861, ?Dbn).

SOURCES

Private source material
47; 89

Unpublished official papers
125 7 no.74, 55(5) no.145, 56 nos.123, 200 and 309, 2244 no.D43, 2245 no.D483, 2286 dated 28.1.1875; 129 5/133, 11/339; 137; 156 71/1882, 88/1894, 49/1897

Official printed sources
166

Newspapers, periodicals, etc.
185 20.6.1855, 6.6.1856, 5.3.1857, 13.8.1857 3.12.1857, 22.4.1875, 17.1.1880; 189 27.4.1875

Later sources
234 pp.200–1, 463

Personal communication
354

ADAMS, John Corbett

Born c. 1821.

Teacher and preacher. Adams arrived on the *Emily* with his 21 year-old wife, Emily. The name of Henry Adams* is linked with theirs on the *Natal Witness* list of *Emily* passengers.

John was listed as a teacher and in Dec. 1850 he advertised his Classical and Commercial School for young gentlemen in Smith Street, Durban. By this time, his wife had set herself up as a milliner and dressmaker. At the end of 1852 Adams was still teaching in Smith Street, and in May 1853 advertised evening classes in 'the English language, writing, arithmetic, etc'.

By the end of Jan. 1854, when Bishop J.W. Colenso* arrived in Durban, Adams's school, which the bishop designated as being 'for children of a higher class' (the Government school being for the 'lower classes'), had just been closed down. Colenso described Adams as an Independent minister, and stated that he had turned to storekeeping.

In the 1854–1855 jury lists for Durban County published in Aug. 1854, Adams is designated as a clerk. By Oct. 1854 he was being employed in that capacity by A. Jacques*, a draper, haberdasher and general storekeeper.

For the next few years Adams continued in this line. About Feb. 1855 he started his own business in Durban, which he called Victoria House. Three years later the *Natal Mercury* carried an advertisement to the effect that a dressmaking establishment would be opened at Victoria House. This could possibly mean that his wife had combined her business with his.

By the beginning of 1860 Adams had given up haberdashery and drapery, and had returned to teaching. He was appointed to the Belmont public school which opened 9 Apr. 1860, at *Clare* (see R. Clarence), a few miles N.W. of Durban. This school was to serve *Clare*, Springfield and surrounding districts. Dr R.J. Mann* in Feb. 1861 expressed great satisfaction with his 'great skill and efficiency' and 'marked aptitude'. This opinion he gave in a letter to the Colonial Secretary recommending that the Government grant to this school be increased from £25 to £50 p.a. Adams had indicated to the school committee that he could not remain as teacher for the 1861 school year unless his salary was increased to £150 p.a. In order to retain his services the committee had agreed to raise their contributions from £55 to £100, if the Government subsidy was also increased. Authorization for the additional amount was granted on 9 February. However, by the beginning of March Adams was advertising for sale his *Belmont Estate*, consisting of 27 acres of 'good sugar land' and a new nine-roomed house. Towards the end of March an advertisement inserted by the auctioneer, R. Acutt*, gives as the reason for the sale Adams's departure from the Colony. He and his wife and four children left Natal on 18 Apr. 1861. They sailed on the *Agnes Jessie*, presumably for Port Elizabeth, as that is where he is next encountered.

In Mar. 1863 he was ordained in Port Elizabeth as a minister of the Baptist Church. From Batts's *History of the Baptist Church in South Africa* one learns that Adams ministered at Port Elizabeth from 1862 until 1866.

Adams had been active in the religious life of Durban and as early as Dec. 1850 he was the agent for the sale of publications of the Religious Tract Society. Both he and his wife were foundation members of the Durban Congregational Church. He acted as preacher for that body from its inception in Apr. 1851 until he resigned in July 1852 and was replaced by Rev. J. Grosvenor*. In Aug. 1853 he was approached by the Baptists to minister to the congregation they were about to form. However nothing seems to have come of this and the Baptist Church in Durban was formally organized only in 1864. When the

Evangelical Alliance was set up in Durban in Feb. 1859, Adams was one of the committee members.

CHILDREN

son born Feb. 1853
daughter born Dec. 1855
daughter born June 1857

SOURCES

Private source material
34 Box 4. *Emily* lists; **48**

Unpublished official papers
125 126 no.49, 129 no.67; **126** 74

Official printed sources
168 15.8.1854

Newspapers, periodicals, etc.
180 28.10.1854, 23.2.1855; **184** 12.12.1850;
185 24.2.1853, 5.5.1853, 12.8.1858, 29.3.1860;
187 31.3.1860, 2.3.1861, 6.4.1861, 16.4.1863;
188 16.7.1852, 7.5.1852; **189** 18.10.1850,
26.8.1853, 21.12.1855, 3.7.1857

Journals, biographies, autobiographies, letters
204 pp.10–11

Miscellaneous unofficial contemporary printed sources
220

Later sources
234 pp.153, 159, 219, 402; **237** pp.31, 49

ADAMS, William

Born *c.* 1820. Died 28 Nov. 1916, Helpmekaar.

Trader and farmer. Adams arrived in Durban from England in 1842. He appears to have made Durban his base until at least 1854.

Shortly after his marriage in that year, he and his wife, his sister-in-law, her husband Piet Hogg (see John Hogg), W.H. Smith*, and a family named Joubert, went on a trading and shooting expedition to Zululand. The party made its headquarters in the Ngoye forest. From Smith's reminiscences one learns something about the lesser-known activities of the ordinary hunter-trader. On one occasion, after some days' hunting, he returned to the camp and found Adams and his wife busy making articles from hide, e.g. 'trektous' (buffalo hide cut into strips and plaited, and used for tow-ropes for wagons), sea-cow whips and sjamboks. Smith noted that the whips would sell at 10/- each, and the sjamboks at 7/6d.

In about 1856 Adams established a trading store on

the Tugela at a spot later to be known as Bond's Drift. A year or two later he and his family settled near Helpmekaar on the 4 000 acre farm *Knostrope*. Since 1850 his brother-in-law, James Rorke*, had been living nearby on the Buffalo river at the drift which still bears his name. While farming at *Knostrope* he also carried on with his trading expeditions. His obituary in the *Natal Witness* states that in over 30 years' wanderings he had visited almost every part of South Africa, and once went as far as the Zambesi.

Adams was one of the casualties of the depression of the 1860s, his trading activities leading to insolvency *c.* 1864. His main asset was *Knostrope*. At a meeting of his creditors in September it was intimated that Adams was expecting assistance from his brother in England to enable him to pay off his liabilities. However in November the trustee reported to the creditors that a 'very unsatisfactory report' had been received from England and recommended the sale of *Knostrope*. The farm was not sold however for in Jan. 1868 a special meeting of creditors resolved that the offer of one J.W. Adams (the brother in England ?) of £300 cash for *Knostrope* be provisionally accepted. The creditors must have confirmed their acceptance because *Knostrope* remained in the Adams family. From Klip River County jury lists of the late 1860s and the 1870s, one learns that Adams was by then renting *Knostrope*.

Adams belonged to the Buffalo Border Guard, and at the time of the Anglo-Zulu War was its quarter-master sergeant. Both he and his son William escaped from Isandlwana, he via Fugitives' Drift, and William by crossing lower downstream.

During the first Anglo-Boer War he was in the Transport service. During the second Anglo-Boer War, he was captured by the Boers, presumably when they invaded Natal, and was sent to Pretoria. After his release he finally arrived in Durban via Delagoa Bay.

In Durban in Oct. 1854 he married Maria Elizabeth Dorothea Strydom (born *c.* 1834), daughter of Hendrik and Maria Elizabeth Strydom. In their old age they left *Knostrope* and lived in Helpmekaar.

CHILDREN

John David (born *c.* 1858, Dbn) m. 10 Aug. 1887, Pmb., Ellen Mary Quirk, d. of P. Quirk*.
William Frederick (*c.* 1862, Dbn – 1951, Jhb.) m. 29 Oct. 1889, Vryheid, Susanna Catharina de Jager (born *c.* 1871, Utrecht).
Charles (Feb. 1863, *Knostrope* – Sep. 1953, Pmb.).
Hendrik (born *c.* 1864, Dundee) m. 14 Oct. 1890, Vryheid, Petronella Hendrika van Rooyen (born *c.* 1871, Utrecht).
Eleanor (Lena) (4 Oct. 1865, *Knostrope* – Aug. 1899) m. Nov. 1885, Rorke's Drift, George Green, son of Joseph Green*.
Hans Frederick (born 23 May 1869, ?*Knostrope*).

? **Arthur** (born *c.* 1870) m. 7 Nov. 1893, Greytown, Susanna Johanna Wilhelmina Koekemoer (born *c.* 1872).

Mary Elizabeth (born *c.* 1879, ?*Knostrope*) m. 27 Feb. 1902, Dundee, Vincent Lovell Whelan (born *c.* 1879).

SOURCES

Private source material
29 Hogg papers; **55**; **77**; **121**

Unpublished official papers
125 2282, 2288; **129** 17/67; **130** 1/30 no.17; **131** IV/7/17 nos.366, 424; **135**; **155**

Official printed sources
168 12.8.1862, 20.8.1867, 17.8.1869, 8.8.1876

Newspapers, periodicals, etc.
180 21.10.1854; **185** 25.10.1854; **189** 15.8.1887, 3.12.1916, 21.9.1953; **197** 1879, 1881, 1882, 1884, 1888, 1895

Portraits, photographs, etc.
189 8.12.1916

ADAMS, William

Born *c.* 1823.

Adams's name is on the passenger list of the *King William*. On Byrne & Co's copy, next to his name and that of Thomas Hill*, is the remark, 'Possibly these parties will not proceed by the *King William*'.

Hill did sail on the vessel, and was allotted land at Mount Moreland. Possibly Adams sailed too and was the William Adams whose land allotments were at Mount Moreland and New Glasgow. By Sep. 1873 these plots, viz. 8 Block B, Mount Moreland (1 acre), and 1 Block G, New Glasgow (½ acre), were unclaimed, and under Law 4, 1872, were liable to forfeiture to the Government.

SOURCES

Private source material
34 Box 4. *King William* lists

Unpublished official papers
125 2263 no.H287; **126** 64

ADAMS, William

Born *c.* 1824. Died 15 Jan. 1894, Ladysmith.

Blacksmith and ferryman. Adams came from Aberdeen. He emigrated to Natal on the *Emily* under W.J. Irons's* Christian Emigration and Colonization Society. With him was his young son, John, his wife having already died.

After landing Adams remained at the coast for nine months and then moved to the Ladysmith district. Here he carried on his blacksmith's trade, and also, from 1855 to 1874, he was the ferryman at the Klip river. After 1874 and until 1890, when ill-health forced him to retire, he continued with his smithy only.

Adams was a member of the Natal Frontier Guard, as was his son, William. Both served during the Langalibalele rebellion.

Sometime in the early 1850s Adams remarried. His second wife was Ellen Franklin (*c.* 1823, Richmond, Surrey – 16 Jan. 1903, Ladysmith), the daughter of John Franklin of Richmond, Surrey. The marriage took place in Ladysmith. She was possibly the Miss Franklin who arrived in Natal on the *Flora*, Sep. 1850.

CHILDREN

John G. (born *c.* 1845, U.K.).

Elizabeth (Nov. 1853, Ladysmith – 27 Sep. 1911, Ladysmith) m. 3 Jan. 1876, Ladysmith, Charles James Jones, son of Samuel Jones*.

William (1 June 1855, Ladysmith – 3 Apr. 1946, ?Ladysmith) m. 21 Mar. 1894, Ladysmith, Elizabeth Malcolm (*c.* 1870 – 15 Nov. 1950, ?Ladysmith), d. of G. Malcolm of the Biggarsberg.

Jessie Ellen (born Apr. 1857, ?Ladysmith) m. 21 Nov. 1877, Ladysmith, William Gray, son of David Gray*.

Emily (born 2 Oct. 1858, ?Ladysmith) m. 13 Nov. 1884, Ladysmith, Cornelius Hanbury Williams.

Annie (20 Apr. 1860, ?Ladysmith – 28 June 1949, ?Ladysmith) unmarried.

Janet (born 24 Dec. 1862, ?Ladysmith) m. 14 Jan. 1886, Ladysmith, Samuel Ellis (born 30 Oct. 1860, Rochdale, Lancs.), son of Thomas Ellis (died 1871) and Mary Ann Ellis (born Hoyle) (*c.* 1835–1909). Samuel was living in London by 1909.

John Howe (born 21 Jan. 1868, Ladysmith).

SOURCES

Private source material
34 Box 4. *Emily* lists; **64**; **66**; **71**; **79**; **97**

Unpublished official papers
125 2245 no. D481, 2286; **126** 73; **129** 9/175, 16/73, 35/124, 43/108; **142**; **143**; **156** 13/1894

Official printed sources
166; **168** 8.8.1854, 12.8.1856, 21.8.1860, 12.8.1862, 15.9.1874, 18.7.1876

Newspapers, periodicals, etc.
185 11.1.1876, 7.12.1877, Supp.22.5.1934; **189** 14.1.1876; **197** 1879, 1881

Later sources
267 p.282; **310** p.82; **330** p.4

Personal communication
342

ADCOCK, Joseph

Born c. 1817, Sheffield. Died 28 Aug. 1880, Wakkerstroom, Transvaal.

Carpenter and joiner. Adcock was the son of George and Elizabeth Adcock. With his second wife, Elizabeth Cullis Oates (c. 1821, U.K. – Jan. 1886, Pmb.), and the two children by his first marriage, Adcock arrived in Natal on the *Hebrides*.

For some months the Adcocks remained in Durban but by at least Aug. 1852 they had settled in Pietermaritzburg where he worked as a carpenter. By the end of 1861 he and a Mr Baxter were in partnership as carpenters and builders. It is not known how long this partnership lasted.

From at least the end of 1852 Adcock was living on erf 44 Burger Street. The 1854–55 Pietermaritzburg burgesses' roll, however, enters him as an owner of property, address, 8 Berg Street and the roll for the following year describes him as an owner, of 44 Burger Street. He appears to have resided on the latter property until shortly before his death.

He died at the home of his son, George, in Wakkerstroom.

His wife Elizabeth may have been related to W.E. Oates* who, in 1855, stood sponsor at the baptisms of two of the Adcock children.

CHILDREN

FIRST MARRIAGE

Catherine Louisa (c. 1839, U.K. – May 1916, Pmb.)
m. (1) Sep. 1865, Pmb., Richard King (born c. 1837)
m. (2) Samuel Brook (c. 1845 – June 1908, Pmb.).
Brook was a platelayer.

Mary Ann (c. 1846, U.K. – 25 Apr. 1916, Pmb.) m. Mar. 1866, Pmb., Charles Roberts*.

SECOND MARRIAGE

Joseph Oates (Oct. 1850, Dbn – 10 Apr. 1907, Ngotche division, Vryheid district) unmarried. Wheelwright.

George Meachen? or **Murchie?** (c. 1852, Pmb. – 4 July 1910, Pmb.) m. Aug. 1873, Pmb., Emma Gesina Worst (c. 1851, Zwolle, Overyssel, Holland – 20 Apr. 1919, Pmb.). Carpenter and blacksmith.

Elizabeth Cullis (c. Sep. 1853, Pmb. – 30 Aug. 1908, Pmb.) m. Oct. 1878, Pmb., Herbert Stutfield (c. May 1833, London – 4 Sep. 1902, Pmb.), widower of Sarah Ann Harrison, daughter of Charles Harrison*.

Thomas Albert (Sep. 1855, ?Pmb. – 27 June 1912, Pmb.) unmarried. Plasterer, mason.

Henry Cope (Apr. 1857, Pmb. – 21 May 1914, Pmb.) m. Sep. 1879, ?Pmb., Bertha Iantha Mansfield (widow) (c. 1850, St Helena – 6 May 1914, Pmb.). Carpenter.

Walter (born 1858, ?Pmb.). Dead by 1880.

Ethel Rosina (Feb. 1861, ?Pmb. – 6 Aug. 1886, Wallace Town [now Inchanga]) m. 29 Apr. 1879, Pmb., Harry James Foord.

SOURCES

Private source material
44; **71**; **72**; **74**; **77**

Unpublished official papers
125 2286; **129** 5/180, 14/171, 29/250, 33/188, 38/228, 46/40; **147**; **156** 7/1886; **157**

Official printed sources
168 10.8.1852, 30.5.1854, 10.8.1858, 14.8.1860, 6.8.1867, 20.8.1872, 29.9.1874, 22.8.1876

Newspapers, periodicals, etc.
189 1.6.1855, 12.12.1878, 3.5.1879, 14.9.1880, 9.8.1886, 8.5.1914, 26.5.1914, 6.5.1916, 25.4.1919; **197** 1863, 1872, 1879, 1881

Miscellaneous unofficial contemporary printed sources
220

ADDISON, Thomas

Born c. 1800. Died Dec. 1856, Mount Moreland.

Addison emigrated on the *King William*, accompanied by his wife, Sarah. According to the passenger list he was a mason. Also on the *King William* was Sarah's sister, Mary, with her husband, Richard Godden* and family. By 1854 Addison was farming on his allotment at Mount Moreland in the Cotton Lands where he died in 1856. By Nov. 1858 his widow was living at *Mount Pleasant*, the home of the Goddens at Mount Moreland.

His wife Sarah appears to have had some nursing experience for she acted as midwife to Mrs Blamey (see J.C. Blamey) in July 1852, and was intermittently employed as a nurse by the family of Hugh Gillespie*. Her association with the Gillespies dated from the arrival of their first child in July 1859, until at least the end of 1865. She accompanied this family on their visit to England from Jan. 1860 to mid-1861.

Mrs Addison died at *Mount Pleasant*, on 15 Jan. 1874 at the age of 69.

SOURCES

Private source material
8 1.7.1852; **9** Marianne C. Gillespie to Isabella Churchill 3.10.1859, 1.5.1861, 6.6.1861, 30.8.1861. Emma G. Churchill to William Gillespie 29.12.1865; **34** Box 4. *King William* lists; **84**

Unpublished official papers
126 64; **131** IV/16/4 no.10

Official printed sources
168 11.7.1854, 29.8.1854

Newspapers, periodicals, etc.
  185 24.1.1874

Later sources
  322 p.31

ADDISON, Dr William Henry

Born 10 Mar. 1820, Offham,[‡] Kent. Died 23 Aug. 1905, *Riet Vallei*, near Howick.

Medical practitioner and sugar planter. Eldest son of Friend Addison.

1842	— MRCS (England)
1844	— Lic. Midwifery (Rotunda)
1845	— M.D. (Edinburgh)
1847	— married Juliana Hallowes at Dolgelley, Merionethshire.
1848	— practising at Ludlow, Shropshire. First child born there.
1849 May	— arrived in Natal on *Lalla Rookh* with his family. Lived in Durban at first.
Nov.	— appointed District Surgeon, Pmb. Allowed to continue private practice.
1850 Feb.	— gazetted as surgeon to Pmb. Yeomanry Corps.
Dec.	— applied for post of 'Kaffir magistrate' at Umlazi location. Appointed.
1851 Jan.11	— went to Umlazi location. Shortly afterwards directed by the Lt.-Governor to hold himself ready to serve as medical officer to an expedition to the Cape frontier. It was intended that this force would assist in the Cape Frontier War. The expedition never materialized.
Apr.10	— *Natal Independent* reported he had relinquished his post as District Surgeon to take up the Umlazi magistracy.
Apr.(end)	Umlazi magistracy abolished. Resumed duty as District Surgeon.
1852	— served on Natal Native Affairs Commission.
1853	— resigned as District Surgeon, Pmb.
1854 Aug.	— his name appears on the 1854–55 jury list for Pmb. County (Ward 4) as pro-

‡ Three neighbouring villages, Offham, Addington and West Malling have, in different sources, each been given as Addison's birthplace. Offham has been preferred as it was stated to be his birthplace in his death notice, filled in by one of his children. Offham also appears on his gravestone.

prietor and occupier of *Riet Vallei*.

1856 Mar.	— proposed to Government that he develop the manufacture of fibre from wild banana, wild hemp and other coastal plants, for cordage, paper and canvas. Wanted the exclusive right, from three to five years, of using the wild fibre-producing plants on Crown lands. The Executive Council recommended this to the Lt.-Governor's 'favorable consideration', but nothing further has been discovered about Addison's scheme.
Oct.1	— title issued to the farm *Addington* (4 756 acres) on the coast near the Umvoti river.
Nov.	— gazetted as a member of the new Natal Medical Committee. Prior to its formation he had been the main adviser to the Natal government on the merits of the qualifications of surgeons and apothecaries applying for licence to practise in the Colony.
1857 Apr.3	— *Natal Witness* reported he had lost his seat on the Pmb. Town Council through non-attendance at its meetings for three months. W.E. Bale* elected in his stead.
1857	— started farming at *Addington*. Experimented with cotton, coffee, indigo and sugar, the last being the only crop with which he was successful.
1858 July	— Steward for the Umhlali Races.
1859 Feb.	— approached the Secretary for Native Affairs with a scheme for erecting sugar machinery to process cane to be grown by mission Africans at Rev. Aldin Grout's mission station near *Addington*. He and William Parnaby* were willing to invest £2 000 in this scheme.
1862	— started using a 12 horse-power steam mill on *Addington* to crush cane.
1865	— advertised *Addington* for lease.
Oct.	— gazetted District Surgeon for Tugela Division, Victoria County.
1865–8	— District Surgeon, Tugela Division.
1866 Nov.	— made a will for the disposal of his English property, particularly land in Kent, and also the inheritance due to him under the will of John Smith Addison, late of Offham, Kent.
1868 Feb.	— gazetted District Surgeon, Durban, in succession to Dr E.W.H. Holland*, deceased. Also appointed Health Officer for the Port of Durban. Farming operations carried on at *Addington* by his son, Friend.

1872 — first President of the newly founded Durban Medico-Chirurgical Society.

1883 Mar. — resigned as Health Officer for the Port of Durban.

1889 Apr. — on pension from the post of District Surgeon, Durban. Retired to his farm *Riet Vallei*, near Howick.

1905 Aug. — died at *Riet Vallei*.

Addison's wife Juliana (*c.* 1826 – 19 June 1892, Pmb.) was the daughter of Capt. Francis Hallowes, R.N. (d.1869) and his wife Mary, of Glapwell Hall, parish of Bolsover, Derbyshire, formerly of Coed (unverified), near Dolgelley, Merionethshire. Her brother, William Hallowes, served in Natal with the 85th Regiment from 1859–1863. He had entered the army in 1853.

CHILDREN

Friend (30 Dec. 1848, Ludlow, Shropshire – 26 Aug. 1925, buried Stanger) m. 5 Mar. 1878, Dbn, Eliza Anna Jackson, d. of W.P. Jackson*. Friend was M.L.A. for Victoria County, 1899–1901. (See *D.S.A.B.* vol.3)

Emily Mary (born 14 Apr. 1850, Pmb.) m. 14 July 1870, Dbn, Frederick Sydney Robinson (1833, U.K. – 3 Feb. 1874, Rondebosch, Cape). He was Archdeacon of Durban, 1869–1874.

William Henry (Mar. 1851, Pmb. – Dec. 1851, Pmb.). William and his nurse died when the Addison home was struck by lightning.

William Henry (1852, Pmb. – 24 Apr. 1939, ?Dbn) m. June 1889, Dbn, Louisa Florence Lloyd, d. of Capt. Walter Lloyd*. William in 1879 gained the qualifications of M.R.C.S. (England) and L.R.C.P. (Edinburgh). He was District Surgeon for Umlazi from 1883 to 1918.

Margaret Juliana (Feb. 1854 – 17 Sep. 1905, Dbn) m. 16 Nov. 1880, Dbn, Alfred Percival Field, son of T.E. Field of Benson, Oxfordshire.

Richard Hallowes (Sep. 1856, Pmb. – May 1921, Pmb.) m. 6 Jan. 1885, Dbn, Florence Lavinia Hirst (*c.* 1859, Liverpool – July 1932), d. of Ira and Adelaide Octavia Hirst of Sydenham, Dbn.

Charles Brabazon (1858, ?*Addington* – 26 Nov. 1910, Dar-es-Salaam) unmarried. Died while on a shooting trip.

Walter Harding Bovell (23 Sep. 1859, ?*Addington* – 7 Oct. 1931, Kloof)

   m. (1) 23 Apr. 1892, Stanger, Rosalie Benoni Colenbrander (Feb. 1870, New Guelderland – 1 July 1901, *Addington*), d. of Theodorus Christiaan Colenbrander (1811–1881)

   m. (2) 7 May 1906, Greytown, Alice Amelia Colenbrander (Dec. 1876 – Sep. 1954), d. of Johannes Arnoldus Colenbrander (*c.* 1822–1907).

Grace (9 Nov. 1861 ?*Addington* – June 1945, ?Dbn)

m. 24 June 1896, Howick, Dr Sidney Nevill Harrison of Durban.

Victor Edward (20 Mar. 1864, *Addington* – 2 Sep. 1897, Dbn) unmarried.

Juliet (15 Oct. 1865, ?*Addington* – June 1945, ?Dbn) unmarried.

Constance Spong (13 Mar. 1867, ?*Addington* – 1953) m. Percy Male.

Francis Hallowes (16 Feb. 1870, Dbn – Oct. 1929, ?Dbn).

SOURCES

Private source material
   16; **29** Fannin papers; **41**; **43**; **44**; **56**; **58**; **71**; **81**; **82**; **101**; **102**; **108**; **114** 5.3.1871, 16.11.1880; **124** 20.1.1858

Unpublished official sources
   125 3(2) no.107, 13 no.155, 21(1) nos.9 and 12; **126** 73; **127** 48 no.95 p.185; **129** 8/36, 9/107, 24/45, 24/99, 32/87, 41/30; **131** IV/16/5 no.32/1866, IV/16/6 no.70; **132** III/12/1 p.84; **133** I/1/9 no.72; **137**; **141**; **147**; **148**; **151**; **156** 42–44/1880, 64/1892, 108/1897, 185/1905, 209/1905

Official printed sources
   166; **168** 8.8.1854

Newspapers, periodicals, etc.
   184 10.4.1851; **185** July 1858, Feb. 1870, 16.7.1870, 14.2.1874, 7.3.1878, 16.11.1880, 2.1.1885; **188** 19.12.1851; **189** 9.11.1849, 3.4.1857, 9.3.1878, 20.9.1892, 28.8.1905, 30.12.1910; **193** Oct. 1854; **195** v.4, 1884 pp.41, 75, 77, vol.5, 1885 p.12; **197** 1863, 1879, 1881, 1895; **199** 1908 p.4

Miscellaneous unofficial contemporary printed sources
   213 p.446

Later sources
   236 *passim*; **242** pp.206–7, 212–3, 222, 224–5; **251**; **254**; **267** pp.102, 288, 316; **271** pp.26–7; **282** pp.5–7; **297** pp.76, 188–9; **320**; **328** *passim*

Portraits, photographs, etc.
   362 (W.H. Addison and Mrs J.H. Addison)

ADLAM, Joseph

Born *c* 1807. Died 6 July 1895, Wandsbeck near Westville.

Carpenter and coffee planter. Adlam came from Bath. He emigrated to Natal on the *Emily* with his wife, Sarah (*c.* 1818 – May 1856, ?Dbn), and five children. His eldest child, Anne, followed the rest of the family in

Oct. 1855 on the *Lady of the Lake.*

Adlam did not take title to his allotments at Richmond, viz., 18 *Little Harmony* (90 acres) and 5 Block F within circle, in Richmond, until Nov. 1872. He remained in Durban and by the end of 1852 was established as a carpenter and builder in Pine Terrace (Street). Like many a carpenter in those less sophisticated days, he also worked as an undertaker. His grandson, Harold (d. 1942), son of Frederick, made this his career, becoming eventually the senior partner of Adlam, Reid & Co.

By the end of 1871 Adlam's business was being run from Queen Street, but it appears that he was still living at Pine Terrace.

By 1874 he had taken up coffee-planting on the farm *Spring Grange*, Wandsbeck near Westville, a property he had owned since at least 1864. He finally retired *c.* 1881, and died at *Spring Grange.*

After the death of his wife Sarah, Adlam married Mary Ann Wilkinson (born Lee), the widow of Richard Wilkinson*. The marriage took place in Durban on 1 Jan. 1858.

CHILDREN

Anne (*c.* 1833 – 4 May 1886, Dbn) m. Nov. 1856, Dbn, Jesse Saveall*.

James (*c.* 1834 – 16 Jan. 1892, Clayton, Sussex)
m. (1) ?Cape, Mary Duffy (*c.* 1835 – 31 Aug. 1871, Dbn).
m. (2) Frances Martin (died Canada).
James was a carpenter, builder and undertaker. It would seem that he spent some years in the Cape, as at least one of his children was born at Port Elizabeth. It is likely he was the Mr Adlam who left Natal on the *Anne* in Mar. 1853. Presumably he was the Mr Adlam who arrived from the Cape with his family in June 1860 on the *Waldensian.*
After his death his widow married a Mr Dales.

Joseph (born *c.* 1839). Joseph was apprenticed as a bricklayer in 1858. By 1866 he was living in Wakkerstroom.

Mary Ann (*c.* 1845, Bath – 27 Apr. 1913, Dbn) m. Apr. 1861, Pmb., George Stephenson (died 4 Jan. 1890, Pmb.).

Sophia (*c.* 1847, ?Bath – 23 Mar. 1928, ?Dbn) m. 7 June 1866, Dbn, William Hurst (*c.* 1841 – 7 Feb. 1893, Dbn).

Emma (1849, Bath – 22 June 1905, Shaka's Kraal) m. 24 Aug. 1871, Dbn, Edwin Essery (8 July 1843, South Petherwin, Cornwall – 21 Feb. 1912, Shaka's Kraal), son of William H. Essery.

Frederick Wilson (*c.* 1851, ?Dbn – 17 July 1892, Jhb.) m. Elizabeth Jane Wells. Frederick was a carpenter.

The Edwin Essery papers in the Local History Museum, Durban, state that Adlam's second wife's name was Hannah Earle, and that her children were Annie, Mary, Sophie, Emma and Fred. This is unreliable as James and Joseph, children younger than Anne, are not mentioned. Furthermore Fred must have been the son of Sarah.

SOURCES

Private source material
3; **10**; **25**; **34** Box 4. *Emily* lists; **44**; **48**; **49**; **52**; **53**; **76**; **109**

Unpublished official papers
125 41 no.74, 55 no.145, 56 nos.139, 200 and 309, 2263 no. H287; **126** 73, 74; **129** 23/228, 45/17, 49/161; **131** IV/2/65 no.142, IV/16/5 nos.6 and 7/1864; **136**; **137**; **156** 18/1892, 19/1893, 71/1895, 154/1905

Official printed sources
168 15.8.1854, 6.8.1867, 10.8.1869, 6.8.1872, 8.9.1874, 6.10.1874, 3.10.1876

Newspapers, periodicals, etc.
185 June 1866, 26.8.1871, 5.9.1871; **189** 18.10.1850, 16.5.1856, 22.8.1856, 25.8.1892, 26.6.1905, 27.2.1912; **197** 1872, 1878, 1879, 1881, 1882, 1884, 1888, 1895

Miscellaneous unofficial contemporary printed sources
220

Later sources
239

AGAR, Charles Artemus

c. 1822, London. Died 11 May 1897, Umgeni, near Durban.

Wine and spirit merchant and condiment-maker. Agar was the son of one Charles Agar. It would appear from W.J. Irons's* correspondence, that he was a cook, but on emigrating, to gain the approval of Her Majesty's Emigration Commissioners, described himself as a 'market gardener'.

Agar came to Natal on the *British Tar* under the auspices of Irons's Christian Emigration and Colonization Society. He was somehow connected with 24-year old Ellen Smith*, a 'domestic servant' as the *British Tar* passenger list describes her. Their possessions were sent up to Verulam on the same wagon. Also, on two occasions, in Dec. 1850 and in the following January, he made contact with Moreland* about the selection of Ellen's Verulam allotment.

By Dec. 1850 Agar was still in Verulam, but had sold his 20 acres to John Atherton*. By May 1852 he was a coffeehouse keeper in Durban, while by the end of that year he had forsaken coffee for stronger stuff, and was running a canteen. This establishment, Agar's Canteen, well-known in early Durban, was in Gardiner Street, on the Market Square. George Russell in his *History of old Durban*, describes it as 'an undersized wooden shanty of the mining camp class'. One can get an idea of what it looked like from James Lloyd's* sketch in the *Illustrated London News* of the first auction, in 1855, of Natal-made sugar. This sugar was produced on the Milner* brothers' farm, *Springfield*. A few months earlier, in May, Agar had taken out a nine-year lease of a ten acre lot at *Springfield*. The terms of his lease with Milner Bros. and J.B. Miller* included planting a third of his land with sugar, and taking his cane to the lessors' mill. By October he had given up this lease.

In 1858 Agar started producing pineapple wine. A year later he was still running his canteen. By mid−1862 he had graduated to dealing in wine and spirits. The 1869−70 Durban County jury list (published in Aug. 1869) describes him as a storekeeper of Durban, but it is known that by the end of that year he was running the Crown Hotel in Verulam. By the end of 1871 he was back in Gardiner Street, Durban, as a wine and spirit dealer. The 1872−73 Durban County jury list has it that he was a canteen-keeper in Durban.

In the 1870s Agar once again tried farming. By mid−1874 he had bought land at the Umgeni in Victoria County and had established himself as a 'planter'. Soon afterwards (the first advertisement found dates to the end of 1874) he launched his 'Diamond', a 'piquant and delicious sauce' prepared especially for the South African diamond and gold fields and 'all hot and tropical countries'. Shades of his pre-colonial days?

In the 1880 *Natal Almanac* he appears as a farmer and sauce-maker of Umgeni, while in the later numbers he is listed as a planter of Umgeni. In his death notice his occupation is stated to be that of 'condiment-maker'.

Agar was married three times. His first wife, whom he appears to have married in Natal, was Margaret Matilda Emily, otherwise called Emily Margaret. She died at Pinetown in May 1862 at the age of 36. In Oct. 1866, presumably in Durban, he married Jane Erridge (*c.* 1832, London − 11 Sep. 1882, Umgeni, Dbn). His third wife was Mrs Emma Julia Leuchars, daughter of Alfred George*. They were married on 29 July 1885 in Durban.

Either Agar or his son Charles painted in water-colour. Two originals have been traced, viz., one of his house, and one entitled 'Seventeen steamers in Durban Harbour, 14th April 1879'.

CHILDREN

Emily Margaret (born Apr. 1852, ?Dbn) m. Henry Deegan.
The Deegans were in Ficksburg, O.F.S., by 1897.
Charles (Aug. 1854, ?Dbn − 30 Dec. 1944, ?Dbn).
    m. (1) Mar. 1888, Pmb., Constance Louisa Hall. This marriage ended in divorce.
    m. (2) 13 June 1900, Dbn, Jessie Willday (widow) (*c.* 1868 − 16 Aug. 1964, ?Dbn).

Ellen (born Apr. 1857, Dbn) m. *c.* 1892, Ladysmith, William Edward Davis (*c.* 1834, Chepstow, Monmouthshire − 29 June 1909, Ficksburg, O.F.S.), a widower, and the son of Rees Davis.

SOURCES

Private source material
34 Box 2. Surveyors' and Immigrants' correspondence book − Agar to Moreland Dec. 1850, Agar to C.T. Littlewort 17.1.1851. Box 4. *British Tar* list; **36** W.J. Irons to Theophilus Irons July 1850; **42**; **43**; **44**; **46**; **70**; **78**; **91**

Unpublished official papers
125 2240 no.B560, 2284, 2288; **129** 9/61, 36/163; **131** IV/7/17 nos.383, 396, IV/19/40 no.59

Official printed sources
168 15.8.1854, 6.8.1867, 13.8.1867, 10.8.1869, 6.8.1872, 20.8.1872, 8.9.1874, 15.9.1874, 6.10.1874, 18.7.1876, 3.10.1876

Newspapers, periodicals, etc.
180 12.8.1854; **185** 16.8.1854, 10.6.1858, 11.8.1859, 12.9.1862; **188** 18.6.1852; **189** 15.5.1857; **197** 1864, 1865, 1870, 1872, 1875, 1879, 1881, 1884, 1888, 1895

Miscellaneous unofficial contemporary printed sources
220

Later sources
234 pp.119, 317, 372; **306** p.1

Personal communication
342

AITCHISON, James Carmichael

Born *c.* 1826. Died Aug. 1854, Cape Town.

He was the second son of Alexander Aitchison of Musselburgh, Midlothian. In Sep. 1848 he came to Natal from the Cape with his brother, John Murray Aitchison*, and T.F. Carpenter on the *Rosebud*. Also on board was a quantity of merchandise with which these three were to launch their general dealers' business in Durban. The firm Aitchison, Carpenter & Co. lasted only until Feb. 1849 when Carpenter withdrew and after a few months returned to Cape Town. For the next two years the business continued under the name of Aitchison Bros., merchants and commission agents, and was then dissolved. James left for Cape Town on the *Vixen* in Apr. 1851.

In Aug. 1853 in Cape Town he married Margaret T.

Gibson. He died a year later at his home in Buitenkant Street.

SOURCES

Unpublished official papers
126 73

Official printed sources
168 27.2.1849

Newspapers, periodicals, etc.
184 15.9.1853; 189 13.10.1848, 2.3.1849, 2.8.1850, 7.3.1851, 8.9.1854

AITCHISON, John Murray

Died Sep. 1855, Cape Town.

Merchant and civil servant. He was the son of Alexander Aitchison of Musselburgh, Midlothian. He came to Natal from the Cape in Sep. 1848 on the *Rosebud*. Accompanying him were his wife, Caroline, (born Gillmer) and child, his brother J.C. Aitchison* and T.F. Carpenter.

Within a couple of weeks of arrival, Aitchison, Carpenter & Co. advertised that the goods they had brought with them to Natal were shortly to be landed and would be open for inspection in Durban. The partnership with Carpenter was short-lived and was dissolved in Mar. 1849. Carpenter left the Colony three months later. The firm Aitchison Bros., merchants and commission agents, continued to operate in Durban for another two years. In Mar. 1851 James pulled out and returned to the Cape, leaving John in business on his own.

Aitchison was a citizen of some consequence and in Feb. 1851 was one of the six Durban men appointed as J.P.s. However, he was later forced to leave Durban for health reasons. In June 1852 he was making preparations to move to Pinetown and relinquished his agency for the *Natal Independent*. Later in the year he gave up active participation in his business and entered the Government service.

By Oct. 1852 he held the appointment of Post Master in Pietermaritzburg. About a year later his health gave way again. In Aug. and Sep. 1853 he had to take leave and A.B. Allison* temporarily acted in his stead.

Before he became ill for the second time Aitchison had, in Apr. 1853, assigned his estate for the benefit of his creditors. The estate of Aitchison Bros. was also assigned, and in Jan. 1854 various properties in these estates in Durban, on the Umhlali river, and at Mount Moreland, were auctioned.

From the Post Office Aitchison was transferred to the office of the magistrate in Pietermaritzburg. Judging from two petitions he sent to the Lt.-Governor, one in Feb. and one in Apr. 1854, this new post seems to have been at a reduced salary. In his second petition he stated that he would have to resign to save himself and his family from suffering 'extreme poverty'. He pointed out that while in the Government service he had always forborne from accepting private business, feeling that as a Government official it would be unfair of him to monopolize agencies and commissions. 'Townsmen', he stated, were often tempted to employ government officers, because in their positions they were able to attend to their clients' business more swiftly than ordinary agents. Aitchison claimed that by not accepting such work he had deprived himself of 'considerable gain'.

Within a month of sending in his second petition, Aitchison was appointed Chief Clerk in the Surveyor-General's office.

Later in the year his health broke down once more and he was compelled to resign his new post and leave the Colony. The Aitchisons returned to the Cape in Dec. 1854 on the *Huma*. He died the following year.

CHILDREN

Alexander William Hay (born before 1848 in the Cape).
George Robert (baptised Jan. 1850.).
Hannah Maria (born Apr. 1854, Pmb.).

SOURCES

Private source material
76

Unpublished official papers
125 16(3) no.146, 56 no.58, 2297 no.666;
126 73; 127 35 no.52; 131 IV/23/21 nos.6, 18

Official printed sources
166; 168 27.2.1849

Newspapers, periodicals, etc.
180 13.5.1854; 184 24.1.1850, 1.1.1852, 15.9.1853, 22.9.1853, 11.5.1854; 187 12.12.1855; 188 29.12.1853; 189 13.10.1848, 2.3.1849, 4.1.1850, 2.8.1850, 7.3.1851, 2.9.1853, 9.12.1853, 14.4.1854, 3.11.1854; 198 1851 p.16

Miscellaneous unofficial contemporary printed sources
220

AITKEN, Robert

Born *c.* 1800, Scotland. Died Sep. 1858 near Richmond.

He was the son of Robert Aitken and Jane (born Bates). In Scotland Aitken had been a small farmer from the neighbourhood of Falkirk. He had had to pay a large rental for the high quality land he farmed. This, combined with the heavy taxes and poor rates then prevailing, was draining his capital. His losses in the two or three years before he came to Natal amounted to between £300 and £400. With 'poverty ahead', as he himself put it, he was compelled to emigrate. He and his family arrived on the *Conquering Hero*.

In Aug. 1850 the Aitkens went to the Richmond district where they were entitled to 90 acres. They appear initially to have found conditions in Natal particularly difficult. In Nov. 1850 a survey was conducted among the inhabitants of the Richmond district to ascertain their impressions of the settlement. Of the 27 immigrants interviewed, Aitken was the only one who could not give a definite 'No' to the question 'Do you regret emigrating?' Furthermore, he alone refused to give his opinion of the settlement.

Part of the reason for this dissatisfaction was the delay in finalizing the selection of his land. As late as Sep. 1851 his position was still uncertain. At the beginning of the month he wrote to Moreland* enclosing the diagram and title deeds of 90 acres which, he claimed, had been given him by mistake. He stated he wanted the land he had originally chosen. He conceded that if Moreland were to appoint someone to show him the boundaries of this other land, and it proved to be as good as that he had originally selected, he would accept it. Aitken asked for an immediate answer to his letter as he wished to begin planting his crops. Sixteen days later, despite a promise from Moreland to have the new land pointed out to him, nothing had happened. As the time for planting was passing, he again approached Moreland. In this exasperated letter, he stated he intended occupying and cultivating the land originally allotted him until such time as he was given land equivalent to it. He threatened legal proceedings for the recovery of expenses and damages for the time he was kept off his land, unless within eight days Moreland had given him the title deeds to his original land, or given him an allotment of equal quality. The Moreland papers, from which this correspondence is taken, give no clue as to further developments. However, by the beginning of 1852, Aitken's problems appear to have been sorted out; by then he was farming his 90 acres, and was also cultivating 2 erfs in Richmond, where he had potatoes, mealies and oats. His oats, he considered, were as good as any in Scotland. He had tried growing wheat from seed he had brought with him, but this had not been successful.

At this stage the Aitkens were living in Zulu huts on their land in Richmond village, but in the following winter they intended moving on to their rural allotment and building a house.

With a brighter outlook ahead, Aitken's views on the Colony had changed considerably. He told Moreland, who in Jan. 1852 made a tour of the Richmond district,

acquiring information from the settlers, that he was 'exceedingly' well pleased with the Colony. He had sent good reports to his 'folks' and hoped they would follow him out in a year or two.

Aitken's name appears on the 1854–55, 1856–57 and 1858–59 jury lists for Ward 5, Pietermaritzburg County as a farmer of *Bonnyside*. This presumably is the name he gave to his 90 acre allotment. He died at *Bonnyside*.

In July 1857 his son James applied for a farm on the Illovo river between Richmond and present Mid-Illovo. On 1 Mar. 1858 title to *Sunnyside* (1 187 acres) was issued to him. Shortly after Aitken's death the family appear to have moved to *Sunnyside* where all four sons farmed. The eldest, Andrew, later had the adjoining farm *Zuur Rug*.

Aitken's wife was Margery (born Betts). According to the *Conquering Hero* passenger lists, she was aged 43 at the time of emigrating. No trace of the date of her death has been found unless she was the Maud [sic] Aitken, whose name appears on the Richmond government register of deaths as having died at *Sunnyside* in Nov. 1880 at the age of 84.

CHILDREN

Andrew (c. 1833, Stirling, Stirlingshire – 25 June 1908, Richmond) m. 19 July 1873, *Cleveland Hill*, Harriet Elizabeth Fell (c. 1841, Stainton, N.R., Yorks. – 30 Sep. 1930, Richmond), d. of Henry and Sarah Fell of *Cleveland Hill*, Beaumont, near present Eston.

John (c. 1835, Scotland – 30 Apr. 1910, Pmb.) unmarried. John had been farming at *Hartebeestefontein* near Umhlongo Nek at the time of his death.

James (c. 1837, Condorrat, Stirlingshire – 14 May 1885, Pmb.) m. 29 July 1863, Richmond, Theresa Moore, d. of Robert Moore*.

George (c. 1839, Scotland – 27 July 1896, *Sunnyside*) m. Dec. 1881, Agnes Sophia Moore, d. of Robert Moore above.

David (c. 1842, Scotland – 14 Nov. 1858 near Richmond) struck by lightning.

SOURCES

Private source material
    34 Box 2. Surveyors' and Immigrants' correspondence book – Aitken to Moreland 2.9.1851, 18.9.1851. Box 4. *Conquering Hero* lists; **60**; **80**; **102**; **106**; **107**

Unpublished official papers
    125 2284, 2286; **126** 64; **129** 3/10 no.57, 3/14 no.A5, 7/280, 8/380, 33/66, 38/72; **132** III/5/24 no.17, III/12/1 p.89; **147**; **150**; **156** 23/1885

Official printed sources
    168 25.7.1854, 29.7.1856, 10.8.1858, 14.8.1860, 6.8.1867, 16.8.1870, 20.8.1872, 25.8.1874, 29.9.1874, 19.9.1876

Newspapers, periodicals, etc.
  181 5.8.1863; **184** 6.5.1852; **185** 25.11.1858,
  Aug. 1863, 24.7.1873; **189** 16.5.1851, 27.2.1852,
  19.3.1852, 16.5.1885, 30.7.1896, 6.7.1908;
  197 1881

Later sources
  267 p.185

AKERMAN, Sir John William

Born 16 Aug. 1825, Plymouth, Devon. Died 24 June 1905, Ealing, London.

Chemist, politician and Speaker of the Legislative Council. He was the son of the Rev. James Akerman (d. 1848, Penzance), a Wesleyan minister of Bromham, Wilts., and his wife Elizabeth Charlotte Long, of Chippenham, Wilts. Akerman received his early education at Kingswood School near Bristol.

c. 1839	— articled to a chemist in Penzance, Cornwall.
1843 Feb.	— Pharmaceutical Society of Great Britain granted a royal charter of incorporation. Akerman a foundation member of the Society.
1850 June 26	— married Jane Stantial (c. 1819 – 13 Dec. 1876, London), daughter of C. Stantial of Corsham, Wilts. The marriage took place at Corsham.
July	— embarked with wife on the *British Tar* under arrangement with W.J. Irons's* Christian Emigration and Colonization Society. Had been advised to seek a warmer climate for the sake of his health. Accompanying the Akermans was his sister Mary and her husband, J.T. Polkinghorne*. Prior to emigrating the Akermans had been living at Corsham.
Sep.	— *British Tar* arrived at Durban.
Oct.	— at Verulam. He and Mr Harvey (probably Francis Harvey*) acted as spokesmen for the *British Tar* immigrants in meeting with Moreland* to discuss the changing of the location of their allotments.
Dec.18	— Akerman and Polkinghorne wrote letters to Moreland from 'Mrs Elliott's boarding house', Durban, complaining of Moreland's alteration of their country allotments on the Umhlanga Estate. Each was supposed to get 100 acres, and had paid survey fees on 100, but only 40

acres were allotted to each of them. Akerman in his letter also protested at being allotted land in dense bush.

Dec.30	— wrote from Verulam to Moreland on the same subject.
1851 Apr.	— wrote to Moreland from Umhlanga complaining his beacons had not been shown him and his land had not been surveyed. Also dissatisfied with the type of land the settlers were being given.
1851	— unsuccessfully experimented with cotton on his Umhlanga land. Moved inland to learn farming from the Boers. Within six months had acquired a knowledge of the Dutch language.
c. Oct/Nov.	— started teaching Dutch children in the Mooi River district.
1852 Feb.29	— wrote to the Government from *Waterval*, Mooi River. Stated he had a large school (17 or 18 pupils), and was content to be thus permanently employed, but the stipend attached was too little to induce a married man of 'character and respectability' to continue in this employment. He believed his school was larger than any other country school in the Colony. Asked for an annual grant which would enable the schoolmaster to establish himself 'permanently and respectably'.
Oct.21	— *Natal Independent* reported that Akerman had been appointed Government teacher at Mooi River.
1853 Apr.13	— teacher, Umvoti. Infant son died on the farm *Pampoen Nek*.
1854	— after three years as a teacher to the Dutch of Umvoti and Mooi River, he had to abandon the post because of the inadequate remuneration. All he had received from the Government was the recognition of his position by the sum of £1 per month, to which was added the very small fees the Boers were able to pay.
1854	— representations made to the Government by the Boers for his permanent appointment, but nothing materialized. Akerman felt this was unjust because other teachers in rural schools no larger than his were receiving £50 p.a. from the Government. After his departure the district was left without a school.
1854 c. Mar.	— started business in Pmb. as a chemist and apothecary.
Sep.	— advertised as a chemist. Also advertised the manufacture of mineral waters,

including effervescing lemonade, ginger-ade, orangeade, etc.

1855 June & Aug. — purchased at auctions the contents of the dispensary and the furniture and fittings of Nicholas van Zweel's business. Van Zweel, Pmb.'s first chemist, had gone insane.

Oct.30 — wrote to Sir George Grey, Governor of the Cape, during the latter's visit to Natal. Recounted his service as a teacher to the Dutch of Umvoti and Mooi River. Stated that during this time he had received assistance from the Government to the value of only £27, and had refused several lucrative offers of employment elsewhere in the belief that the Government would make him a bigger grant-in-aid. Asked for pecuniary compensation. Answer: not in the Governor's power to make such compensation.

1857–1862 — served on the Pmb. Town Council. During his term was, with others, instrumental in establishing Alexandra Park.

1857 Aug. — by this time was the owner of one third (1 291 acres) of the farm *Onverwacht* near Table Mountain.

1859 Aug. — elected Mayor of Pmb.

1861 Mar. — wife Jane's relation Rachel Curtis Tucker (born Stantial) and her husband, James Tucker, from Corsham, Wilts., arrived on the *Leila* as government-assisted immigrants. Akerman had stood surety for the repayment of their passage money.

1862–1892 — served in the Legislative Council as member for Pmb. Borough except for short breaks between May and Dec. 1868, and Sep. 1873 to Mar. 1875.

1863 — wife Jane's nephew, Edward S.T. Stantial, and his sister, Hannah Elizabeth (later wife of James Chatterton*), arrived in Natal.

1864 — made a J.P. for Pmb. County.

1870 May — appointed as a member of the Natal Executive Council.

1876 — retired from business as a chemist. Wife's nephew, Edward Stantial, took over the firm.

1876 Aug. — London Conference on confederation for South Africa opened. Akerman was one of the two Natal delegates.

Dec. — wife, Jane, died in London.

1877 — his book *Native government in Natal* published in London.

1878 Jan. — married in Pmb. Emma Elizabeth Brock (c. 1851, Bath — 27 Dec. 1909, Ealing, London), widow of William Brock, and daughter of W.H. Brumby, auctioneer and estate agent, Bath.

1878 — appointed a member of the newly-established Natal Council of Education.

1880 Oct. — elected Speaker of the Legislative Council (9th Council).

1881–2 — served on the Natal Native Commission.

1882 — elected Speaker (10th Council).

1883 — elected Speaker (11th Council).

1884 — Chairman of the Customs Conference with the O.F.S. at Harrismith.

1886 — represented Natal at the Colonial and Indian Exhibition in London.

1886 — elected Speaker of Legislative Council (12th Council).

1887 — created K.C.M.G. on the occasion of Queen Victoria's Golden Jubilee, the first Natal person in elective office to receive this honour.

1888 Jan. — a Natal delegate at the Cape Town Customs Conference.

1888 — *Decisions of the Hon. Sir John William Akerman, Speaker of the Legislative Council (from 28 Oct. 1880 to 28 July 1887)*; compiled by F.W.A. Watson, published in Pmb.

1890 — elected Speaker of the Legislative Council (13th Council).

1892 Apr. — retired from the Legislative Council, owing to ill health.

1893 — *Decisions of the Hon. Sir John William Akerman, Speaker of the Legislative Council (from 19 July 1888 to 4 Aug. 1891)* vol.2 published in Pmb.

1905 June 24 — died at his home in Ealing, London.

Akerman was prominent in various bodies, eg. the Natal Society, the Natal Rifle Association and the Pietermaritzburg Botanic Society. He was also a member of the Royal Colonial Institute.

CHILDREN

James (4–13 Apr. 1853) born and died on the farm *Pampoen Nek*, Umvoti County.

Sarah Jane (born and died May 1854, buried in Pmb.).

Elizabeth Charlotte (16 Oct. 1855, Pmb. – 1926)
m. (1) 17 Dec. 1878, ?Pmb., Thomas Daniel Barry (21 Nov. 1833, Swellendam – 18 Oct. 1890), son of Joseph Barry (1796–1865) and his wife Johanna Martina v. Reenen. Thomas was a Cape M.L.A.
m. (2) 25 Feb. 1895, Mowbray, Cape, Robert Crosby, M.L.A. for Albany, Cape.

Katherine Stantial (Feb. 1858, Pmb. — June 1859, ?Pmb.) died in childhood.

Conrad (Oct. 1878, ?Pmb. — Aug. 1975, Pmb.)
  m. (1) 1915, ?Pmb., Ethel Marion Harwin (c. 1880, Pmb. — Feb. 1918, Pmb.), d. of John and Eliza Harwin of *Sans Souci*, Pmb.
  m. (2) 1920, Vera Florence Stott (Jan. 1898, — 27 Nov. 1978, Pmb.), d. of Clement Horner Stott.

SOURCES

Private source material
  4; **17**; **29** Akerman papers; **34** Box 2. Surveyors' and Immigrants' correspondence book — *British Tar* immigrants to Moreland 26.10.1850, Akerman to Moreland 18.12.1850, 31.12.1850, 17.4.1851, E. Tatham to Moreland 26.5.1851. Box 4. *British Tar* list; **77**; **102**

Unpublished official sources
  125 16(1) no.7, 103 no.R275, 2242 no.C348, 2244 no.D284, 2247 no.D770, 2286; **126** 65; **127** 52 no.6, p.95; **129** 37/18, 37/214; **131** IV/3/67 nos.37, 57, 65; **132** III/5/25 no.180; **147**; **156** 103/1898, 156/1905
  132 III/5/25 no.180; **147**; **156** 103/1898, 156/1905

Official printed sources
  166; **168** 5.5.1868, 12.1.1869, 24.5.1870, 2.9.1873, 16.3.1875; **171**

Newspapers, periodicals, etc.
  179 17.10.1855; **184** 21.10.1852, 28.4.1853; **185** 19.5.1853, 20.1.1877, 7.1.1878; **189** 11.9.1854, 22.9.1854, 29.9.1854, 20.7.1855, 18.10.1855, 5.2.1858, 6.8.1858, 5.8.1859, 12.8.1859, 16.1.1877, 28.1.1877, 5.1.1878, 5.3.1895, 17.5.1916, 3.12.1962, 8.10.1968, 28.11.1978; **197** 1863–1874, 1879–1882, 1888; **200**

Miscellaneous unofficial contemporary printed sources
  218 v.2, p.778

Later sources
  240 p.157; **243** p.267; **250**; **252**; **261** p.357; **267** pp.172–3, 327; **276** pp.121–2; **307** p.257; **308** p.362; **309** p.25; **321**

Personal communication
  334

Portraits, photographs, etc.
  305 p.29

ALBOROUGH, William

Born c. 1808, Forncett St Mary, Norfolk. Died 7 Aug. 1878, *New Forncett*, Boston.

Farmer. Alborough and two of his three children, William and Jane, came to Natal with Bishop Colenso's* missionary party. They landed in May 1855 on the *Jane Morice*. They were not members of the missionary group, but had been parishioners of Colenso, who had been rector of Forncett St. Mary before accepting the see of Natal.

After two years in Natal Alborough was still with the Bishop, probably as a tenant farmer. In July 1857, when he applied to the Government for a land grant, he described himself as an 'agriculturist' of *Ekukhanyeni* (the Bishop's mission station).

Alborough was successful in his bid to get a government farm. On 2 Nov. 1857 he was issued with the title to Lot 91, Ward 5, Pietermaritzburg County. This property, which he named *New Forncett*, is near Boston.

Alborough married for the second time on 15 Sep. 1866. His wife was Agnes Graham (c. 1843, Carlisle, Cumberland — Dec. 1922, buried Boston), the daughter of James Graham of Carlisle, and presumably the sister of Rowland Graham*. The marriage took place on Rowland Graham's farm, *Greenwood Park*, near Boston.

After Alborough's death, Agnes remarried in Feb. 1882. James Noble, a Carlisle man, was her second husband. His sister married Thomas Chaplin, son of William Chaplin*.

CHILDREN

A daughter who remained in England.

William (c. 1836, Forncett St Mary — 13 Apr. 1892, Boston) m. June 1863, Pmb., Anne Eliza Sleightholm (c. 1846, Sleights, Yorks. — 19 Aug. 1877, Pmb.), d. of John Sleightholm. This family came to Natal on the *Barbadoes* in June 1861. William farmed at *New Forncett* in the 1860s and early 1870s. By 1876 he was on the farm *Highlands* in the same district.

Jane (c. 1838, Forncett St Mary — Nov. 1901, Cato Ridge) m. Sep. 1862, Pmb., Robert Bloy (born Jan. 1838, Stratton St. Michael, Norfolk), brother of F.R. Bloy*. Robert Bloy had come to Natal in June 1858 on the *Lady of the Lake*. At the time of her death (during the second Anglo-Boer War) Jane was a refugee from the Transvaal. According to her estate papers she owned a small house in Elsburg, Transvaal.

Edward (17 July 1867, Boston — 10 Mar. 1952, buried Bulwer) m. Blanche Mildred ?— (c. 1886 — Nov. 1952, buried Bulwer).

James Rowland (born 21 Mar. 1869, ?Boston) m. 23 Nov. 1893, Pmb., Gertrude Annie Mare (born c. 1873), d. of Samuel Mare.

John Graham (23 Oct. 1870, Boston – Aug. 1949, buried Malton) m. Oct. 1897, Pmb., Amy Elizabeth Smith (June 1870 – July 1926, buried Malton), d. of William and Sarah Ann Smith and grand-daughter of William Smith (died 1876)*.

Isabella Alice (born *c*. 1873, ?Boston) m. 25 Sep. 1890, Boston, Henry Tarboton (*c*. 1871 – 4 Jan. 1920, Eshowe), grandson of Henry Tarboton*.

George Nunn (born *c*. 1874, ?Boston) m. July 1901, Pmb., Fanny Shackleford (*c*. 1875, Natal – 29 Jan. 1942, New Hanover).

Agnes (born Mar. 1875, ?Boston) ?died young.

SOURCES

Private source material
  54; **59**; **71**; **76**; **77**; **78**; **87**; **88**; **98**

Unpublished official papers
  125 2283. 2284. 2287; **126** 73; **129** 11/447;
  131 IV/23/2 no. 190; **132** III/5/24 no. 6, III/12/1
  p. 91; **134**; **141**; **145**; **147**; **149**; **156** 364/1878,
  43/1892

Official printed sources
  168 14.8.1860, 6.8.1867, 16.8.1870, 20.8.1872,
  25.8.1874, 29.9.1874, 15.8.1876; **174** p. 322

Newspapers, periodicals, etc.
  185 Aug. 1867; **189** 31.8.1877, 17.8.1878,
  13.2.1882, 30.9.1890, 21.4.1892, 14.1.1920;
  197 1879, 1881

Later sources
  280 p. 52; **310** p. 9; **321**

ALDER, Charles

Born *c*. Jan. 1819, England. Died 19 May 1905, Durban.

Bricklayer. Alder was in Natal by Dec. 1848. How and when he arrived in the Colony is not known.

By Dec. 1851 he was living in Durban and working at his trade. From a power of attorney he gave to a firm of London lawyers at this time it emerges that he was in some way connected with a certain John Williams Alder, deceased, late of 28 Duke Street, Lincolns Inn Fields. This presumably indicates a relationship with John Williams Alder*.

By May 1853 he was living at 'the Umlaas', possibly near Richmond. This assumption is made from the fact that early in 1860 two of his children were baptised in that village.

Information about Alder's movements is sketchy. It appears that *c*. 1861 he was at the Umvoti. 'The Umvoti'

is an ambiguous term, it could mean the Greytown district, or it could be the coastal area at the Umvoti river mouth.

He is next heard of at Verulam in 1869, when his eldest daughter was married. He remained in Verulam earning a living as a bricklayer until about the mid–1880s.

By the end of 1887 both he and his son James were working as bricklayers at Groutville.

Alder's wife's name was Ann, and she died in about 1865.

CHILDREN

Alice Ann (born Sep. 1851) m. 25 Oct. 1869, Verulam, Joseph Brandon [*sic*], son of Thomas Brennan*.

Esther (born May 1853, ?Umlaas) m. May 1871, Verulam, George Williamson.

James Charles (June 1855 – 9 Nov. 1915, ?Dbn) m. Apr. 1878, Verulam, Agnes Huntley Johnson, d. of William Johnson*.

Rosa Cassandra (Mar. 1857 – 11 Nov. 1905, Dbn) m. 18 Dec. 1875, Verulam, Isaac Oliver*.

Rosa Ann (born July 1859)

Jessie (*c*. 1861, Umvoti – 27 July 1909, Dbn) m. Mar. 1887, Verulam, John Josiah Paskin (*c*. 1835, Grahamstown – June 1900, ?Verulam), widower of Hendrina Johanna Catharina v.d. Merwe, widow of James Melville*.

Emily (1863 – 1947, buried Ladysmith) m. Mar. 1882, Verulam, James Mill Adam (born *c*. 1856).

Charles William

SOURCES

Private source material
  77; **80**; **84**; **85**; **91**; **97**

Unpublished official papers
  125 2237 no.994, 2283, 2288; **129** 23/143, 24/225,
  36/107, 41/74; **131** IV/23/21 no.11; **137**

Official printed sources
  168 15.9.1874, 18.7.1876, 22.8.1876

Newspapers, periodicals, etc.
  185 Oct. 1869, 23.12.1875, 13.4.1878;
  189 28.12.1875, 16.4.1878;
  197 1879, 1881, 1882, 1884, 1888.

ALDER, John Williams

Born *c*. 1828.

A bricklayer who arrived on the *Minerva* with his wife, Sarah, (born *c*. 1829). Three months later their first child was baptised in Durban. Alder did not take up his 40 acre allotment, viz. 144 *Dunbar* nor his village erf at Byrne (7 Block M). This land eventually became liable to forfeiture to the Government in Sep. 1873 under Law 4, 1872.

The last reference to him is the fact that an unclaimed letter was awaiting him at the Durban Post Office in Mar. 1851.

It would seem that he was related to Charles Alder* as a power of attorney executed by the latter in Dec.1851 reveals his connexion with one John Williams Alder, deceased, late of Lincolns Inn Fields, London.

CHILD

James Abel (born Sep. 1850, ?Dbn).

SOURCES

Private source material
44

Unpublished official papers
125 2263 no.H287; **126** 64; **131** IV/23/21 no.11

Newspapers, periodicals, etc.
189 21.3.1851

ALDRICH, George

Born *c.* 1816.

He arrived on the *Devonian*. According to the passenger list Aldrich was a farm servant. He did not claim his 20 acres at *Harmony*, Illovo (no.125), nor his Richmond village allotment (8 Block E within circle). This land finally became liable to forfeiture in Sep. 1873 under Law 4, 1872.

In Mar. 1857 he was in custody for 'feloniously' taking possession of 'securities' addressed to Dr C.M. Aldridge*, which had come by steamer from the Cape and were to be left at the Post Office until called for. In the following month he was acquitted on a charge of fraud and theft arising from this occurrence. Nothing further has been discovered about his movements. Perhaps he was the Mr Aldrich of Zwaart Kei, Cape Colony, whose death on 9 Jan. 1881 from the effects of snakebite was reported in the *Natal Mercury*.

SOURCES

Private source material
34 Box 4. *Devonian* lists

Unpublished official papers
125 2263 no.H287

Newspapers, periodicals, etc.
185 15.1.1881, **187** 21.3.1857; **189** 24.4.1857

Later sources
271 p.64

ALDRIDGE, Dr Charles Miller

Born 1813. Died 5 Apr. 1885, London.

M.D., M.R.C.S. (Edinburgh). He was the son of Edward Bright Aldridge and his wife, Rachel.

Aldridge and his wife, Caroline Amelia, came to Natal in Mar. 1857 on the *Rory Brown*. He was in Natal for over two years before he sought a licence to practise medicine in the Colony. The Government Notice granting him this permission was dated 6 May 1859.

Aldridge built up his practice in Pietermaritzburg. He became the medical referee for the Natal Fire Assurance and Trust Company until it went into liquidation in 1867, one of the many casualties during the depression of the mid–1860s. The Prophet Ignoramus in his unique phraseology puts it thus, 'As for the Heffanhay [F. and A.], it has gone to Gehenna, and left the Rabbi Turncow [its Secretary, J.W. Turnbull, a lawyer] and the Hakim Newridge in the lurch.'

In 1866 Aldridge became the Surgeon of Grey's Hospital. Shortly after, he presented the hospital with a library of about 600 volumes for the use of the patients.

From *c.* January to *c.* June 1869 Aldridge acted as District Surgeon, Pietermaritzburg County, during the absence on leave of Dr Samuel Gower*. He resigned preparatory to returning to England and was succeeded by Dr Charles Gordon as Acting District Surgeon, while Dr W.J. Otto acted as Hospital Surgeon. The Aldridges left in August on the steamer *Natal*. Before he left Pietermaritzburg Aldridge was presented with an inscribed plate and a purse of 200 guineas 'for services extending over ten years'. This indicates that his connexion with the Hospital, albeit in an unofficial capacity, dated back to the beginning of his practice in the Colony. His obituary in the *Natal Witness* describes him as 'a constant attendant at, and valuable helper to, Grey's Hospital in its early days'.

The Aldridges came back to Natal in Feb.1871 on the *Beethoven*, and he resumed his post at Grey's. He finally resigned and returned to England in the latter part of 1876.

By Sep. 1883 the Aldridges were living in Pemberton Terrace, Upper Holloway. Here it was that he died.

Dr Aldridge's ledger, a massive tome covering the years 1862 to 1869, is housed in the Natal Society Library,

Pietermaritzburg. It contains full details of his patients' accounts.

CHILD

Rachel (born 18 Jan. 1859, Pmb.).

SOURCES

Unpublished official papers
   126 73, 74, 75; **129** 4/120; **131** IV/23/2
   no.15/1867; **156** 40/1885

Official printed sources
   163 29.9.1874; **168** 26.1.1869, 22.6.1869

Newspapers, periodicals, etc.
   185 27.1.1859; **189** 21.1.1859, 12.5.1885;
   197 1863–67, 1872, 1874

Miscellaneous unofficial contemporary printed sources
   219 Book 1, Chapter 10

Later sources
   242 pp.216, 225; **271** pp.64, 67

ALISON, Frederic William

Born c. 1825, Liverpool. Died 3 Apr. 1866, Mauritius.
Clerk. He was the son of one J.W. Alison.

Alison and his wife emigrated to Natal on the *Henrietta*. He did not take up his allotments at Byrne, but settled in Durban. He sold his claim to the Byrne land to H. Tarboton*. In 1863 Tarboton tried to take title to this land, viz., 81 *Dunbar* (40 acres) and 8 Block K in Byrne, but as Alison had not been an approved emigrant his land had reverted to the estate of J.C. Byrne & Co., and Tarboton was unable to get any assistance in the matter from the Natal government. This land appeared on a list of unclaimed Byrne allotments subject to government forfeiture compiled in 1873 by the Registrar of Deeds office.

By Jan. 1854 the Alisons were living near Pine Terrace in Durban. When their first child was baptised in May 1851, Alison, in the parish register, was stated to be a 'gentleman'. Despite this, in those days, meaningful appellation, Alison was not a man of means, and both he and his wife worked. Mrs Alison nursed in various private Durban homes, and Alison was a clerk.

Prior to June 1863 Alison went through a period of unemployment. He eventually decided to try his hand at trading to help support his wife and children, a decision which was to bring much hardship to the Alison family.

Dickinson, Munro & Co. (i.e. R.W. Dickinson* and W. Munro*) agreed to let Alison have goods on credit if his promissory note was signed by a person of standing.

As Mrs Alison had been nursing the wife of E.P. Lamport*, Alison got her to approach Lamport for his signature. Lamport understandably declined. Very soon afterwards he left on a voyage to Mauritius, and Alison succumbed to the temptation to forge his signature on a promissory note for £35. The merchandise was handed over and Alison set off from Durban. Unfortunately the goods were so damaged by water in the rivers he had to cross that they were rendered unsaleable. Eventually he returned to Durban without having disposed of a single article. The few unspoilt items were sold in Durban by the Alisons to procure the bare necessities for their family. When, after four months, the bill became due, Lamport repudiated it, and Alison gave himself up. In Feb. 1864 he was sentenced to two years' hard labour.

This placed his family in a distressing situation and they were almost wholly dependent on public charity. After petitions for clemency submitted in Aug. 1864, Oct. 1864 and Feb. 1865, Alison's sentence was finally remitted in March 1865.

Until this lapse Alison had borne a good character. The fact that 70 Durban residents drew up a petition which was submitted together with Mrs Alison's petition (Oct. 1864) for her husband's release, would seem to substantiate this. Also noteworthy is the fact that two of those who had suffered through Alison's action, came to the aid of the family. William Munro and his wife paid Mrs Alison's rent for several months, while E.P. Lamport, in Feb. 1865, submitted a letter expressing his belief that Alison's case should be favourably treated. It ran into ten pages and stressed the appalling conditions in the Durban Gaol, where, because of lack of security, prisoners were kept in chains at night, as well as in the daytime. Lamport claimed to be able to speak with authority, having more than ten years previously been a member of a commission that reported on the Durban Gaol. He also referred to the case of a 'systematic swindler' who had taken in people to the amount of several hundred pounds, and who, after a long period awaiting trial, was sentenced to only six months' imprisonment. One reason for this was the judge's opinion that his confinement in the Durban Gaol before trial was in itself a severe punishment.

Alison was released shortly after Lamport's appeal. He died in Mauritius just over a year later.

Alison's wife was Mary Ann Oliver Rimmer (c. 1827, Liverpool – 6 Feb. 1879, Pinetown). After his premature death she remarried. This marriage took place in Durban on 5 Oct. 1868. Her second husband was a boatman named Caleb Allen who in the early 1870s was a canteenkeeper of Umgeni near Durban. From 1876 to 1877 Mrs Allen was the postmistress at Queen's Bridge, Umgeni.

CHILDREN

Frederick William (1 Jan. 1851, ?Dbn – Jan. 1920, Pmb.)
   m. Apr. 1877, Dbn, Elizabeth McNicol, d. of Archibald

McNicol*. Frederick was a hotelkeeper of Umgeni, in the 1870s.

Lydia Jane (born 21 Sep. 1853, Dbn) m. June 1881, Pmb., James Patrick, son of Edwin Patrick*.

Mary Fanny (born 3 May 1856, ?Pinetown) m. 23 July 1878, Dbn, James Logan, probably the son of J.F. Logan*.

Alice Onslow (20 Oct. 1858, ?Dbn – 23 July 1944, Hillcrest) m. 13 Jan. 1885, Dbn, Thomas William Winn.

Meta Cecilia (27 Aug. 1860, Dbn – 26 Apr. 1891, Greenwood Park, near Dbn) m. 18 Dec. 1884, Dbn, Robert Fullerton Logan, son of J.F. Logan above.

Ellen Patience (born 1 Jan. 1864, ?Dbn)

SOURCES

Private source material
34 Box 4. *Henrietta* lists; **41**; **43**; **44**; **74**; **104**

Unpublished official papers
125 2242 no.C351, 2253 nos.F166, F308, F332, 2254, no.F377, 2263 no.H287, 2286, 2287, 2288; **129** 4/231, 5/33, 9/123; **137**; **147**; **148**

Official printed sources
166; **168** 20.8.1872, 1.9.1874, 15.9.1874, 18.7.1876, 22.8.1876

Newspapers, periodicals, etc.
185 4.1.1854, Supp.22.5.1934; **189** 12.7.1850

Portraits, photographs, etc.
362 (Mrs Alison)

ALLAN, John

A Yorkshireman who arrived in 1851 with his wife and daughter on the *Jane Morice*. Accompanying them were Thomas Allan* and family. Perhaps he was the John Allen [*sic*], a farmer of 16 Church Street, Pietermaritzburg, listed in 1854 in the *Natal Government Gazette* list of voters, and the John Allen [*sic*], a farmer of 28 Burger Street, entered in the 1860–61 Pietermaritzburg County jury list.

In all probability the Mrs Martha Allen [*sic*] who died on 5 July 1878 aged 80 was his widow. She died at her Burger Street residence. According to the *Natal Witness* her husband had been John Allen [*sic*] of Exby [*sic*] Grange, Yorkshire. The name Exby cannot be verified. There is however an Exelby very near Burneston from where Thomas Allan came. Query – was Thomas Allan the son of this couple? Further proof linking Martha with John comes from the *Natal Almanac*. From 1871 issues carried an entry for Mrs Allen [*sic*], a widow of 28 Burger Street.

CHILDREN

Martha (*c.* 1833, Yorks. – 31 Dec. 1910, Normandien, near Newcastle)
  m. (1) Nov. 1851, Frederick William Good, son of James Good*.
  m. (2) Dec. 1856, Pmb., Alexander Jacques*.
  m. (3) 27 Apr. 1895, *Upper Gourton*, Weenen County, James McNicol Gorrie.

?Thomas (born *c.* 1825) (see Thomas Allan below)

SOURCES

Private source material
26 21.4.1851, 2.7.1851

Unpublished official papers
125 2282; **129** 3/4 no.23, 40/187; **147**

Official printed sources
168 8.8.1854, 14.8.1860

Newspapers, periodicals, etc.
184 10.7.1851; **189** 11.7.1851, 11.7.1878; **197** 1871–72, 1874, 1876

ALLAN, Thomas

Born *c.* 1825, Yorkshire. Died 2 Jan. 1897, Ladysmith.

Constable and builder. Allan arrived in Natal on the *Jane Morice* in July 1851. His wife, two children, and a relation, John Allan*, and his family accompanied him. It is possible that John Allan was his father. In the passenger lists both were described as labourers.

By at least Apr. 1853 the Allans were in Ladysmith, where Thomas was employed as a constable. He remained in this post until about the end of 1856. From Nov. 1854, after the resignation of H. Urquhart*, he had the additional responsibility of being poundmaster at Ladysmith.

During 1857, 1858 and part of 1859 Allan worked in Ladysmith as a labourer. For a short time thereafter he was a baker. By Aug. 1860 he was a bricklayer, and from at least Jan. 1862 was working as a mason. The 1862–63 Klip River County jury list (published Aug. 1862) describes him as a builder. Thereafter he appears to have stuck to this trade. It was he who built the earliest school buildings at Hilton College. G.A. Lucas*, magistrate at Ladysmith and co-founder of Hilton, arranged for Allan to go to his farm *Upper Hilton* in Jan. 1872, when the school first opened, and erect the necessary buildings.

The Allan family's connexion with Hilton thus dates from the school's earliest days. Allan's eldest son, Thomas, was the first pupil entered in the school register, and his youngest child, born within two years of the school's beginnings, was given 'Hilton' as a second name. After Tom junior's school career was completed he worked at Hilton, supervising farming operations for Lucas. When, in 1882, Lucas finally disposed of his interest in the farm, Tom became the owner of 600 acres of it. To this day Thomas senior's portrait hangs in the Campbell Hall at the school.

By 1888, when their daughter Alice was married, the Allans were living on the farm *Geluk* near Colenso, where another daughter, Annie Laura Robinson and her husband farmed.

Allan's wife was Ann Robinson (*c*. 1825, Ripon, Yorks. — 23 Sep. 1902, Ladysmith).

CHILDREN

Mary (*c*. 1847, Burneston, Yorks. — ?O.F.S.) m. Nov. 1864, Pmb., Samuel John Friday*.

Elizabeth (*c*. 1851, Burneston, Yorks. — 9 Mar. 1909, Estcourt)
  m. (1) 5 May 1866, Ladysmith, Samuel Edward Shackelton*.
  m. (2) 3 July, 1889, Dbn, James Glenn (born *c*. 1855) an inspector on the N.G.R.

Thomas John (Jan. 1853, Ladysmith — 11 Aug. 1908, Pmb.)
  m. (1) 10 Oct. 1876, *Vearsdale*, near Howick, Mary Vear, d. of William Vear*.
  m. (2) 18 June, 1891, Pmb., Alice Henrietta Laurens (4 Mar. 1862, ?Jersey — June 1922, Pmb.), d. of Philip and Ann Laurens (born Le Sueur) of Mid-Illovo, formerly of Jersey.

Martha Ann (born 30 June 1855, ?Ladysmith) m. 7 Aug. 1875, Ladysmith, Philip Andrew Border (born *c*. 1854).

William Lawson (3 Feb. 1857, Ladysmith — 22 Jan. 1879, Isandlwana) unmarried.

Edwin George (23 Mar. 1859, ?Ladysmith — 7 Apr. 1861, ?Ladysmith) died in childhood.

Annie Laura (born 22 May 1861, ?Ladysmith) m. 1 Nov. 1882, Ladysmith, John Robinson, son of Charles Robinson (*c*. 1815 — 1883)*.

Henry Lawson (born 21 Nov. 1863, ?Ladysmith).

Alfred Friday (?Jan. 1866, ?Ladysmith — 16 June 1896, Pretoria) m. May 1894, Indaleni, Mary Emma Bowman (born May 1867, ?Pmb.), d. of Thomas Bowman (*c*. 1830–1925) of *Antiford*, Mid-Illovo, and his wife Jane (born McCulloch). Alfred was a farmer of *Geluk Drift*, Ladysmith when he married.

Alice Jane (born 7 Oct. 1869, Ladysmith) m. 7 Mar. 1888, *Geluk*, near Colenso, Charles Henry Robinson, son of Charles Robinson above.

Sophia Robinson (born 11 Sep. 1871, Ladysmith) m. ? Dahl.

Lilly Hilton (19 Sep. 1873, Ladysmith — 14 Mar. 1875, ?Ladysmith) died in childhood.

SOURCES

Private source material
  57; **60**; **64**; **66**; **71**; **72**; **76**; **79**; **97**; **99**

Unpublished official papers
  125 2245 no.D481, 2284, 2286; **126** 73;
  129 5/135, 6/249, 7/145, 14/219, 33/154,
  35/77; **131** IV/19/46 no. 4; **142**; **143**; **147**; **150**;
  156 58/1902, 180/1908, 121/1909

Official printed sources
  166 1856; **168** 2.8.1860, 12.8.1862, 15.8.1865,
  20.8.1867, 17.8.1869, 13.8.1872, 15.9.1874,
  18.7.1876

Newspapers, periodicals, etc.
  189 13.10.1876, 15.2.1879, 12.3.1888, 20.6.1896,
  17.8.1905; **197** 1881, 1884, 1888, 1895

Later sources
  270 pp.26, 44; **295** p.7; **305** p.564; **310** p.10

Personal communication
  347

Portraits, photographs, etc.
  360

ALLANSON, George G.

Born *c*. 1810.

Allanson emigrated on the *Henrietta*. His occupation was given in the passenger lists as 'labourer'. He did not claim his Byrne allotments, viz. 132 *Dunbar*, and 10 Block M in Byrne village and this land eventually became liable to forfeiture to the Government in Sep. 1873.

Presumably he was the George Allanson, a man of a 'most respectable' Lancashire family who, early in 1852, had been in the employ of R.C. Rawlinson*. Shortly after leaving Rawlinson he was, in Apr. 1852, prosecuted for forgery and in June, sentenced to five years' imprisonment with hard labour. In Aug. 1853, Rawlinson, one of the parties who had prosecuted him, petitioned the Lt.-Governor for mitigation of Allanson's sentence. He maintained that when he had left his service, Allanson had been a man of 'unblemished character', who had been 'much emaciated' in body and 'entirely disabled' from supporting himself by labour, and was 'absolutely houseless and hopeless'. Rawlinson considered that the state of despair he was in had affected his mind and that this was the reason for his crime. He explained that although Allanson had been in prison only a short time, he, Rawlinson, was leaving the Colony and wished his memorial to be taken into account should Allanson's case come up for review some time in the future.

Allanson remained in the Pietermaritzburg Gaol until about the end of 1855, or early 1856. In Feb. 1856, a report appeared in the press cautioning people against him, as he had attempted to borrow money from Durbanites, maintaining that E.P. Lamport* had received funds from England on his behalf.

It would appear that in later years he once again fell foul of the law. A George Allanson, aged about 60, was sentenced, in Aug. 1868, to three years with hard labour for horse-stealing. In Apr. 1870 he petitioned the Lt.-Governor from the Pietermaritzburg Gaol for a remission of sentence. In this memorial he stated that, if released, he intended returning to the O.F.S. where he had a little property and 'a few friends'. He was given the usual remission — i.e. release after serving two-thirds of his sentence.

Possibly he was the George Allanson, who, when the Weenen School was established in 1859, was appointed first schoolmaster. He appears to have remained there until about 1864. From Nov. 1860 to Dec. 1861 he was also the village postmaster, and in 1861 acted as poundmaster. This George Allanson married Lucy Emily, the daughter of J.D. Gregory*, and died c. 1875. The only child born to him and Lucy, Robert (Feb. 1861, Weenen — May 1921, ?Dbn), was later in the firm Allanson & Sommer, sanitary engineers, in Durban. Robert's wife was Jane, who died in Apr. 1949 aged 76.

SOURCES

Private source material
   76; 92

Unpublished official papers
   125 2242 no.C510, 2258 no.G226, 2263 no.H287;
   126 64; 129 23/246

Official printed sources
   168 20.11.1860, 15.1.1861, 24.12.1861

Newspapers, periodicals, etc.
   185 22.2.1856; 197 1865, 1866

Journals, biographies, autobiographies, letters
   212 p.14

Later sources
   318

ALLEN, James

This settler was in Natal as early as 1846. On 2 April of that year he married Georgina Sophia Christina Muller. One child, Johanna Petronella, was born on 12 Jan. 1849 and was baptised in Pietermaritzburg on 28 January.

Possibly he was the James Allen who later went to Utrecht. This James Allen's wife died at Utrecht on 17 May 1879 aged 49 years, 5 months, 11 days. A month earlier, on 21 April, Sara Cornelia Allen (born c. 1857) had been married at Utrecht to Edwin Dixon (c. 1852 — 29 Oct. 1901, Newcastle). This couple afterwards lived in Frankfort, O.F.S.

Another child was possibly James Christiaan Allen of *Grootvlei*, Utrecht, who married Hester Johanna Magdalena Jordaan (8 Jan. 1857 — 18 Dec. 1905, *Grootvlei*), daughter of Peter Willem and Anna Jordaan (born de Winnaar).

SOURCES

Private source material
   75

Unpublished official papers
   153; 156 74/1902, 139/1906

Newspapers, periodicals, etc.
   189 17.4.1846, 21.3.1851, 25.5.1878, 2.11.1901

ALLEN, Philip

Died 1 July 1865, ?Pietermaritzburg.

Colonial Treasurer, later Resident Magistrate, Newcastle. He was the youngest son of William and Mary Allen (c. 1778–1870), of Liscongill (unverified), Co. Cork, Ireland.

Allen was appointed Treasurer for Natal on 7 Aug. 1852. He was living in Woolwich at the time. He arrived in the colony on 7 November on the *Sir Robert Peel*, and took up his post on the 11th.

By the end of 1852 he was residing on erf 32 Church Street. However by Apr. 1854 he had purchased part of erf 35 Pietermaritz Street. His wife and four children joined him only in Oct. 1854, having arrived from Liverpool on the *Rydal*. Travelling with them was Allen's sister, Christabella, and her maid. Christabella later married G.A. Lucas*.

In Allen's job as Treasurer the first major crisis he had to deal with, the outcome of which was to blight the rest of his career, was the robbery of the Treasury chest. This took place over the week-end 29–30 Oct. 1854. At the end of June, when there had been over £4 000 in the large chest after the collection of native hut tax, Allen had raised the question of security. After some delay it was decided that the large chest be kept in the commissariat office at Fort Napier and that only money for current expenditure be kept in the smaller one in the Treasury.

This was the one that was burgled. Of the £633-odd

stolen, £109-odd, mostly in silver, was discovered on the following Wednesday when a proper search was made of the two rooms comprising the Treasury Office. Idle rumour fastened suspicion on various people, Allen and his clerk, J.P. Symons*, being two of these. One of the pointers against Allen was the fact that since he had taken over as Treasurer there had been no checking of the balances in the chest by the Auditor. Official instructions required this to be done every three months. Another was his weak financial position, and the refusal of his recent application for an increase in his £300 p.a. salary.

However the authorities, despite his negligence re the audits, took his integrity for granted and appointed him to carry out the official investigation into the robbery. With the Secretary of State for the Colonies breathing down their necks the Natal officials bestirred themselves to an unusual degree. Eight hours a day for nine days the Acting Crown Prosecutor, H. Cope*, the Pietermaritzburg Resident Magistrate, Sir T. St George* and Allen examined witnesses, and Allen's report when finally submitted was accompanied by 177 pages of evidence. Furthermore, Allen and St George had been 'out at night watching persons'. The search later moved to Durban and departing passengers had their luggage searched. Moreland* in particular was one on whom suspicion fell. Not only his baggage, but he himself was searched. He was about to sail to Cape Town on the steamer and had with him a fully-grown lion he was taking to England. The lion's cage was a suggested cache, but no one felt enough motivation to investigate. The money was never found. The indignities to which he had been subject made an indelible impression upon Moreland, of which more anon.

Allen as Colonial Treasurer was second in importance only to the Colonial Secretary. In Nov. 1856, under the Natal Charter, he took his place as a member of the Executive Council. During the interval between the departure from Natal of W.C. Sargeaunt and the arrival of Major D. Erskine, viz. July 1857 to June 1858, Allen was acting Colonial Secretary, while John Bird* took over the Treasury.

In June 1858, just before the first settlers under the new government immigration scheme began arriving, the *Natal Star* announced Allen's appointment as Emigration Agent. In July the *Natal Mercury* reported that Allen and J. Henderson*, the Emigration Commissioners, had arrived in Durban to meet the second emigrant ship to arrive, the *Phantom*. Allen also on occasion acted as the Secretary for Native Affairs and as the Resident Magistrate for Pietermaritzburg.

Allen took an active part in the life of the community. At the first general meeting of shareholders of the Natal Bank in May 1854 he was elected to the Board of Directors. Afterwards he became its first Chairman. He committed an indiscretion in regard to the Natal Bank for he deposited government funds therein before it had even received its charter of incorporation and without the knowledge of the Lt.-Governor. Other interests included the Pietermaritzburg Agricultural Society of which he was the President from July to Dec. 1857, and the Victoria Club. Allen was one of the ten 'Originators' when it was founded in 1859. He was also one of the foundation members of the Natal Carbineers. In 1855 he was elected the first lieutenant of the Pietermaritzburg troop and in 1858 became the Lt.-Colonel of the corps. In this year when a government force of Europeans and Africans was sent against the chief Matyana, Allen was appointed its commander.

Allen was one of Prince Alfred's aides-de-camp during the latter's passage through Natal in Sep. 1860. During the visit he gained the impression during conversation with Sir George Grey, the High Commissioner, that it might be necessary to appoint a commissioner of the country south of Natal. In the following month Allen petitioned the Acting Lt.-Governor about this, having understood that in all probability the salary for such a post would be higher than his £450 p.a. He requested that he be recommended to the High Commissioner for this appointment. He stressed his experience with the indigenous tribes both as Acting Resident Magistrate, as Acting Secretary for Native Affairs and as commander of the Matyana expedition. Allen did not make any headway with this application. He was informed that at the time no such appointment was contemplated.

During his first years in Natal, Allen had acquired, besides his Pietermaritz Street property, a small farm outside Pietermaritzburg which he named *Allendale*. By Jan. 1856, however, he had disposed of this latter property. Between 1857 and 1859 he engaged in large-scale property speculation. Besides part of erf 26 Burger Street, Pietermaritzburg, an erf in Fort Nottingham and 45 acres on the Umhloti river, he bought the farms *Vinks River* (4 504 acres), *Spring Grove* (3 066 acres), *Springvale* (3 033 acres) – the two latter abutting on the Mooi river – *Groen Veldt* (2 lots, viz. 2 263 and 3 127 acres) in Weenen County, and *Woodstock* (3 065 acres). These farms had cost him £890, and as was the usual practice in Natal, he bought them on credit. His plan was to sell them by advertising them in the United Kingdom and to this end he issued a prospectus. However, his financial position, never strong, deteriorated still further before anything came of his plan, and he tried unsuccessfully to have these farms sold by auction. Allen in his pre-Natal days had had a history of financial embarrassments. He had been insolvent in Ireland; later he had been arrested for debt in Bangor, Carnarvonshire, and imprisoned for a short time in Carnarvon Castle; then in 1849, to escape his creditors, he had gone to France. In 1851 he returned to Ireland and in 1852 got benefit from the Insolvent Act.

In Apr. 1861, the month after the scheduled auction of his farms, at a board meeting of the Natal Bank at which

Allen was not present, certain of his liabilities came to the notice of the directors. As a result Joseph Henderson came to him and told him, that as certain of the directors recognised that the bank was under obligations to him, it was suggested that the bank pay off his liabilities and take out mortgages on his landed property. To this end Henderson suggested he make a detailed statement of his assets and liabilities that could be laid before the directors. Should the proposal not be carried the documents would be returned. The information therein would be treated as strictly confidential. On 2 May, before Allen had had an answer from the directors, his affairs 'became a topic of general conversation' and it was obvious that there had been a leak from the Board of Directors. He taxed them with it and called on them to make good the arrangement. This they refused to do. Also on 2 May, and again a few days later, according to Allen, Judge Lushington Phillips had taken an active part in discussing his affairs, and among other remarks had referred to him as 'a fraudulent insolvent'. Allen now found himself called on to meet all his liabilities, and in fact to wind up his affairs. He attributed this sudden emergency to the leak by the Board and the 'circulation of scandal' by a person 'in the high position of a judge'. On 13 May Allen came to an agreement with his creditors whereby they would receive landed and other property in lieu of cash. On the 17th a deed of assignment of all his property to a trustee (P. Ferreira) was drawn up. No portion of his salary, however, was assigned. On the following day he resigned as Chairman of the Natal Bank.

To return to the Treasury chest robbery — Moreland, as a member of the Legislative Council, annually brought up a question on the progress being made in finding the culprits responsible for this robbery and also for that of public monies at Ladysmith. Then in Sep. 1858 he openly stated to J.P. Symons and T.G. Crowly* that Allen had robbed the Treasury chest. On 5 Nov. anonymous letters, signed Guy Faulkes, and laying the robbery at Allen's door, were sent to various prominent people. The result of this was the case *Regina* v. *Moreland*, the charges being those of libel and slander. Judgment was given in Jan. 1859. Moreland's authorship of the letters was not proved, but he was found guilty of slander. As the presiding judge, Lushington Phillips, was unsure whether slander was a crime in Roman-Dutch law no sentence was passed. Allen then sued Moreland for damages, but was awarded only a token £1. Moreland had, however, to give surety for £200 to be of good behaviour to all, and particularly to Philip Allen, for the next twelve months. A couple of months later, Allen sued J.W. Akerman* for heavy damages for libel. Akerman, a recipient of one of the letters, had shown it to one or two friends before destroying it. This case was settled out of court.

In June 1861 Moreland renewed his persecution of Allen when he presented to the Legislative Council the petition of one of Allen's creditors, Thomas Hind*, a builder and bill

discounter, to whom Allen owed £567-odd on promissory notes. Hind had signed Allen's deed of release without fully understanding it and when he realised he would not be paid in full he became difficult. Allen was convinced that Phillips was the author of Hind's petition, but in fact it later came to light that Moreland and James Archbell* had prepared it and then approached Hind. On the Legislative Council's refusing to discuss it Moreland then brought specific charges against Allen and a select committee of the Council was appointed to consider these. After the select committee had submitted its report, Lt.-Governor Scott had the Executive Council deliberate on the charges. They were:

1 Allen had assigned his estate for the benefit of his creditors.
2 He had obtained its release under circumstances highly discreditable to himself.
3 He had speculated in land, chiefly on credit, and was indebted to the Government for large arrears in quitrent.
4 He had damaged the colony by issuing in England a false and coloured prospectus to further his land speculations.
5 He had obtained endorsements to accommodation bills from a clerk in the Colonial Office (viz. T.G. Crowly).
6 He had contravened the spirit of the Natal Bank charter by continuing as chairman after he was disqualified (i.e. having mortgaged his shares).
7 He had sat and voted in the Legislative Council, being at the time a 'notorious defaulter'.
8 That all these circumstances were calculated to create a feeling of distrust and apprehension as to the security of public monies.

The Secretary of State, Lord Newcastle, to whom both the report of the proceedings of the select committee and the minutes of the Executive Council were forwarded, in his answering despatch, dated Feb. 1862, noted with 'great regret' a 'strong indication' of the charges having been influenced by personal feeling. Of the eight only three were substantiated by the select committee, viz. 1, 3 and 5, whereas the Executive Council considered that only numbers 1 and 5 were proved. Both the Executive Council and the Secretary of State took a very serious view of charge 5. Newcastle stated that notwithstanding the freer attitude appertaining in Natal towards such transactions, Allen's conduct was 'highly reprehensible'. Scott was instructed to see that the bills had been liquidated and that Crowly's liability had been terminated. Then he was to convey to Allen a 'grave admonition' and to keep an eye on his proceedings in order to ascertain that he extricated himself honourably from his difficulties and avoided any embarrassment which might render it improper to leave him in a position of such trust as that of Treasurer.

Hind, finding that the Legislative Council would not consider his petition, then sued Allen for the amount of his promissory notes. The case was scheduled to be tried by the Chief Justice, Walter Harding*, and Lushington Phillips on 16 July. A. Walker*, Allen's advocate, recused Phillips on the grounds of his prejudice and hatred towards the defendent, his interference, and the advice given by him to Thomas Hind. He read a petition to the Court by Allen and an affidavit Allen had made, stating that Phillips was prejudiced against him because he, as a member of the Executive Council, had voted for Phillips's suspension from office in Dec. 1859. This had occurred after a difference of opinion between himself and the Lt.-Governor over the case of Thomas Bingham*.

The trial was then deferred. In the meantime Phillips made an affidavit before the Resident Magistrate charging Allen with perjury, and sought a warrant for his arrest. This was refused on the grounds of lack of sufficient evidence. Phillips then went as an advocate before the bar of the Supreme Court and moved for process of court to compel the magistrate to arrest Allen. The Court turned this down. At a subsequent sitting on 25 July, Walker was called upon to prove Allen's petition, and state on what grounds he brought it before the Court. This he did on the following day and without further enquiry the court decided that Phillips should not try the case. On 30 July the case *Hind* v. *Allen* was tried and Hind lost. On 3 September Hind's advocate gave notice that Hind was to withdraw from all further proceedings.

Lushington Phillips was not going to let the position stand. On 12 August he wrote to the Secretary of State on Allen's allegations against his legal impartiality, stating that he had exhausted the means at his disposal for quashing Allen's allegations. Scott, in fairness to Allen, allowed him to see this letter before forwarding it in order that he might also present his side. Allen's letter stated that he had been unable to obtain the enquiry for which he had petitioned before the Court, and said it was his intention to proceed against Phillips for perjury. These two letters were forwarded to London on 30 August. In his answering despatch, dated 30 November, Newcastle instructed Scott merely to inform Phillips that he had received his letter.

Allen instituted proceedings against Phillips, claiming damages for slander. Phillips put in a similar claim against him, the trial being set for 31 Mar. 1862. On 4 April the verdict was given in Phillips's favour, each party to pay its own costs. On the following day Allen sent in to the Lt.-Governor his resignation as Colonial Treasurer. On the same day he resigned as Lt.-Colonel of the Carbineers.

Scott, in reporting the verdict to Newcastle on 1 May, forwarded at Allen's request a letter in which Allen asked that if Newcastle thought the circumstances were not strong enough to require his resignation, he would gladly resume office. If, on the other hand they were, he requested that he be given another post of 'less political importance'. Scott expressed his regret to Newcastle that Lushington Phillips had not also resigned. He considered Allen had

done well to resign as the Government had to contend against much, and to have one of its members before the public in the 'objectionable position' in which the trial had placed Allen, would be a source of weakness. He expressed the opinion that however reprehensible his conduct in his private affairs, Allen had always done his work well. He suggested his appointment as incumbent of the new magistracy beyond the Biggarsberg. Allen, he stated, had frequently acted as magistrate and exhibited a 'peculiar aptitude' for such office. The Secretary of State, in answer, opined that Allen could not have done otherwise than resign. In consequence of Scott's 'highly favourable testimony' he would not object to his being given the new magistracy.

After the Supreme Court verdict Allen once more tried to prove his allegations against Phillips. At the end of May Scott forwarded a letter to Newcastle in which Allen endeavoured to corroborate the truth of his assertions. Newcastle replied that if he could submit specific charges, supported by detailed evidence of misbehaviour against Phillips, he should take the matter to Scott and his Executive Council. If he was not in a position to substantiate his charges, neither he nor the Natal authorities were competent to take any action. Newcastle stated, as his personal opinion, that the matter had reached a point at which it would be best for all parties that it be dropped. As no further correspondence on the subject has been found, it would seem that it was in fact allowed to lapse.

Allen's financial affairs in the meantime were still in the process of being sorted out. In Jan. 1862 Scott had sent to Newcastle an account of the progress made in the liquidation of his liabilities. However, in July he reported to London that Allen's property had failed to realise the expected amount, there being a deficit of about £1 700. He stated that in the circumstances he was postponing any steps on Allen's reinstatement in the public service pending Newcastle's decision. The Secretary of State replied that if Allen was acting with the full knowledge and assent of his creditors and Scott had no reason to suppose there was any 'want of honest and open dealing' in his proceedings, he could use his discretion in maintaining him in his office. In December Scott acknowledged this directive and reported he had provisionally conferred on Allen the magistracy beyond the Biggarsberg. Allen was confirmed in his new post by a despatch from London dated 27 Feb. 1863.

Allen's magistracy came to be known as Newcastle. Here he remained until his death. His last days are vividly depicted in the diary of Theophilus Shepstone*. On Sunday 25 June 1865 Shepstone recorded that Dean Green* had preached a strong sermon in which he alluded personally to members of the congregation and condemned their conduct in 'unmeasured and unwarrantable terms'. Allen walked out of the church. In the evening Allen visited Shepstone and told him he had been troubled in mind and body for months past without a chance of going to church, and that he went that morning craving for comfort but had found none — he had asked for bread and been given a stone — 'he burst into tears and wept like a child'. The entry for the following day records that Shepstone had heard that Allen's mind was quite thrown off balance and that it had been necessary to remove his pistols and razors. James Rorke* had been sent to sit up with him. On 27 June Shepstone wrote that Allen had eluded Rorke, found his pistol and shot himself in the head, 'stunning mournful news — there is no hope of his recovery'. He died four days later.

Within two days of his death his executor dative, William Martin*, surrendered his estate. Only in May 1868 was the final liquidation account filed.

As a member of the public service Allen had been 'zealous' and 'active.', two of Scott's adjectives. On one occasion Scott wrote of him to the Secretary of State as an 'honourable and meritorious public servant', while on another he stated Allen had discharged his duties so as to merit his 'confidence and approval'. Allen seems however to have had a difficult personality. An example of the sort of image he presented to most colonists comes from an entry in the diary of H.E. Knight* dated 8 Apr. 1861. Commenting on the case of Dr T.T. Kelly*, Resident Magistrate for Klip River, he wrote, '*Allen* has without doubt been prime mover in the enquiry against Kelly and as a result Lucas (Allen's brother-in-law) sits in Kelly's place — which is *suggestive* at least — I shall now be curious to mark how *Allen* fares, he has attained apparently his object, and poor Kelly at any rate will never thwart him more, now let us mark how it will go with the *victor*.' Prophetic words perhaps, seeing that it was in the same month that the directors of the Natal Bank came to learn about his liabilities, an event which marked the beginning of his downfall.

The politics and society of the small Natal community were at this time riddled with cliques and animosities. Allen had many enemies. He was impatient and tactless with the private members of the Legislative Council. In particular, in acting as Colonial Secretary, and thus spokesman for the Government, he had antagonized them. In his own words, written in Sep. 1861, this time was the 'most stormy period that has marked the restless career of that body', with himself 'fearlessly' endeavouring to do his duty as a member of the Council and on occasion to 'expose the unscrupulous attempts of some of the elective members to mislead the public with regard to the acts of the Government'. Moreland's enmity towards him, as we have seen, was of long standing. Proceedings of the House were on more than one occasion adjourned to allow tempers to cool after clashes between the two of them. Lushington Phillips too was a powerful enemy. Having had a brush with the executive himself, he was popular with the anti-government faction in the Council, who attacked the government generally and in particular those of its members who were also in the House. In reporting Allen's resignation as Treasurer to Lord Newcastle Scott stated that his enemies had worked secretly and often unscrupulously to bring about his downfall. A significant observation he made in this despatch was to the effect that there were many people in Natal, who if they had had to pass through the same ordeal, would not stand in any better position than Allen. He deprecated the system of credit and bill accommodation that permeated the entire colony.

Allen's wife was Frances Cocks, daughter of the Hon. Philip James Cocks (1774–1857), of Stepple Hall, Shropshire, Lt.-Colonel of the 1st Foot Guards and M.P. for Reigate, and his wife Frances Herbert (died 1871). The Hon. Philip was the second son of Lord Somers, Baron of Evesham, and his second wife, Anne Pole. Allen and his wife were married on 17 Oct. 1847.

Little is known of the later history of Allen's immediate family. His wife Frances appears to have been in Natal as late as Nov. 1867. By 1874 however she was living in Portland Road, London. In 1876 and 1879 when T. Shepstone visited her in London her address was Norland Square, off the Bayswater Road, London.

Other members of Allen's family besides his sister Christabella came to Natal. His sister Louisa came on the *Woodlark* in July 1859. She married R.B. Struthers* in Mar. 1861. Two nephews also made their careers in Natal. One was Dr James Franklin Swithin Allen (1852–1913), M.D., M.Ch. (Queen's College, Ireland), who came to the colony in 1874 directly after qualifying. He practised in Pietermaritzburg from 1876–1900. (See *D.S.A.B.*, vol. 3)

James's brother Francis Christopher Bland Allen (*c.* 1847–1912) settled in the Biggarsberg district. In the 1880s (from 1882 on) and in the 1890s he was postmaster there. The 1873–77 *Natal Blue Books* record C. Allen or John [*sic*] Christopher Bland Allen as Excise Surveyor, Little Umhlanga. Possibly these entries all refer to the same person. Dr J.F.S. Allen and F.C.B. Allen were sons of Philip's brother, William Allen, J.P., a magistrate of Co. Cork. Another of Philip Allen's nephews, Robert (*c.* 1853–1874), the son of his brother Robert, died on his way to Natal on the *Durban*. This vessel docked in Jan. 1875. Two Messrs Allen were listed as passengers.

CHILDREN

Allen had six children. Only five have been identified.

Arthur. He was dead by 1906.

William Cocks

Jane Somers m. Gretton.

Christabella (born July 1855, ?Pmb., dead by 1906). m. Kerr.

Walter Harding (born Apr. 1858, ?Pmb. – dead by 1906)
In 1880 and 1881 Walter was serving in the 32nd Pioneers in India, in Bombay in 1880 and Rawalpindi, Punjab,

in 1881. In this year he asked T. Shepstone to sell for him an erf he had in Newcastle.

SOURCES

Private source material
31 30.4.1862; 33 8.4.1861, 10.8.1862;
35 25.6.1865, 27.6.1865, 1.7.1865, 25.9.1874,
2.9.1876, 14.9.1879, 8.11.1880, 11.7.1881; 69;
71; 72; 102; 124 Part 4, Chapter 3 p. 324

Unpublished official papers
125 126 no. R1124, 135 no. R1192, 136 No. R1315,
147 no. R632, 2245 no. D379, 2283; 126 73, 74;
127 22 no. 34, 39 nos. 202, 231, 247, 254, 38
nos. 158 and 195, 40 no. 291, 1213 no. 59 p. 107,
no. 107 pp. 244–60, no. 6 p. 272, no. 47 p. 318,
and no. 144 p. 510, 1324 p. 7; 129 8/395, 28/181,
47/33; 130 1/30 no. 24, 1/84; 131 IV/2/65
nos. 213 and 236, IV/23/2 no. 23 dated 17 May 1861

Official printed sources
166; 167 1897; 173 pp.38, 220, 300; 174 pp.9,
19, 24

Newspapers, periodicals, etc.
185 18.3.1858, 29.6.1858, 17.7.1858, 5.1.1860,
Mar. 1861, 15.4.1862, 9.12.1862, 7.7.1870,
26.1.1875; 187 2.3.1861, 29.3.1862; 189
1.6.1855, 25.1.1856, 13.6.1856, 11.6.1858,
24.12.1858, 29.1.1875, 26.1.1875, 13.8.1896,
15.8.1913

Miscellaneous unofficial contemporary printed sources
220; 221 pp.590–1; 226 p. 21

Later sources
234 p. 189; 242 p. 217; 246 pp. 158, 162–6,
178–9, 181; 255; 266 pp.106, 199, 268 p. 8,
269 pp.135–149; 271 p. 73; 277 p. 24

Portraits, photographs, etc.
364 Accession 110/6, C.108

ALLEN, William Hill

He was an intermediate passenger on the *Iris*. The only other information about him forthcoming was that he was one of the signatories to a letter to the Captain of the vessel expressing appreciation of the good treatment the passengers had received during the voyage.

SOURCES

Newspapers, periodicals, etc.
188 16.1.1852

Personal communication
342

ALLERSTON, Alfred (born *c.* 1828) and William Francis (born *c.* 1830)

These two young men were from Bridlington, Yorkshire. They were probably related to William Allerston*, also a Bridlington man. Both came on the *Haidee*. Their occupations as given on their emigration certificates were 'gardener' and 'grazier' respectively.

Both were landowners in Pietermaritzburg Division by Aug. 1852, and were on the 1852–53 jury list. F.W. [*sic*] was entered as a gentleman and an owner and occupier of his property. All the information given of Alfred was that he was a landowner.

One of them may have been the Mr Allerston who sailed for Cape Town in Aug. 1853. He travelled steerage on the *Sir Robert Peel*.

SOURCES

Unpublished official papers
126 73; 157; 159

Official printed sources
168 10.8.1852

Newspapers, periodicals etc.
184 17.10.1850

ALLERSTON, William

Born Apr. 1811, Bridlington, Yorks. Died 28 July 1897, Pietermaritzburg.

Market gardener, clerk, carter. He was the son of Francis and Ann Allerston (born Woodcock). His father was a ship's carpenter, and in the naval dockyards at Chatham and Sheerness had worked on the construction of men-of-war later under Nelson's command. Allerston senior retired to Bridlington Quay, where he became the innkeeper of the 'Cock and Lion'.

William at the age of eight was sent to school in London. He later returned to Bridlington, and, with a brother, went into business as a linen draper. They lost their savings in railway share speculation, and William decided to emigrate. He and his family arrived in Natal on the *Henry*

Tanner. They were delayed three weeks in Durban while the luggage was being off-loaded. During this time the Government housed the emigrants in the still uncompleted Customs House at the Point.

After a few weeks in Pietermaritzburg, the Allerstons moved on to Ladysmith where William had obtained the post of constable. Ladysmith then consisted of only four wattle and daub houses, and the representatives of law and order for the whole of Klip River Division comprised the magistrate, James Melville*, Allerston the constable, and about 25 Natal Native Police.

Conditions were hard and Allerston's health began to suffer, so after about seven months the family returned to Pietermaritzburg. Here Allerston took on any work that he could get until he was able to afford to buy land and build a house. Then he started a market garden. By at least June 1851 this was what he was doing. The last reference found to him as a gardener dates to July 1856.

As a Byrne emigrant he was entitled to 65 acres at *Slang Spruit*. By April 1851 he had taken title to this allotment, but did not settle on it. He remained in Pietermaritzburg where by the end of 1852 he was the owner and occupier of erf 15 Greyling Street. By Aug. 1858 he was living in Church Street, possibly on erf 11, which was his address two years later. He was working as a storekeeper by mid-1860. By 1867 he was employed as a clerk, address, erf 22 Boom Street. By the end of 1870 he was living at 20 Boom Street, and still working as a clerk.

In about 1871 Allerston and his sons, his daughter Rosina, and her husband, George Denby, went to try their luck at the diamond fields and stayed in Kimberley about two years. After his return to Pietermaritzburg, Allerston went into business as a carter, again at 20 Boom Street in which occupation he remained until at least the early 1880s. However, when his wife died in 1884, he was described in the Pietermaritzburg death register as a clerk.

In 1834 Allerston had married Mary Ann Cranswick (*c.* 1813 – Jan. 1884, Pmb.), daughter of John Cranswick (died 1862), an ironmonger of Bridlington.

CHILDREN

Mary (*c.* 1835 ?Bridlington – 31 Dec. 1917, Pmb.) m. Oct. 1853, ?Pmb., David Knapp*.
Francis (*c.* Feb. 1838, Bridlington – 22 Nov. 1889, Barberton) m. Nov. 1861, Pmb., Harriett Lavender, d. of George Lavender*. Francis was a bricklayer and builder.
John (*c.* 1840, ?Bridlington – 3 Jan. 1871, O.F.S.).
William (born *c.* 1842, ?Bridlington).
Elizabeth (Apr. 1844, Bridlington – 27 Dec. 1888, Pmb.) m. Dec. 1862, Pmb., Benjamin Ireland, son of Mrs Ann Ireland*.
Rosina (22 Feb. 1849, Bridlington – 2 Apr. 1905, Pmb.) m. 9 Sep. 1870, Pmb., George Denby (*c.* 1841, U.K. – 6 Sep. 1883, Pmb.), son of Samuel and Rebecca Denby of Cowick, Yorks. Denby was a grocer.

Laura (May 1851, Pmb. – May 1898, Pmb.) m. June 1870, ?Pmb., Charles Douglas (*c.* 1840, Aldgate, London – Mar. 1899, Pmb.).
Harriet (May 1853, Pmb. – May 1898, ?Pmb.) m. 1 Feb. 1883, Pmb., James Edwin Beard (*c.* 1843, Manchester – June 1917, Pmb.), son of James R. and Mary Ann Beard. In his early days Beard was an itinerant photographer. In 1885 he was of *Waterfall*, Mid-Illovo. He was later a bookkeeper.
Agnes Cranswick (born Feb. 1856, ?Pmb.).

SOURCES

Private source material
34 Box 1. General correspondence book – Moreland to Macleroy 8.4.1851. Box 2. Surveyors' and Immigrants' correspondence book – Allerston to Moreland 12.5.1850. Box 4. *Henry Tanner* lists; **71**; **77**; **102**

Unpublished official papers
125 2282–2287; **129** 7/75; **131** IV/2/67 no.417, IV/2/68 no.559, IV/2/69 no.575; **147**; **156** 67/1883, 49/1887, 14/1896, 82/1905, **157**

Official printed sources
168 10.8.1852, 8.8.1854, 29.7.1856, 10.8.1858, 14.8.1860, 6.8.1867, 16.8.1870, 20.8.1872, 1.9.1874, 29.9.1874, 22.8.1876

Newspapers, periodicals etc.
185 29.2.1856, 4.3.1865 (the latter is the Pmb. edition with which is incorporated **181**), Oct. 1870, 17.1.1871, 12.9.1883; **189** 16.11.1880, 5.2.1883, 31.12.1888, 30.7.1897, 12.5.1898, 4.4.1905, 21.6.1917, 7.1.1918; **197** 1871, 1872, 1874, 1876, 1879, 1881, 1882, 1884, 1888

Miscellaneous unofficial contemporary printed sources
220

Later sources
231 pp.163–5; **267** pp.158–9; **272** pp.156–7

ALLISON, Albert Bidden

Baptized 5 Aug. 1823, Lowestoft, Suffolk. Died 3 Aug. 1903, Johannesburg.

Magistrate and farmer. Zulu name: Gweba[‡]. He was the son of Francis Bidden Allison and Mary Rix, and brother

---

[‡] Two of the three meanings of this word could be applicable, viz., to pass judgment or decide; or, to round up, turn, guide with whip-cracks.

of J.T. Allison* and Marion Phillis Rix, who married J.M. Foley*.

Allison, with his first wife Marianne Weyman (c. 1824 – May 1854, ?Pmb.) and two children, arrived in Natal on the *Sovereign*. Shortly after landing he and eleven others were given permission by Moreland* to squat on the Cotton Lands pending the survey of the *Sovereign* emigrants' land there.

Although designated a farmer on the *Sovereign* passenger list, Allison did not settle on his allotment. Towards the end of July 1850 he engaged himself to Moreland in Durban as clerk and draughtsman at £7 per month. Twelve months later he was invited to go trading in the Zulu country. Not being in a financial position to do so, he suggested to Moreland that he hire Moreland's wagon and oxen for the trip, and do some business on his (presumably meaning Byrne & Co.'s) behalf, with the unsold goods Moreland had.

Nothing came of this suggestion, and by Apr. 1852 Allison, what with the bankruptcy of Byrne & Co., and Moreland's difficulties, was out of a job. He then applied for, and was given, the post of Assistant Clerk in the Pietermaritzburg Post Office at £50 p.a. Thus began ten years of Allison's life as a government clerk. He remained in the Post Office until Sep. 1853, when he gained the position of Clerk to the Secretary for Native Affairs. In May 1854 he was made First Clerk in the Audit Office. It was while he was in this post that, in Nov. 1855, he and Joseph Burrup*, his future brother-in-law, were both suspended from office and salary for about six months. The reason was that Allison tried, with Burrup's aid, to provoke Edmund Tatham* to a duel over a family matter. Tatham at the time was the Acting Resident Magistrate at Richmond, with Burrup as his clerk.

In June 1859 Allison was transferred to the Surveyor General's office as Government Draughtsman at the same salary. In Oct. 1860 his promotion to Chief Clerk and Draughtsman in the same department was approved by the Secretary of State. It was while he was in the Surveyor General's office that he executed the map of Natal that appears in R.J. Mann's* *Colony of Natal* (1859).

Before moving from Allison's life in Pietermaritzburg, it may be of interest to learn that, at least by 1859, the Allisons were living on the Umsindusi, in the 'very neat residence' attached to Milton mills. Allison had leased the house and 45 acres for five years. In Sep. 1861 the house was burnt down.

In 1862 Allison's working life underwent a big change. He was chosen by Lt.-Governor Scott to go to England to procure men, arms and accoutrements for a Mounted Police Corps. Scott considered Allison a suitable choice because he had been in the Army before emigrating, and in the Colony had always shown an active interest in volunteering. Allison left Natal in Sep. 1862 on the *Waldensian*. Six months later he had completed his task, and was aboard the *Natal Star*, waiting to sail with his recruits for Natal. He had signed up 30 men, and, as instructed, most of them came from light cavalry regiments. Scott, in his despatch on Allison's departure for England, stated that he had selected him to have command of the corps. Lord Newcastle approved this appointment in a despatch dated Feb. 1863.

Allison was made a J.P. for the Colony in Aug. 1863. By Nov. 1864 he was established with his Mounted Police in camp on the Umzimkulu river, near Hancock's Drift. The prevention of gun-running was one of their main tasks here. Although the Mounted Police Corps was still in existence at the beginning of 1866, it was disbanded shortly after.

From Captain of the Mounted Police, Allison's next appointment in the government service was as Border Agent in the Upper Tugela region, at Olivier's Hoek. This post was created to control movement across the Natal-Basutoland border, and to keep the Natal government informed of what was happening to the west of its borders. The O.F.S.–Basuto War and the Basuto raid into Natal on its outbreak in June 1865 had made the Natal government sensitive to infiltration from that quarter. Allison himself gives the date for this appointment as 1864, but the first reference to his holding the post is in the *Natal Blue Book* for 1869. Be that as it may, Allison certainly appears to have been in the area by June 1868 when he commanded a small force of Africans pursuing Bushmen into the Drakensberg.

In Sep. and Oct. 1869 he again led an expedition against Bushman raiders. 120 cattle and 60 horses were stolen from William Popham of *Meshlynn*, Kamberg, and an African settlement nearby. Allison's two-pronged pursuit, consisting of eight whites and 200 Africans, eventually surrounded a Bushman party in a gorge in the reaches of the upper Orange river. The Bushmen showed resistance and 16 or 17 were 'dispersed', as Allison put it in his official report. 'Extirpated' is the word he used on a later occasion. Only four or five escaped. The Bushman raid that had led to this retaliation was the last large raid Natal was to suffer.

Because of economic stringency the Border Agency was discontinued, and from July 1872 to Apr. 1874 Allison was on the pension list on half pay. He volunteered to carry on the agency without remuneration until better times came. With government permission he re-engaged the six African police and the interpreter, whom he clothed, fed and paid himself. This cost, plus the other expenses of the agency, he later averred, was greater than the sum the government paid him as a pensioner.

It was during this period that the Langalibalele rebellion took place. Allison was placed in command of one of the two flying columns that were intended to head off the Hlubi tribe before they reached the Bushman's river pass. He had 500 loyal Africans in this command and the intention was to ascend the Drakensberg near Champagne

Castle. Knowledge of the topography was scant, and there was no pass in this region. Allison was therefore not able to rendezvous with the column under Major Durnford.

After the skirmish at Bushman's river pass, Allison, with a flying column consisting of 100 whites and 1 500 Africans, pursued Chief Langalibalele into Basutoland. The chief, five of his sons and the captured tribesmen were brought to Pietermaritzburg under Allison's escort.

In 1874 Allison was appointed Administrator of Native Law at Olivier's Hoek, and in the August of the following year, the Upper Tugela magistracy was established with Allison as magistrate.

In Nov. 1879 charges were brought against him and a two-man commission was sent to investigate. Their report showed the accusations to be so serious as to make it a question as to whether or not he should be suspended. In the meantime he was interdicted from carrying out the duties of his office. The Executive Council considered the report and Allison's reply to the allegations, and decided that five of the charges were substantiated. These mainly concerned the use of prisoners to do private work on his farm, sometimes without any guard set over them. One stated that he had used Zulu refugees on his farm, while they were rationed at public expense. The last charge concerned a Zulu refugee, who was Allison's house servant, who was sentenced to seven days' hard labour in chains. In this case no evidence was called, and no record written up in the books of the office. In Apr. 1880 Allison was suspended by decision of the Executive Council. The Council found him guilty of grave dereliction of duty, but in view of his length of service, advised the Lt.-Governor to grant him a year's sick leave; not to allow him to return to his magistracy, but to keep him on half-pay until another post could be found for him, or until he was retired.

The Legislative Council refused to vote his salary in the 1881 Supply Bill. This plus a dispute with the Government about the granting of title to his farm, *Rosenstein*, in the Upper Tugela, led to endless correspondence between Allison and the Natal authorities, and even the Secretary of State for the Colonies. Nine years later the Allison affair was still unsolved. Allison had the distinction of having, not one, but two blue books published relating to his claims. In 1889 *Papers relating to the case of Mr A.B. Allison (late Resident Magistrate, Upper Tugela Division)* (289p.) appeared, and this book was followed in the next year by *Further papers in the case of Mr A.B. Allison. . .* (22p.).

Allison was not again employed in the government service, and for a number of years in between visits abroad, farmed first at *Rosenstein*, and later at another of his farms, *Groot Geluk*.

During the Second Anglo-Boer War he and his family had to leave their farms and seek refuge in Ladysmith. All five sons served as British intelligence officers during the conflict, one, Marthinus, being killed.

By Mar. 1903 Allison was living at Troyeville, Johannes-

burg. He died a few months later at Bellevue, Johannesburg.

Allison, presumably because of his military background, was a keen volunteer. In Dec. 1854 he served in the commando against the chief Dushane, who was resident in the Upper Umkomanzi magistracy. When the Natal Carbineers were organized in 1855, Allison became the Lieutenant and Adjutant. In Mar. 1856 he served with the regiment in the Drakensberg in pursuit of Bushmen. By the beginning of 1858, when the corps was used against the chief Matyana, he was the captain of the Maritzburg troop. He held the same commission at the time of the Zulu invasion scare in mid–1861, during which the Carbineers were called up. Allison in 1862 became the Major of the corps and remained as such until his resignation in Feb. 1871.

Both Allison and his second wife appear to have had an interest in zoology. Dr J.W. Matthews in his *Incwadi yami*, refers to their small 'but carefully selected menagerie' at Olivier's Hoek. Their son, Marthinus, collected botanical specimens, particularly orchids, some of which were named after him.

Allison's second wife was Cornelia Stuart (24 Dec. 1832, Velsen, Holland – 15 Mar. 1913, Klip River, Transvaal), the daughter of Jacobus Stuart and Meinoude Elia de Vries Robbé. They were married in Sep. 1856, presumably in Pietermaritzburg.

Allison's mother was in Natal, and living with him in Pietermaritzburg in 1855. It is possible she was the Mrs Mary Allison who is buried in the Commercial Road cemetery, Pietermaritzburg. She died in Jan. 1861 at the age of 71.

CHILDREN

Charlotte Katherine Rix (7 Mar. 1851, Dbn – 5 May 1914, Pmb.) m. 8 July 1873, Olivier's Hoek, Albert Thurlow Allison, son of her uncle J.T. Allison.

Rosa Eliza Mary (born Mar. 1853, Pmb.) m. 26 May 1874, ?Olivier's Hoek, John David Taylor (10 Mar. 1849, George, Cape – May 1919, Pmb.), son of David Taylor (1808–1850) and his wife Sophia Elizabeth Moodie, and grandson of Donald Moodie*.

James Stuart (born *c.* 1858, ?Pmb.) m. 4 Nov. 1885, Winburg, O.F.S., Cora de Kok, his cousin, d. of K.J. de Kok and his wife Agatha Maria Elia Stuart of Winburg.

Elia Maria Theodora (born Feb. 1859, ?Pmb.) m. 11 Oct. 1883, *Hoffenthal* Upper Tugela, Eduard Willem van Musschenbroek, son of Jean Gisberto Pierre Herman van Musschenbroek and his wife Marie Teding van Berkhout, of *Groot Geluk*, Upper Tugela.

Theodore Stuart (born *c.* Feb. 1861, Pmb.) m. 24 Nov. 1885, Harrismith, O.F.S. Susan Cecilia Bland, d. of John Bland of Harrismith.

son (14 Nov. 1862, Pmb.) born and died the same day.

Albert Bidden (born *c.* 2 Feb. 1864, Pmb.) m. 7 Jan. 1886, ?Upper Tugela, Anna Marie van Musschenbrock, d. of

J.P. van Musschenbrock of *Groot Geluk*, Upper Tugela, presumably the sister of E.W. van Musschenbrock.

Arnold A. (born 1 Apr. 1867, Pmb.) m. Jacoba van Muscchenbrock.

Marthinus Stuart (born 13 Aug. 1869, Pmb.) killed in 2nd Anglo-Boer War.

Theophilla (born 3 Mar. 1872, Ladysmith) m. Herbert Aldwynckle.

SOURCES

Private source material
  5; **34** Box 2. Surveyors' and Immigrants' correspondence book — Allison to Moreland 23.7.1851. Box 4. *Sovereign* lists, and Document S67; **44**; **71**; **72**; **102**

Unpublished official papers
  125 15 no.43, 16(3) no.146, 2241 no.C107, 2249 no.E347, 2253 no.F347, 2282, 2286; **126** 74; **127** 28 no.21 p.199, 30 no.69 p.242, 34 no.23 p.132, 36 no.82 p.123, 40 no.298 p.106 and no.300 p.122, 1211 no.64 p.8, 1213 no.129 p.465; **132** III/5/26 no.277; **146**; **147**; **156** 73–4/1890, 50/1904

Official printed sources
  162; **163**; **166**; **168** 11.8.1863, 28.2.1871; **169**; **170**; **173** pp.27–8, 30–1, 216–7

Newspapers, periodicals, etc.
  181 11.9.1861, 14.10.1863; **184** 1.9.1853, 11.5.1854; **185** Feb.1861, Nov.1862, Feb.1864, Apr.1867, Aug.1869, 19.3.1872, 19.8.1873, 16.6.1874, 17.10.1883; **187** 19.5.1860, 14.9.1861; **189** 29.3.1850, 19.5.1854, 15.4.1859, 13.1.1860, 17.10.1883, 16.12.1885, 13.1.1886, 26.3.1913, 8.5.1914; **197** 1863–71, 1879, 1881, 1882, 1884, 1888, 1895

Journals, biographies, autobiographies, letters
  211 p.58; **216** p.204

Miscellaneous unofficial contemporary printed sources
  220; **223**; **226** pp.21, 29–31, 36–9, 42–3, 360–3

Later sources
  233 p.16

Later sources
  233 p.16; **263** pp.206, 268, 296, 310; **274** p.139; **279** pp.19–21, 43, 45; **286** *passim*; **299** pp.74 *et seq*; **311** pp.169–176

Personal communication
  335; **343**; **348**

ALLISON, Rev. James

Born 4 July, 1805[‡], Carlisle, Cumberland. Died 1 Apr. 1875, Pietermaritzburg.
Missionary. Zulu name: Mneli (possibly meaning 'one who showers blessings on others'). Son of James Allison (*c.* 1775–1820), a British army officer, and his wife Ann Maxwell (*c.* 1778–1865). James senior had seen service in the East Indies and in the Peninsular campaign. In the British Isles he had been stationed at Carlisle, Bury St Edmunds, Inverness and lastly at Cork. It was from Cork in Jan. 1820 that James and Ann Allison and their family left for the Cape. They were members of one of the Irish parties of settlers, and sailed on the *East Indian*.

1820 Apr. — *East Indian* arrived at Simon's Bay — diverted to Saldanha Bay from whence the settlers travelled to the Clanwilliam district.

May — James Allison senior's brother, Francis, and his family arrived at Algoa Bay in the *Albury*.

1820 — Allison senior died near Clanwilliam. Shortly afterwards the Irish settlers were relocated in the Albany district.
— soon after his father's death Allison was apprenticed to a Dutch farmer in 'the interior of the Colony', who was also a hatter.

1825 Oct. — by this time Allison was on a Wesleyan mission station in Little Namaqualand where he had been engaged to teach the Namaquas hat-making.

1827 Jan.9 — Rev. Haddy reported to the Secretaries of the Wesleyan Mission Society that Allison, 'the young man who is teaching the Namaquas the hat-making business' had that day come to him and asked to be 'instructed in relation to the state of his soul'.

1827 — Allison married Dorothy Thackwray (*c* 1804, ?U.K. – 23 June 1864, Pmb.), daughter of William and Dorothy Thackwray, 1820 Settlers ex *Northampton*, originally from Sheffield, Yorks. According to the postnuptial contract executed by the Allisons in Sep. 1860, they were married in Grahamstown. One source gives 4 Jan. 1827 as their marriage

‡ Some sources give 1802, others 1804. The year 1805 has been fixed upon as this corresponds with his age at death as given on his death certificate, and also on his gravestone.

date, but Rev. Haddy's letter from Namaqualand quoted above lays this open to query.

1829 July — Allison's father-in-law, William Thackwray, was killed near the Umzimvubu river with Lt. F.G. Farewell*.

1832 July — Allison began his career in the mission field, starting as a catechist.

— among the stations where he laboured were Buchaap, Thaba Nchu, Thaba Kuruhele and Imparane where he worked for seven years among the Mantatees (Tlokwa) under Chief Sikonyela.

1838 Jan. Piet Retief met Sikonyela in Allison's garden at Imparane. Despite Allison's opposition he had Sikonyela handcuffed until the Mantatees produced the cattle they had stolen from King Dingane.

1839 July — Allison was visited at Imparane by the Quaker traveller James Backhouse — see his *A narrative of a visit to Mauritius and South Africa.* (1844)

1841 — Allison's wife's ill health forced him to leave Imparane. He was temporarily at Thaba Nchu, Ratabani, and then Lishuane.

1845 Aug. — he arrived in what is now Swaziland accompanied by 30 converts, including four African teachers and their wives. In the previous year he and Rev. R. Giddy had visited the country to investigate its possibilities for missionary work, the Paramount Chief Raputse, and later his son Mswazi, having requested missionaries.

— he established a mission at Mount Mohamba.

1846 — his translations into Swazi dialect of four portions of the Gospels of St John and St Matthew, and also the Wesleyan first catechism were published at Platberg by the Wesleyan Mission Press. These were the first translations attempted in Swazi.

Sep. — by this time, besides Mohamba, he had five sub-stations, manned by teachers.

Sep.14 — civil strife in the Swazi country resulted
— 16 in Mount Mohamba being attacked by Chief Mswazi's impis and some Boers. 50 of Allison's people were killed. The immediate cause was the flight of some of Mswazi's enemies to the protection of one of Allison's sub-stations.

Sep.17 — Allison, his teachers and followers, and many Swazis left Mohamba.

Oct.6 — they crossed the Pongola river on their way to Natal.

— eventually Allison reached Pmb. with about 200 Africans.

1847 Jan. — at the district meeting of the Albany and Kaffraria District (of which Natal was then a part), Allison and Rev. W.J. Davis* were appointed to work among the Natal Africans.

Mar. — Davis wrote to the Government requesting that he be permitted to start a mission station in the Zwartkop region and that Allison be able to establish one in the intended reserve in the region on the Umkomanzi (Umkomaas) river.

— Allison chose the site for a station and established it, naming it Indaleni.

1848 June — meeting in Pmb. of a special committee of the Albany and Kaffraria district to investigate the complaints against one another by the brethren of the Natal mission. Revs. J. Richards*, W.C. Holden* and Allison were concerned with the worldly avocations of Revs. Archbell* and Davis. Archbell retired as a result of this meeting but Davis emerged unscathed.

July — Allison received an annual grant of £50 for his industrial school.

1850 Jan. — Revs. Holden, G. Parsonson* and Allison wrote to the General Secretaries of the Wesleyan Mission Society about Davis's behaviour.

Dec. — Lt.-Governor Pine reported to the Secretary of State his loan to Allison of £100 for ploughs and oxen for his people — this was to be repaid in five years.

1851 — by this time Indaleni was the most flourishing mission station in Natal. It had a village laid out in the European style, a temporary mission house, outbuildings and a chapel. Mrs Allison was training Africans as tailors and dressmakers, while Allison's manual labour school had 25 pupils. Besides the 3 Rs they were taught building, carpentry, blacksmithing and agriculture. He was different from most missionaries in that he did not only evangelise but also put a strong emphasis on practical education.

1851 Jan. — Edward London* teaching in the school
— June at Indaleni.

1851 June 20 — resigned all connexion with the Wesleyan mission — from 'conscientious motives' as Capt. R.J. Garden, who interviewed Allison, puts it.

His long term protests at the behaviour

of Davis and Archbell had brought forth scathing attacks on him by these two, and he had been unable to get any redress from the Chairman of the Natal District, Rev. H. Pearse*.

July 30 — Allison purchased *Welverdient* (6 123 acres) the farm of Andries Pretorius. This was renamed Edendale.

Aug. — Allison left Indaleni. About 450 of his people followed him.

— 99 heads of households among his followers were partners with him in the purchase of *Welverdient*. He however assumed sole legal and financial responsibility for the transaction. The price was £1 300 to be paid over four years at 6% interest. The property was divided into 100 shares at £16 each (£10 for suburban lots of about one acre, and £6 for town lots of about one rood). This scheme, whereby Africans were able to buy their own lots in the mission property to be paid for by the fruits of their labour, was something new on the Natal missionary scene.

1852 June — London teaching at Edendale. Left shortly afterwards.

1853 Feb. — Bishop Colenso* visited Edendale — see his *Ten weeks in Natal*.

1854 May — petitioned Lt.-Governor for the renewal of the grant of £50 p.a. which had ceased when he left Indaleni. Grant resumed.

1855 — Allison found he could not meet the purchase price of the farm owing to the losses his people had suffered from lung-sickness among their cattle. Sir George Grey, High Commissioner for South Africa, when visiting Natal, lent him £200 free of interest. The town area of the mission was named George Town in his honour.

1857 — corn and grain mill erected at Edendale for Allison by John Anderson (1812–1898)*. This appears to be the second mill Allison had had built at Edendale. He and his Africans had built the first one themselves.

1857 June — Allison's niece Elizabeth Allison Simpson*, married T.W. Fannin (see Thomas Fannin). For a number of years she had run the infant school at Edendale. For the rest of 1857 Allison took over the school.

1858 — final payment made for the farm. By this time the population of Edendale numbered about 600. George Town consisted of 62 houses erected by the Africans, each with its own enclosed garden.

1858 Sep.24 — Allison and his wife made their will. Re the lands purchased in his name for a mission station, this document stressed that he and his wife had no right or claim upon them other than to such subdivisions they had already or might later purchase, including the site on which the mill stood, which Allison had purchased in the same manner as subdivisions had been purchased by others on the station.

1859 Jan.9 — D.H. Tarboton* signed a lease on Allison's corn mill at Edendale plus the part of the farm on which it stood (about 40 acres). The lease was to run for 100 years at £180 p.a.

1859 Mar. — William Bennitt* was by this time running the Industrial training institution.

1860 — by this time Allison's station was in receipt of government aid to the tune of £220 p.a., £70 for the infant school and £150 for the boys' day school and the Industrial training institution.

1860 early — in his report for 1859 on the Industrial training institution Allison stated that Bennitt was not satisfactory and he had accordingly given him notice of dismissal. At the time the station was in a state of 'great unsettledness', as Allison put it, in consequence of his being in the process of distributing the lands to his followers, and from 'other causes'.

1860 Feb.27 — a meeting of 60 of the most influential landowners and inhabitants of the mission was held at George Town. Allison was asked to open communication with the Wesleyan Church in order to effect a union with that body. Also it was agreed that the ecclesistical property on the estate be transferred to the Wesleyan Church. A committee of ten was appointed to assist Allison in carrying out the above resolutions.

1860 Mar.26 — Allison wrote to the Secretary for Native Affairs re Bennitt's appeal that the Lt.-Governor cause an investigation as to the correctness of the grounds on which he was dismissed. Allison stated that an inquiry at the present time would be injurious to his position. It was indispensable for him, for the completion of the distribution of the titles and for 'order and harmony' to be restored at the station, that his influence and position among the natives remain unimpaired. He stated that if the Lt.-Governor would agree not to have an inquiry, he would for the present withdraw his dismissal of Bennitt. He added that he was considering leaving the station, but wanted to get the titles question settled first.

1860 Mar.29 — the Secretary for Native Affairs informed Allison that the Acting Lt.-Governor did not wish to interfere in matters at the station, but in view of the unsatisfactory state of affairs, felt it his duty to withdraw the annual grant of £150 to the boys' day school and the Industrial training institution with effect from 1 May 1860, and until matters had returned to a more 'favourable condition'.

1860 Sep. — by this time Allison had left Edendale and was resident in Pmb. In this month he and his wife made separate wills. Each document stated that the surviving spouse was to be sole heir and executor. The extent of property was not specified and therefore there was no mention of the land at Edendale.

1860 Oct. — the Wesleyan Church Conference in Pmb. resolved to accept Allison's people back into the Wesleyan communion and to take over Edendale. At this meeting the station was described thus. 'There are 120 members, about 800 residents, a good staff of local preachers and leaders, an industrial and infant school supported by a government grant of £225 [sic]; all things considered it is the most advanced and promising station in the colony...' (Allison had requested in May that the government grant be resumed, stating that Bennitt 'had corrected the negligence complained of'.)

— one theory advanced for the break between Allison and his people is that he would not agree to their reconciliation with the Wesleyans. Another is that his followers found that the titles were worthless and that all the land was in Allison's name. They therefore rectified the situation and drove him out. Unless circumstances had altered since his 1858 will had been made, its terms would seem to contradict this view.

— in Pmb. Allison commenced a mission among the Africans of the city, including a night school.

1861 — Allison reached an accord with the Edendale community. Points of agreement included the issuing of freehold titles to individual residents once the purchase price, survey fees, etc. on their allotments had been paid in full, the transfer to the Wesleyan Church of town lots in George Town, the formation of a trust to administer the commonage, the market place and the cemetery, and the payment to Allison of £258 odd for his ministerial services during the period 1858–1860. This sum was to be paid by the Wesleyan Methodist Missionary Society.

1863 — erected a small chapel, seating 80 to 100.

1864 June — wife died in Pmb.

1865 May — wrote to Secretary for Native Affairs for assistance with the chapel he was building. It had reached roof level, but funds had run out. As he was desirous of roofing it before the rainy season, he asked for a bond. He disclosed that he had offered it, when complete, to the Free Church of Scotland, and the matter was under consideration. Should the Free Church decide against it, he would offer it to some other denomination. A bond was arranged.

This chapel was his Ebenezer Chapel from which Ebenezer Street takes its name. It is still standing (1981).

1865 c. July — his mother died at Mowbray in the Cape.

1867 July — wrote to the Secretary for Native Affairs asking for an increase in his grant of £25 from the Reserve Fund for his night school — had 120 pupils.

Oct. — entered the Free Church of Scotland at a meeting of the Presbytery of the Free Church held at Pinetown. Accepted as a missionary agent.

c. Dec. — wrote to Secretary for Native Affairs asking for his grant from the Reserve Fund to be increased to £100. He intended to use it for a tutor in a farming school, not for the night school.

1868 Jan.18 — married Mary McCarthney Dunn (c. 1843, Raefield [unverified] Dumfriesshire – 18 July 1897, Dbn), born Rae, and supposed widow of Robert Dunn of *Shallow Spruit*, Umgeni. The marriage took place at her residence, *Groot Hoek*, Umgeni.

1868	– J. McLaren (son of J. McLaren*) was appointed catechist and teacher at the mission training school in connexion with the Ebenezer Chapel.
1869	– founded the Impolweni mission station on *Groot Hoek*.
	– retained his Pmb. property on erf 15, Loop Street.
1872 Jan.	– Allison and his wife had to remarry, she under the name of Rae. According to the special licence dated 25 Jan. Mary had married Allison on 18 Jan. 1868 under the name of Mary McCarthney Rae Dunn 'but which name of Dunn it is now ascertained she was not legally entitled to'. It appears that Dunn had been a bigamist.
c. 1874	– Rev. J. Stalker appointed Free Church of Scotland resident missionary, Pmb.
1875 Jan.19	– the date of the last entry Allison made in the church registers at Impolweni.
Apr.1	– died at Pmb. His brother-in-law, Rev. James Cameron (1805–1875), General Superintendent of Wesleyan missions in Natal, delivered the address at his funeral.

CHILDREN

ADOPTED DAUGHTER

Elizabeth WARREN (*c.* 1833 – 23 May 1895, *Liddesdale*, Boston) m. 1 Jan. 1850, Indaleni, Robert Lindsay*. Elizabeth came originally from Grahamstown. She had been with the Allisons in the Swazi country and journeyed with them from there to Natal.

CHILDREN BY HIS SECOND MARRIAGE

Thackeray James (20 Mar. 1870, Impolweni – 12 Sep. 1923, Pmb.) m. 2 Sep. 1897, Pmb., Marianne Price (born *c.* 1877), d. of Henry J. Price of *Brookby*, Zwart Kop Valley, Pmb., formerly of Shropshire. This marriage ended in divorce. Thackeray was an advocate.
Maxwell Francis (May 1871, Pmb. – 25 Dec. 1871, Impolweni) died in infancy.
Dora Agnes (born 23 Nov. 1874, died Johannesburg) m. 21 Dec. 1898, Pmb., Aubrey Samuel Langley (born 25 June 1871, Pmb.) son of Rev. James Langley (1834–1910), Wesleyan missionary in Natal 1860–1880. A.S. Langley was headmaster of Durban High School from 1910–1931.

SOURCES

Private source material
  12 28.9.1851; **28** 6/2 pp.21–2; **32** pp.216, 765; **37**; **38**; **60**; **72**; **76**; **102**; **119**

Unpublished official papers
  125 16(2) no.118, 27(2) no.158, 37(2) no.59, 2244 no.D235, 2283, 2284, 2285, 2295 no.330; **127** 1209 no.19 p.149; **129** 9/88; **131** IV/2/65 no.206, IV/3/67 nos.42, 43, 44, IV/16/4 no.11, IV/19/64 no.70; **133** I/1/10 nos.24, 37, 41, 151–2, I/1/15 no.31, I/1/17 nos.74–5; **137**; **141**; **146**; **147**; **156** 81/1897

Official printed sources
  166 1857; **174** p.12

Newspapers and periodicals
  184 31.7.1851; **185** 30.7.1857, July 1865, 14.9.1865, 24.3.1870, 20.1.1872; **189** 4.1.1850, 27.11.1851, 1.4.1853, 12.6.1857, 4.3.1859, 5.11.1867, 2.4.1875, 6.4.1875, 24.12.1875, 6.6.1895, 20.7.1897, 3.9.1897, 29.12.1898; **197** 1866, 1878, 1881, 1884, 1888, 1895; **199** 1910 pp.6, 269

Journals, biographies, autobiographies, letters
  201 pp.394–404; **204** pp.50, 52. 66; **206** pp.193, 197; **212** p.14

Later sources
  234 p.315; **238** p.9; **248**; **256**; **262** p.142; **267** pp.89–90; **281** pp.203, 246; **284** pp.13, 22, 73, 84, 160; **288** p.31; **291** *passim*; **294** pp.1–8; **302** p.140; **315**; **332** *passim*

Personal communication
  340; **344**; **356**; **357**

Portraits, photographs, etc.
  359 p.62

ALLISON, John

Born 1826, Scotland. Died 18 Sep. 1896, *Milichan*, near Ladysmith.

Farmer. Allison came from Duntocher, Dunbartonshire. He emigrated to Natal on the *Isle of Wight*, landing at Durban in Sep. 1851. Fellow passengers were William Anderson (1790–1873)* and family.

To begin with both Allison and the Andersons went to Pinetown where one of Anderson's daughters, Jessie, and her husband, A.K. Murray*, had settled. Not much is known of Allison's days in Durban Division. In 1852 he won the ploughing match in Durban at the second Show of the Natal Agricultural and Horticultural Society. Later in the year (6 September), in Pinetown, he married Christiana, one of Anderson's daughters. In 1853 Allison was farming in Pinetown, and it was here that his and Christiana's first child was born. They were living in Klip

River County by the time of the birth of their second child in 1855.

At first Allison farmed at *Matuan's Kop*. On 1 Apr. 1859 he was granted title to the quitrent farm *Hamburg* (3 006 acres), north of Ladysmith. In about the middle of the same year he bought the adjoining *Klipfontein* from a Mr van Rooyen. This he renamed *Milichan* or *Milichan Hall*. He and his wife lived there for the rest of their days. *Milichan* remained in Allison ownership well into the 20th century.

CHILDREN

Elizabeth (13 Aug. 1853, Pinetown – 5 May 1926, Ladysmith) m. 18 June 1874, *Milichan*, David Gray, son of David Gray*.

Margaret (27 Feb. 1855, near Ladysmith – 10 Nov. 1927, Ladysmith) unmarried.

Isabella (29 Sep. 1856, near Ladysmith – 10 May 1916, Pmb.) m. 24 Aug. 1881, Ladysmith, James Hamilton Templeton (died June 1900, Pmb.), son of Rev. John Lynn Templeton of Duntocher, Scotland.

Mary Lavinia Jessie (11 July 1858, near Ladysmith, died ?Pietersburg, Tvl.) m. 15 Jan. 1894, Utrecht, Johannes Hendrickus Oosthuizen (born *c.* 1868, Cape Colony).

James William (5 June 1860, *Milichan* – 12 July, 1860, ?*Milichan*) died in infancy.

James (born 18 June 1861, ?*Milichan*) m. Dec. 1895, Pmb., Kate St Clair Templeton (*c.* 1861 – 29 Apr. 1936, Ladysmith), d. of Rev. J.L. Templeton, above.

Christiana (27 Apr. 1863, Ladysmith – 1 Aug. 1912, *Milichan*) unmarried.

William (16 Jan. 1865, Ladysmith – 1941, buried Ladysmith) m. 26 Dec. 1894, Dbn, Helen McWilliam (died 1952, buried Ladysmith), d. of A. McWilliam.

● **John Andrew** (5 Oct. 1868, *Milichan* – 24 Dec. 1946, buried Ladysmith) m. Mary Jane (Mollie) Milne (*c.* 1865 – 21 Mar. 1942, buried Ladysmith).

● **Agnes Moreland** (5 Oct. 1868, *Milichan* – 29 July 1954, buried Ladysmith) unmarried.

●● **Ellen Franklin** (22 Oct. 1869, *Milichan* – 7 Apr. 1941, buried Ladysmith) unmarried.

●● **Selina Salmon** (born 22 Oct. 1869, *Milichan*) m. 11 Aug. 1896, *Milichan*, Arthur Hunt Spring, son of Arthur Spring*.

Ann Sproul (15 Jan. 1872, *Milichan* – 12 June 1917, Dundee, buried Vryheid) m. a Mr McWilliam. Possibly he was the George Robb McWilliam who died at Vryheid on 8 June 1920, aged 60.

● and ●● denotes twins

SOURCES

Private source material
33 12,7.1858, 12.6.1859, 16.6.1859, 10.7.1860,

12.7.1860, 20.6.1861; **49**; **64**; **65**; **66**; **76**; **79**; **97**

Unpublished official sources
125 2258 no.G305, 2286; **129** 9/256, 33/148, 46/241; **132** III/5/25 no.144, III/5/27 no.343, III/12/1 p.95; **142**; **143**; **147**; **153**; **156** 98/1908

Newspapers, periodicals, etc.
185 20.8.1860, Apr. 1863, Jan. 1865, Oct. 1868, Oct. 1869, 23.1.1872, 27.6.1874, 2.9.1881; **187** 10.9.1852; **189** 28.12.1894, 24.9.1896, 11.5.1916, 14.6.1920; **197** 1879, 1881

Later sources
234 p.133

Personal communication
337; **346**

ALLISON, John Thurlow

Born *c.* 1824, Norfolk. Died Apr. 1889, Pietermaritzburg.

Accountant. Son of Francis Bidden Allison and Mary Rix, brother of A.B. Allison*, and Marion Phillis Rix, the wife of J.M. Foley*.

Although born in Norfolk, Allison, in the late forties, appears to have been resident in Suffolk, at Eye and Ipswich. Possibly he was the J. Allison, who, in 1850, was J.C. Byrne & Co.'s agent at Ipswich.

Allison, a Mrs Allison and four children, are listed as *Lady of the Lake* passengers, arriving in Durban in Dec. 1854. In fact only three children reached Natal, the youngest, Laura, dying at sea.

Allison's first wife, Elizabeth Chambers, died after only a few years of marriage, but it has not been ascertained whether she died before or after the family left England. The Mrs Allison on the *Lady of the Lake* could either have been his wife, or his mother, who was definitely in Natal by the end of 1855. The only Mrs Allison who appears in the Port Captain's shipping lists between 1851 and 1855 is the one who accompanied John Thurlow.

Allison settled in Pietermaritzburg. From Dec. 1855 he was employed as a clerk in the Natal Bank, and in Dec. 1859 was appointed Acting General Manager. He held this position during some of the period between Carl Behrens's resignation in Dec. 1859 and the appointment of George Macleroy* in Apr. 1861.

In July 1858 Allison was given a government grant near the Umlaas river. This was the farm *Belgium* (1 008 acres). In 1870 he notified the authorities that he wished to abandon this land.

During most of the 1870s and throughout the 1880s,

Allison appears in the *Natal Almanac* street directory of Pietermaritzburg as an accountant. In the mid–1860s he was one of the two auditors of the Natal Fire Assurance & Trust Co.

Allison was a foundation member of the Natal Carbineers in 1855. During the mid sixties he was a committee member of the Victoria Club.

His second wife was Elizabeth Mayne, daughter of Charles W. Mayne*. They were married in Jan. 1856, in Pietermaritzburg.

CHILDREN

Albert Thurlow (14 Feb. 1842, ?London or ?Suffolk – 6 June 1898, Pmb.) m. 8 July 1873, Olivier's Hoek, Charlotte Katherine Rix Allison, d. of A.B. Allison, and his cousin.

Joanna Eliza (c. 1847, ?Ipswich or ?Eye, Suffolk – 24 Nov. 1911, near Bethlehem, O.F.S.) m. 17 Sep. 1874, Pmb., John Edwin Priest Burniston (c. 1845, Doncaster, Yorks. – 11 Nov. 1911, near Bethlehem, O.F.S.).

Maria Theresa (c. 1848, Ipswich, Suffolk – 22 Jan. 1917, Dbn) m. Sep. 1874, Pmb., George Frederick Hall, son of George Hall*.

Laura (died 1854) died at sea, in childhood.

Mary Elizabeth (c. 1857, Pmb. – Dec. 1897, ?Dbn)
m. (1) 14 Feb. 1878, Pmb., Thomas Smallwood (c. 1842, Cheshire – 3 June 1879, Pmb.), formerly of Wirksworth, Derbyshire.
m. (2) Oct. 1880, Pmb., Robert Troy (born c. 1852).

Alice Sarah (born 21 Feb. 1858, Pmb.)
m. (1) 28 Dec. 1880, Pmb., Charles Pitman (born Glos.)
m. (2) Feb. 1918, Pmb., Alfred Thomas Holmes (c. 1857 – Aug. 1919, Pmb.).

Frank Mayne (19 May 1859, Pmb. – Feb. 1932, Pmb.)
m. (1) 5 Feb. 1884, Pmb., Mary Jane Williams (c. 1863, Helston, Cornwall – 17 Jan. 1895, Pmb.), d. of John Williams of Helston, Cornwall.
m. (2) Dorothy Dolphin.

John William (1861, Pmb. – Mar. 1936, Pmb.) m. ?May 1887, ?Ladysmith, Mary Elizabeth Huber (1853 – Apr. 1943, ?Pmb.). John was the founder of the Pmb. saddlery firm J.W. Allison & Co.

Philip Rix (13 Mar. 1864, Pmb. – Aug. 1941, Pmb.) m. Aug. 1889, Pmb., Susan Jessie Thompson (c. 1869 – 3 Aug. 1927, Ladysmith).

SOURCES

Private source material
6; 58; 64; 71; 72; 76; 92; 102; 111

Unpublished official papers
125 2258 no.G256, 2282, 2286–2288; 126 73; 129 9/184, 44/116 and 117; 132 III/5/25 no. 168, III/12/1 p.91; 137; 143; 147; 148; 156 11/1895

Official printed sources
166

Newspapers, periodicals, etc.
181 23.3.1861; 185 25.2.1858, 26.5.1859, Mar. 1864, 19.8.1873; 187 6.2.1856; 189 26.2.1858, 8.10.1858, 20.5.1859, 23.12.1859, 16.2.1878, 21.6.1879, 15.1.1881, 6.2.1884, 18.1.1895, 14.6.1898, 16.11.1911, 22.11.1911, 27.1.1917, 19.8.1919; 191 27.12.1855; 197 1864–67, 1870–71, 1876, 1879, 1881–82, 1884, 1888, 1895

Miscellaneous unofficial contemporary sources
226 p.26

Later sources
246 p.273

Personal communication
335

ALSTON, Edmund

Born c. 1813.

He emigrated to Natal on the *Edward*, and is described in the passenger list as a farmer. Next to his name in Byrne & Co's *Edward* list, forwarded to Moreland*, are the words 'will probably not proceed'. He must have 'proceeded', however, as his name appears in Moreland's list of allotments. He did not take title to his land viz. 152 *Beaulieu* (20 acres), and 7 Block V within circle, in Richmond. This land in Sep. 1873, under Law 4, 1872, became liable to forfeiture to the Government.

SOURCES

Private source material
34 Box 1. Survey record book. Box 4. *Edward* lists

Unpublished official papers
125 2263 no.H287

Official printed sources
168 17.6.1851

Newspapers, periodicals, etc.
189 10.5.1850

ANDERSON, Alexander

Born 24 Sep. 1813, Auchterarder, Perthshire.

He was the son of James Anderson (*c*. 1774–1853) and Helen Stewart (*c*. 1782–1831), and brother of John Anderson (1816–1889)*.

In Mar. 1850 he bought land in Greyling Street, Pietermaritzburg from his brother. Four years later, on 10 Feb. 1854, the *Natal Witness* carried a notice of a 'peremptory sale' of his two pieces of ground in Greyling Street. On 24 February an account appeared in the same newspaper of his arraignment on a charge of the murder in Dec. 1853 of Mrs Jane Meek Thompson (wife of Charles Thompson*), with whom he had been living.

The jury concluded that she had been murdered, but there was no evidence to show that Anderson had done it.

Almost immediately Anderson left the Colony, deserting the infant of Mrs Thompson's of which he was the reputed father. After its mother's death the child had been handed to Margaret Forbes, the estranged wife of A.R. Forbes*, to wet-nurse. From Dec. 1853 to Anderson's acquittal in Feb. 1854 the attorney, A. Walker*, had paid maintenance on Anderson's behalf. After Anderson's departure Walker no longer had the necessary funds for this purpose. Mrs Forbes was thus forced to undertake the sole support of the child until its death in May 1854. She submitted two petitions on the subject to the Lt.-Governor but was unable to get any compensation.

SOURCES

Unpublished official papers
125 2239 no.B547, 2241 no.C196, 2243 nos.721 and 781

Official printed sources
168 10.8.1852

Newspapers, periodicals, etc.
189 10.2.1854, 24.2.1854

Miscellaneous unofficial contemporary printed sources
220

Personal communication
350

ANDERSON, James

Born *c*. 1812.

Carpenter. Anderson was carrying on his trade in Cape Town in 1839. On 10 December of that year he married Amelia Elizabeth Warner Knipe (*c*. Nov. 1818, Middlesex –

7 Feb. 1908, near Estcourt). The ceremony took place in St Andrew's Presbyterian Church in Cape Town.

It is not known when the Andersons came to Natal. References have been found to a James Anderson who bought some land in Oct. 1846 in the insolvent estate of George Winder*. Also there was a James Anderson who in June 1847 was carrying out a contract for the Natal government. On the other hand, according to his daughter Eliza Jane's evidence, she had come to South Africa as a child (*c*. 1850–1851).‡

In his later years in Natal Anderson 'gave himself over to inebriety and idleness'. At the end of June 1851 he deserted his wife and four children and 'quitted' the 'district'. (Possibly he was the Mr Anderson who left for East London on the *Albinia* in Aug. 1851.) His wife was left in great poverty and had to support her family by working as a monthly nurse.

In Nov. 1852, the Anderson children had a horrifying experience. Mrs Anderson, who at the time was working in the home of Rev. Grosvenor*, had, as usual, locked the children into their cottage before leaving for work in the evening. Shortly before midnight, an intruder forced off the staple and lock, entered the cottage, and endeavoured to cut the throat of one of the children, Robert. In the darkness he missed and cut off the lobe of the left ear, through the left cheek, and across the child's chin. The screams of the children brought Mrs Anderson and Rev. Grosvenor running from the Grosvenor house nearby, but the assailant had fled. As Robert shared a bed with the other children and was closest to the wall, the attack was obviously intended for him. Joseph Welford* was later charged with the assault, and evidence was led that about a week before, in a state of intoxication, he had charged Robert and one of S. Beningfield's* sons with throwing stones at him, and threatened to shoot them, brandishing a loaded gun.

In about 1853 the Andersons moved to Verulam, where Mrs Anderson continued to work as a nurse. In 1855 she started proceedings for divorce. A fact that emerges from her sworn affidavit made in June 1855 was that she believed that Anderson had returned to Cape Town or certainly to the Cape. Her divorce was finalized *c*. Mar. 1856. In May she married James Miller*. In the marriage register of the Durban Wesleyan church her marital status is entered as 'widow by law'.

It is worthy of note that Mrs Anderson kept a record of all the births and deaths of her patients. This fact emerges from an affidavit she made in 1901 in connexion with establishing the date of death of one of them, the wife of Josiah Harvey*. She gave the approximate date of Mrs Harvey's death (1866) to within a few days, and stated that she had recorded births and deaths in a book,

---

‡ Eliza Jane's statement in *Women of South Africa*.

which, however, had been destroyed by fire in the 1880s. When it is considered that only in 1868 was it mandatory in Natal for births and deaths to be registered, it is realised what a potentially valuable source this book of hers would have been, had it survived.

Mrs Anderson died at 'Beacon Hill' Upper Zaai Laager, near Estcourt.

CHILDREN

Robert Frederick (born c. 1841).

Eliza Jane (born 1844, Edinburgh)‡ m. Mar. 1861, Verulam, Peter Foster*.

Sarah Ann (c. 1844 – 23 Mar. 1916, Dbn) m. Mar. 1864, Verulam, John Alfred Stevens (c. 1842 – 22 Feb. 1923, Dbn).

Joseph John Basset (Nov. 1850, ?Dbn – 16 Oct. 1854, ?Dbn) died in childhood.

SOURCES

Private source material
44; 53

Unpublished official papers
125 7 no.65, 41 nos.50, 61 and 74, 2239 no.B280; **126** 73; **129** 11/191, 32/40; **130** IA no.1; **131** I/5/41 no.445 (reference supplied by Mr P. Spiller, Faculty of Law, University of Natal, Durban); **137**

Newspapers, periodicals, etc.
177 9.11.1852; **180** 21.10.1854; **183** 11.3.1856; **187** 21.5.1856; **188** 5.11.1852, 19.11.1852; **189** 11.1.1856

Journals, biographies, autobiographies, letters
217 p.101

ANDERSON, John

Born 20 Dec. 1812, Auchenfad (unverified), parish of Renwick, Kirkcudbright. Died 30 June 1898, Pinetown.

Millwright and engineer. Before emigrating to Natal Anderson was employed in Her Majesty's steam engine factory at Portsmouth Dockyard.

On 6 Apr. 1850 at Portsmouth he married Mary King (Aug. 1823, St Erth, Cornwall – 14 Sep. 1912, Pinetown), daughter of John and Mary King. A month later they sailed for Natal on the Minerva.

The Andersons' emigrants' allotments were in the Byrne valley, and this is where they made their first home. Their eldest daughter, Elizabeth, was the first settler child to be born in the valley.

Anderson's trade as a millwright necessitated frequent absences from home. Moreland* noted, on visiting the Byrne valley in Jan. 1852, that Anderson had not been able to do much on his land because he had been working at his trade. During most of 1852 he was engaged in constructing the machinery for E. Henning's* windmill on the Berea in Durban. This, Natal's first windmill, was completed in October of that year. Also in 1852 he had constructed a corn mill at Richmond for H.J.C. Hutton*, while in 1857 he completed a corn and flour mill for the Rev. James Allison* at Edendale.

With the development of cane growing in Natal and the consequent need for mills and other sugar-making machinery, the bulk of Anderson's business became centred on the coast. As a result the family left Byrne early in 1859 and settled in Pinetown. Here he worked as an engineer, mill-wright and wheelwright. He later added wagonmaking to his business. He retired in about 1881.

Although Anderson was in Byrne only a short while, he left his mark there. He was the builder of the small yellow-wood church in which the settlers and their descendants worshipped from 1856 to 1923. In 1929 it was dismantled and the materials sold to meet the expenses of the erection of a cairn to the memory of the early pioneers. The purchaser reassembled the church as a shed on his farm Hamilton at the top of the Byrne valley. It was still intact in the early 1970s.

CHILDREN

Elizabeth Margaret (Apr. 1851, Byrne – 1932) m. 11 July 1872, Pinetown, William Arthur Mallandain, son of Robert Mallandain*.

Mary Clementine (1853, Byrne – 2 Dec. 1910, Pinetown) m. 14 Mar. 1874, Dbn, William Augustus Barrington Dales, son of William Dales*.

John (1855, Byrne – ?23 Oct. 1934, ?Donnybrook) m. 18 June, 1894, The Reproach, Klip River County, Annie Matilda Bloy, d. of Francis Bloy*.

Ellen (1858, Byrne – 1928) m. June 1882, Pinetown, Edward William Evans (May 1859, Manchester – 1923), later of Johannesburg.

Thomas Maxwell (9 Aug. 1859, Pinetown – 17 Mar. 1916, Pinetown) m. 1890, Lucy Elizabeth Bloy, d. of Francis Bloy above.

William King (29 Aug. 1861, Pinetown – Jan. 1942) m. Mar. 1893, Pinetown, Mary Jane Kirk, d. of Joseph Kirk*.

Augusta Agnes (26 Sep. 1864, Pinetown – 1938) m. Apr. 1890, Pinetown, Harry Higgins Boden (1860 – 30 Nov. 1902, at sea), of Durban.

Alfred Joseph (22 Jan. 1868, Pinetown – 1934)
m. (1) 7 Nov. 1894, Ladysmith, Minnie Susannah Hayes (1873 – 30 Mar. 1897, Cape Town), d. of H.S. Hayes of Ladysmith.
m. (2) 1899, Josephine Mary O'Callaghan (1874–1942), d. of W.T. O'Callaghan of Cape Town.

Anderson's sons, John, Thomas and William, all farmed in the Donnybrook district, while Alfred, the youngest, went to Johannesburg in 1891 and went into mining.

SOURCES

Private source material
12 9.5.1851, 26.12.1858, 22.5.1859, 27.2.1868; 28 6/1/3; 29 Anderson papers; 34 Box 4. *Minerva* lists; 62; 63; 64; 71; 78; 80; 105; 113

Unpublished official papers
125 2285, 2286; 126 64, 129 40/159, 47/46, 49/67; 136; 147; 148; 156 86/1898, 236/1902

Official printed sources
168 25.7.1854, 29.7.1856, 10.8.1858, 14.8.1860, 6.8.1867, 6.8.1872, 25.8.1874, 8.9.1874, 3.10.1876

Newspapers, periodicals, etc.
177 5.10.1852; 184 14.10.1852; 185 3.2.1859, 17.2.1859, Oct. 1864, 16.7.1872, 17.3.1874; 188 23.4.1852, 8.10.1852; 189 20.2.1852, 30.4.1852, 18.6.1894, 6.4.1897, 4.12.1902, 23.3.1910; 197 1865, 1866, 1876, 1878, 1879, 1881, 1882, 1884, 1888, 1895; 199 1908 p.7, 1910 p.148

Later sources
267 p.247; 300 p.8; 310 p.14

Personal communication
336

Portraits, photographs, etc.
358

ANDERSON, John

Born 1 June 1816, Auchterarder, Perthshire. Died 17 Oct. 1889, Pietermaritzburg.

Shoemaker. He and Alexander Anderson* were brothers, and scions of the Anderson family of Glen Ogle, Perthshire. Their parents were James Anderson (c. 1774–1853) and Helen Stewart (c. 1782–1831) of Sneddyhaugh (unverified).

Anderson served his apprenticeship as a shoemaker. In Nov. 1836 he enlisted in the 45th Regiment. His regimental number was 1007. He rose to the rank of sergeant, but in 1843 was tried by court martial and reduced to private, and retained this rank for the remainder of his army career. Anderson was a member of one of the first two companies of the 45th to arrive in Natal in July 1843.

Four years later, in June 1847, he received his discharge from the regiment and in the same month he established

himself as a boot and shoemaker at 6 Greyling Street in Pietermaritzburg. Within six years he had prospered amazingly. In Apr. 1850 he advertised vacancies for no less than six journeymen. At roughly the same time, the Perthshireman James Ellis*, newly arrived in the Colony, commented in a letter home, that Anderson was worth a great deal of money and property. His marriage in 1851 further cemented this prosperity, as his wife took an active part in building up the family business.

By 1851 Anderson had moved his premises to erf 11 Church Street. In the 1890s when Pietermaritzburg streets were renumbered, the address was changed to 113 Church Street. Here the Andersons, and later their two sons, conducted a large business. By the mid–1890s they had a factory at 113 Church Street, and outlets for their products outside Pietermaritzburg.

In about 1879 or 1880 Anderson retired and his sons took over, the firm's name then changing to Anderson Bros. Shortly after this Anderson went to live in Richmond on a property named *Cyprus Villa*. However, by the end of 1883 he was back at 11 Church Street.

Anderson took an active interest in local affairs. In the 1850s he was much involved with the formation of the Natal Rifle Corps, of which he was a foundation member. In the early 1860s he was a councillor for Pietermaritzburg and was one of those instrumental in the establishment of the city's Alexandra Park.

His wife was Catherine Whitson (1822, Edinburgh – 12 Jan. 1903, Pmb.), the daughter of Robert Whitson. She had come to Natal in Sep. 1851 on the *Isle of Wight*. They were married in Pietermaritzburg, on 5 December of the same year.

CHILDREN

Helen Stewart (Sep. 1852, Pmb. – June 1924, ?Pmb.) m. 5 Apr. 1881, Pmb., Thomas William Turner (1853, Burghill, Hereford – Mar. 1932, Pmb.), son of J. Turner of Stocks House, Wellington, Herefordshire.

Robert Whitson (Nov. 1854, Pmb. – 3 July 1913, Pmb.) unmarried. Died as a result of a carriage accident. He was a Pmb. city councillor at the time.

John James (5 Nov. 1857, Pmb. – Mar. 1925, Pmb.) unmarried.

It is amusing to note that to the young fry of Pietermaritzburg, Robert, the senior partner, and John James, were respectively known as 'Boots' and 'Shoes'.

SOURCES

Private source material
76; 79; 102

Unpublished official papers
125 2239 no.B547, 2245 no.D523, 2282, 2287; 126 73; 129 15/218, 50/27; 131 IV/18/13 no.165;

132 III/5/12 dated 4.5.1848 and 24.5.1848; **147**;
156 70/1889, 17/1903; **158** 12/5751 July–Sep.
1843, 12/5756 Apr.–June 1847

Official printed sources
168 10.8.1852, 8.8.1854

Newspapers, periodicals, etc.
184 11.4.1850, 11.12.1851; **188** 19.12.1851;
189 25.6.1847, 7.4.1881, 18.10.1889, 14.1.1903,
5.7.1913; **192** July 1850 p.60; **197** 1863, 1873,
1879, 1881, 1882, 1884, 1888, 1895

Miscellaneous unofficial contemporary printed sources
220

Later sources
267 p.188

Personal communication
345

Portraits, photographs, etc.
358; **363**

ANDERSON, Robert

Labourer. He was employed by A. Macnab* in the Karkloof
from 2 July to 28 Nov. 1850. A dispute between the two
men ended with Anderson suing Macnab. Anderson claimed
wages plus expenses outlaid for subsistence and lodging
on a journey to Durban on Macnab's behalf. The case was
due for trial on 15 Jan. 1851 but Macnab, in attempting to
reach Pietermaritzburg to attend court, drowned while
crossing the Umgeni river.

The last reference found to Anderson is at a meeting
in July 1851 of creditors in Macnab's intestate estate.
Here James Millan* acted as Anderson's agent, Anderson
being at sea.

SOURCES

Unpublished official papers
130 1/9 no.37

ANDERSON, Robert

Born c. 1818. Died 14 August 1878, Pietermaritzburg.

Civil engineer and land surveyor. Anderson commenced
practice as a surveyor c. 1842, and before emigrating to
Natal had worked in both England and Ireland, possibly
in Co. Armagh. He arrived in the Colony on the *Herald*

as the surveyor to the settlers sent out by John Lidgett
on that ship, and later on the *Nile* and *Choice*. His wife
and three children followed him to Natal on the *Nile*.

In Aug. 1850 Anderson sought permission of the government to practise as a surveyor in Natal. He and T.W. Fannin
(see Thomas Fannin) had, by Nov. 1850, completed the
survey at Hout Bosch Rand of the settlement to be known
as Lidgett's Town (now Lidgetton). The agency in Natal
for the Lidgett and Hackett settlers appears to have been his
for a short while after J.E. Methley* gave it up. Anderson
was succeeded by James Archbell* and Richard Lawton*.
By Sep. 1852 Anderson was handling another agency,
that of the settlers at York.

Anderson made Durban his headquarters, his address
there being Pine Terrace (Street). By Sep. 1851 he also had
an office in Church Street, Pietermaritzburg, and agents
in both centres. A year later, finding his income as a government surveyor insufficient, he applied, unsuccessfully it
would seem, for a vacant government post.

He is next heard of in Jan. 1854 when he announced
in the press that he had resumed business as a civil engineer
and government surveyor. His address here was given as
Smith Street, Durban. What he had been doing between
the end of 1852 and the beginning of 1854 has not come
to light.

Anderson continued in private practice in Durban until
May 1858 when he obtained the position of Special
Surveyor attached to the Department of the Secretary for
Native Affairs. His particular task was the fixing of the
boundaries of Natal's native locations. Although as a special
government surveyor he was not on the fixed establishment,
he was not allowed to undertake any private work, but
had to depend on his government salary. By mid–1861 he
found his salary and allowances were insufficient to support
his family and petitioned the Lt.-Governor for an increase.
He stated that his living expenses and the wages of his
African labour were double what they had been when he
was first appointed. Furthermore, he averred, he had
experienced heavy losses in oxen and wagons. This memorial
appears to have resulted in an increase of £50 per annum.

His memorial had been addressed from Durban but at
some period between then and 1868 the Andersons moved
to Pietermaritzburg. Up to the time of his death Anderson
retained the post of Special Government Surveyor.

Anderson died at his home *Park View* on erf 14 Burger
Street – the house is now numbered 146 Loop Street.
This property was bequeathed by his widow to their daughter Louisa, wife of Leighton Baylis. Presumably this is how
the adjacent street, Leighton Street, came by its name.

Anderson's wife was Mary Mitchell (c. 1822 – 10 Oct.
1880, Pmb.).

CHILDREN

William Alfred Blackburn (born Ireland – died 1 July
1893, Jhb.) m. 20 Feb. 1878, Pretoria, Grace Jessie

Violet Murray, d. of William Murray*. William was a land surveyor, and at one time was manager of Moodies Goldmining and Exploration Company. Anderson Street in Pretoria is named after him.

Sophia (c. 1845, ?Ireland – 29 Aug. 1894, Pmb.) m. 22 Mar. 1877, Pmb., Henry Cooke Campbell, son of Rev. William Campbell*.

Louisa Martha (c. 1850, Co. Armagh, Ireland – Feb. 1923, Pmb.) m. 31 July, 1880, Verulam, Leighton Baylis (c. 1849, Oxfordshire – 20 Apr. 1904, Pmb.), a dentist and son of George Lawrence Woodroffe Baylis and his wife Annie.

● **Robert Charles** (born Mar. 1852, ?Dbn).

● **Henry Mitchell** (Mar. 1852, ?Dbn – 17 Apr. 1908) m. 28 Nov. 1881, Potchefstroom, Julia Ada Knight (11 July 1855 – 27 Feb. 1941), d. of George Knight (died 1858) of Colchester, Essex and Julianna Acutt (died 1878), sister of Robert Acutt*, W.H. Acutt* and Mrs Beater*. Henry was a land surveyor and settled in Pretoria.

Mary Elizabeth (born Feb. 1854, Dbn) m. 1 June 1876, Pmb., Dr Samuel Kyle Cotter (born 1841, Charleville, Co. Cork, Ireland), a surgeon in the Army Medical Corps.

● denotes twins

SOURCES

Private source material
29 *Nile* list; 30 Letter dated 6.4.1857; 53; 72; 76; 77; 85; 114 1.10.1880

Unpublished official papers
125 2239 no.B488, 2241 nos.C197 and C244A, 2244 nos.D1 and D81, 2286, 2287; 129 8/202, 27/52; 133 I/1/11 no.70, I/1/32 no.134; 147; 156 373/1878, 52/1880, 8/1894, 81/1894

Official printed sources
168 15.8.1854

Newspapers, periodicals, etc.
184 14.11.1850, 19.1.1854; 185 8.2.1854, 24.5.1854, 6.5.1858, 3.6.1876, 24.3.1877, 14.3.1878, 16.8.1878, 4.8.1880, 16.10.1880, 7.12.1881; 188 29.9.1851; 189 31.5.1850, 2.6.1876, 23.3.1877, 14.3.1878, 15.8.1878, 16.8.1878, 10.8.1880, 7.10.1880, 4.7.1893, 30.8.1894, 23.10.1897; 197 1868, 1869, 1871–1873, 1881

Miscellaneous unofficial contemporary printed sources
220

Later sources
231 pp.184–5; 293 pp.157–60

ANDERSON, William

Born 20 July 1790, Torryburn, Fifeshire. Died 22 Oct. 1873, *Milichan Hall*, near Ladysmith.

Farmer. For some years Anderson worked either as estate manager or gardener on the Earl of Caledon's estate in Co. Tyrone, Ireland. While in Tyrone he married Elizabeth Smith (5 Sep. 1797, Cambridgeshire – 8 Apr. 1878, Ladysmith). They were married at Caledon on 28 Apr. 1817.

Judging from the birthplaces of their children, they changed their place of residence fairly frequently. Some time between 1820 and 1823 they left Caledon and went to Scotland. Here they appear to have lived firstly at Edinburgh, then at Castle Semple in Renfrewshire. By Sep. 1830 they had moved to Garnkirk in Lanarkshire. At the time they came to Natal they were enrolled as members of the Presbyterian church at Chryston, near Garnkirk.

The Anderson family emigrated to the Colony in stages. First to come was their eldest son Robert, two unmarried daughters, Esther and Martha and their married daughter Jessie, with her husband A.K. Murray*. This party arrived on the *Ina*. The Murrays went to live in Pinetown and the young Andersons followed suit. Mr and Mrs Anderson with six of their remaining seven children sailed from Glasgow on the *Isle of Wight*, landing at Durban in Sep. 1851. Their sixth daughter, Elizabeth, and her husband came to Natal only in July 1857, on the *Lady of the Lake*.

At first the Andersons settled at Pinetown. Shortly after their arrival, Murray endeavoured to obtain for his father-in-law the position of poundmaster in the village. In Mar. 1852 Murray again approached the Acting Secretary to Government on the subject. From the press it would appear that only in November of that year was Anderson officially appointed to the post. An item in the *Natal Mercury* a month later noted that he was managing Murray's farm at Pinetown, and described him as an 'experienced and professional horticulturist'. Also in 1852, in May, Anderson was appointed to the Committee of Management of the Pinetown Presbyterian Church.

Anderson and his wife appear still to have been living in Pinetown by mid–1853. By Sep. 1857 it would seem they were living at Assegai Kraal on the Durban-Pietermaritzburg road on the Pietermaritzburg side of the boundary between Pietermaritzburg and Durban Counties. They were still there in Mar. 1858, but by May 1860 were back in Pinetown. It would appear that in their old age they were taken into the home of their son-in-law, John Allison*, near Ladysmith.

The Anderson family brought about a strong link, particularly in the 1850s, between Pinetown and Ladysmith. All the children with the exception of one, Jessie, lived in or near Ladysmith at one time or another. Also, it was through Anderson's future son-in-law, Captain Struben*, that Rev. Charles Scott* and his family moved from Pinetown towards the end of 1854. Struben was the Resident Magistrate for Klip River County and made possible the appointment of Scott as minister and teacher at Ladysmith.

CHILDREN

Isabella (2 Apr. 1819, Caledon, Co. Tyrone – 13 Apr. 1900, Ladysmith) unmarried.

Harriet (Sep. 1820, Caledon – Feb. 1848, Scotland) unmarried.

Elizabeth (Mar. 1822, stillborn).

● **Esther** (26 Apr. 1823, Edinburgh – 12 Dec. 1899, Pmb.) m. July 1851, ?Dbn, Edward William Tilney/Tinley*.

● **Jessie** or **Janet** (26 Apr. 1823, Edinburgh – 30 July 1911, Pmb.) m. 26 or 28 Mar. 1841, Scotland, Archibald Keir Murray*.

Elizabeth (28 Apr. 1825, Castle Semple, Renfrew – 9 Nov. 1896, Ladysmith) m. May 1851, Scotland, David Newton*.

Christiana (7 Feb. 1828, Edinburgh – 12 Nov. 1898, Ladysmith) m. 6 Sep. 1852, Pinetown, John Allison*.

Robert Shand (24 Sep. 1830, Garnkirk, Lanarks. – 15 Aug. 1878, Pmb.) m. 20 Sep. 1860, Camperdown, Frances Wright, d. of Leonard Wright*. Robert was a transport rider and farmer.

Catherine (20 Aug. 1832, Garnkirk – 19 Sep. 1914)
m. (1) 25 July 1855, Ladysmith, Johannes Hermanus Marinus Struben.
m. (2) James Brooks (1841, Scotland – 21 Nov. Nov. 1901, Pretoria), son of James and Margaret Brooks (born Taylor). Brooks was a Transvaal surveyor, after whom the Pretoria suburb of Brooklyn was named.

Mary Ann (Polly) (20 June 1834, Garnkirk – 14 Oct. 1911, Dbn) m. 6 Sep. 1852, Pinetown, Humphrey Evans Knight*.

Martha (Patty) (30 Sep. 1836, Garnkirk – Mar. 1900, Worthing, Sussex) m. 7 Nov. 1855, Ladysmith, William Field*.

William Smith (born 7 Nov. 1839, Garnkirk)
m. (1) 10 Apr. 1860, Colenso, Maria Charlotte Johnstone, d. of A.J. Johnstone*.
m. (2) Annie Charlotte Richards (c. 1863 – 12 Sep. 1905, Volksrust, Tvl), d. of E.R. Richards and grand-daughter of Edward Richards*. William was a transport-rider.

Archibald Murray (6 Feb. 1843, Garnkirk – Sep. 1936, Pmb.) m. 21 Mar. 1870, Harrismith, Adrienne Johanna van Maltitz (Mar. 1852, Colesberg, Cape – Oct. 1945, ?Pmb.), d. of Pieter J.M. van Maltitz of Colesberg. Archibald was a transport-rider.

● denotes twins

SOURCES

Private source material
18; 33 1.9.1857, 2 to 4.3.1858, 26.2.1859, 10.4.1860, 12.2.1861, 20.9.1861; 34 Box 4. *Ina* lists; 66; 76; 77; 79; 97; 103; 123

Unpublished official papers
125 14 no.115, 16(2) no.135, 2239 no.B514, 2282, 2283; 126 73; 129 9/256, 42/211, 43/146, 43/211; 131 IV/23/2 no.135; 137; 143; 147; 156 363/1878, 76/1896, 84/1900

Newspapers, periodicals, etc.
184 18.11.1852; 185 30.12.1852, 16.11.1855, 3.5.1860, 27.9.1860, 28.10.1873, 10.4.1878, 13.4.1878, 12.11.1896; 188 10.9.1852; 189 16.4.1878, 17.8.1878, 13.12.1899, 29.11.1901, 22.9.1905, 17.10.1911; 197 1881

Journals, biographies, autobiographies, letters
217 p.258

Later sources
300 p.7

Personal communication
337

ANDERSON, William

Born c. 1818.

He arrived on the *Conquering Hero*. Judging from their dates of birth there is a possibility that he and William Pringle Anderson* are one and the same. By the beginning of August 1850 he was earning a living in Durban as a plasterer.

Possibly he was the William Anderson who was employed as a labourer by A. Macnab* from 21 Oct. 1850 until 6 Jan. 1851. This supposition rests on the fact that the labour force on Macnab's farm consisted almost entirely of emigrants who had been fellow-passengers of his on the *Conquering Hero*.

Presumably he was the William Anderson who did not claim his Richmond allotments viz. 174 *Beaulieu* (20 acres) and 7 Block E in Richmond. In Sep. 1873 this land, under Law 4, 1872, became subject to Government forfeiture.

SOURCES

Unpublished official papers
125 2263 no.H287; 126 64; 130 1/9 no.37

ANDERSON, William

Born *c.* 1818, Glasgow. Died 21 Aug. 1898, Durban. Station-master, N.G.R. Anderson had served in the 27th Regiment and had been discharged in Dec. 1845, in Cape Town.

By Mar. 1849 he had arrived in Natal. As a discharged soldier he applied for an erf in Pietermaritzburg. Half of erf 111 [*sic*] Burger Street was granted him in Apr. 1849.

By 1857 he was living in Durban. In July of that year he again petitioned for a piece of land. This he did under the Proclamation dated 29 Apr. 1857, offering grants of Crown lands. The farm he applied for was between the Umpambinyoni and Umzimai rivers. He described it as adjoining the boundary of the farm *Umbelli Belli* (see R. Joyce) and between Mrs Higham's and the coast lands applied for by Henry Milner*.

His request to be near the Highams (see J.H. Higham) identifies him as the William Anderson, a labourer, who had married Mrs Higham's mother, Isabella, widow of Henry Caldwell*. They were married in Apr. 1856 in Durban. He was a widower at the time.

Similarly it can be established that he was the William Anderson, the first station-master of Berea Road station, Durban, who, according to A.M. McCrystal's *Dawn of Durban*, was related to William Pigg, son of A. Pigg*. William Pigg's wife was Janet Caldwell, another daughter of Isabella Caldwell.

Although Anderson was unsuccessful in his application for land in the vicinity of Umzinto, he was, by mid–1859, living in this area. He was still there in Aug. 1862.

By 1881 he was the station-master of 'West-end' station (later Berea Road), a position he held until at least 1887. It is possible that he was the William Anderson who appears in the 1876–77 Durban borough voters' roll as a railway guard of Smith Street and in the 1879 *Natal Almanac* as a railway guard of Ordnance Road, Durban.

SOURCES

Private source material
44

Unpublished official papers
125 2249 no.E247, 2250 no.E584, 2252 no.F99; **129** 9/258; **131** IV/12/13 no.104; **132** III/5/12 dated 13.3.1849, III/5/18 no.407; **137**

Official printed sources
168 3.10.1876

Newspapers, periodicals, etc.
197 1879, 1882, 1884, 1888, 1895

Later sources
289 p.16

ANDERSON, William

Born *c.* 1823.

A farmer from Port of Spittal near Stoneykirk, Wigtownshire, who emigrated to Natal on the *Unicorn*. Possibly he was the William Anderson whose land in the Richmond district, viz. 85 *Harmony* Illovo (20 acres) and 12 Block R within circle, Richmond, was never claimed. This land, by Sep. 1873, had, under Law 4, 1872, become subject to government forfeiture.

SOURCES

Private source material
34 Box 4. *Unicorn* lists

Unpublished official papers
125 2263 no.H287

Newspapers, periodicals, etc.
189 27.9.1850

ANDERSON, William Henry

Supercargo and part-owner of the *Minerva*, one of the Byrne & Co. emigrant vessels. Anderson sailed for Natal on his ship. From the letters of Ellen and George More McLeod* one gets an insight into Anderson's character, and a complex one it was too. Whenever spoken to his answer was prefaced with 'D––n your eyes' (as spelt by George McLeod with true Victorian propriety). He was 'a stout gentleman' and bore a resemblance to Tom Spring (the professional name of Thomas Winter (1795–1851), champion English pugilist). This likeness Anderson accentuated in his dress, keeping up the illusion until the *Minerva* reached Durban. Another facet of his personality manifested itself during the voyage. He helped the little girls to pass the time by thoughtfully providing quantities of bits of coloured material for them to make into patchwork quilts.

In Feb. 1851, some months after landing, Anderson wrote to the Secretary to Government for the certificates of location of the *Minerva* emigrants. He had been advised by his joint owners that the production of these to the Land and Emigration Commissioners would be necessary to enable them to receive the return of the £2 000 they had deposited with the Commissioners on despatching the emigrants. The substance of the answer he received was that most of the certificates were in Byrne's name and could not be issued to him. They would have to be either given to the assignees of Byrne's estate or transmitted in duplicate to the Emigration Commissioners.

Anderson was still in Natal, and living in Durban, in

Aug. 1851. It is not known when he left the colony.

The last piece of information about him comes from a July 1854 issue of the *Natal Commercial Advertiser*. It was reported that Anderson, 'formerly a resident in this colony', had been convicted of forgery and sentenced to seven years' penal servitude.

SOURCES

Private source material
> **12** 17.5.1850, 31.12.1854; **34** Box 1. Moreland to Byrne 5.7.1850, 23.7.1850

Unpublished official papers
> **125** 13(1) no.19; **131** IV/12/13 no.11

Newspapers, periodicals, etc.
> **180** 22.7.1854

Later sources
> **247** p.1425

ANDERSON, William Pringle

Born *c.* 1817, Berwick Upon Tweed, Northumberland. Died 1892, Berwick Upon Tweed.

Pilot. Anderson was a master mariner and came from a sea-faring family. One of his ancestors had fought on the *Victory* during the Battle of Trafalgar.

When Anderson emigrated to Natal has not been discovered. Taking into account his age and that of William Anderson* (born *c.* 1818), ex *Conquering Hero*, there is a possibility that they are one and the same.

Anderson was followed by his wife and three of their children in 1852. They reached Durban in August of that year on the *Rydal*. The eldest son, John, was left in the care of one of Mrs Anderson's sisters. He came to Natal only in May 1859 on the *Lady of the Lake*. Anderson stood surety for the repayment of John's passage money under the government emigration scheme then in operation. Also on board was Anderson's sister-in-law, Charlotte, and her husband, George Moffitt, a chainmaker from Seaham Harbour, Durham. Anderson stood surety for them as well. Charlotte eventually became the third wife of Alexander Smith (1818–1893)*.

Anderson worked in Durban Bay as a pilot, but it would seem from the Natal Blue Books that he was appointed to the permanent establishment only in 1859. He was pensioned during 1878. About 4 years later he returned to Berwick Upon Tweed.

Anderson was twice married. His first wife was Jane Wardle or Wardell (*c.* 1817, Sunderland, Durham – 19 Sep. 1873, Durban), the daughter of Thomas Page Wardle/ Wardell. His second wife was a Mrs Janet Colquhoun Whiting (*c.* 1834, Paisley, Renfrew – 24 May, 1917, Durban). She had come from Adelaide, Australia.

CHILDREN

John Thomas (*c.* 1841, Sunderland, – 14 Mar. 1881, Dbn) m. 9 Dec. 1866, Dbn, Emma Todman (*c.* 1847, ?Surrey – 1 Jan. 1919, ?Dbn), d. of Richard and Hannah Todman.

Alexander (Mar. 1844, Sunderland – Apr. 1938, buried Dbn) m. 23 June 1876, Umzinto, Clara Joyner, d. of William Joyner*. Alexander was a master shipwright and mariner. He wrote *Windjammer yarns: some incidents in the life of a South African seaman. . .* (1923)

Charlotte (*c.* 1845, Sunderland – 28 May 1866, Dbn) m. 24 Jan. 1862, Dbn, Archibald Borland (*c.* 1839, Glasgow – 10 Dec. 1878, Pmb.), son of Archibald and Mary Borland.

William Henry (*c.* Mar. 1850, – 19 Dec. 1915, Dbn) m. 24 Mar. 1874, Dbn, Agnes Aingworth (*c.* 1853, Dudley, Staffs. – 14 Oct. 1889, Dbn), d. of Richard Reed Angell Aingworth. William Henry was a marine engineer.

Frances (May 1853, Dbn – June 1931, Pmb.) m. 10 Sep. 1874, Dbn, James Arbuckle Richardson, son of J.A. Richardson*.

Jane (Jenny) (born Jan. 1858, ?Dbn) m. 2 Nov. 1876, Dbn, Joachim Heinrich Graumann, proprietor of the Criterion Hotel, Durban. By 1893 Jane was living in Hamburg, Germany.

SOURCES

Private source material
> **19**; **40**; **44**; **45**; **48**; **53**; **83**; **92**; **113**

Unpublished official papers
> **125** 2283, 2285, 2286; **126** 65, 73; **129** 3/20 no.T16, 5/19, 5/236, 6/223, 7/138, 21/79; **137**; **147**; **156** 23/1881, 17–18/1882, 9/1916

Official printed sources
> **166**

Newspapers, periodicals, etc.
> **185** 4.3.1858, May 1866, 30.9.1873, 9.4.1874, 12.9.1874, 9.3.1875, 27.6.1876, 23.3.1881; **188** 13.8.1852; **189** 12.3.1875, 30.6.1876, 24.5.1890, 7.5.1892; **197** 1879, 1881

Later sources
> **228** *passim*, especially pp.74, 88, 96–7, 112–3, 128, 147; **229**; **234** p.153; **321**

ANDRADE, A.F.

Born *c.* 1821.

He emigrated to Natal on the *Edward*. It would appear, as Professor Hattersley suggested, that he was the Antonio F. Andrade who became Secretary and General Manager of the Natal Railway Company. He was appointed on 15 Sep. 1868 and replaced A. McArthur*.

During Andrade's managership the whole Colony was in a depressed state. Campbell's *The birth and development of the Natal railways* well describes the lean period the Point-Umgeni railway went through at the time. The wages of the Indian labourers were, at one stage, twelve months overdue. The white staff also had to wait several months for their pay. Payment of salaries and wages depended on the debts collected, and this activity was part of Andrade's duties. Money was so scarce that railway staff were often given orders by the Management on grocers, butchers, etc. for goods on account per contra the money these firms owed the railway. Campbell records that the staff was so reduced that besides being General Manager, Secretary and Debt Collector, Andrade was his own secretary and correspondence clerk.

On more than one occasion Andrade had been praised for the competent manner in which he attended to the Company's affairs and books. Towards the end of 1870 it became apparent that his handling of the latter had been a little too accomplished, in that he had misappropriated about £200.

At the meeting of shareholders of the Company in Apr. 1871, the directors, in their report for the half-year ending 31 Dec. 1870, announced these defalcations, and stated that Andrade had been dismissed. Although there was a warrant out for his arrest, he had not, at the time of the meeting, been apprehended.

J.H. Russell was appointed in his place. Russell later married the widow of R.P. (Dick) King*.

SOURCES

Private source material
  34 Box 4. *Edward* lists

Unpublished official papers
  126 64

Newspapers, periodicals, etc.
  185 22.4.1871

Later sources
  244 pp.38–9; 325 pp.46, 49

ANDREWS, George

Born *c.* 1833. Died 4 Aug. 1911, Durban.

Clerk and storekeeper. Andrews emigrated to Natal because he had a weak chest but his origins and the date when he arrived are a matter of surmise. From circumstantial evidence it would appear that he came from Hampshire, possibly landing in Natal in Oct. 1853. In that month a Mr Andrews appears on the passenger list of the *Princeza*.‡

Presumably he was the George Andrews who, by at least Aug. 1854, was renting *Holderness Farm* in the Pinetown area. He was still there at the end of that year but by Oct. 1855 he appears to have been living in Durban. In that month his fiancée arrived on the *Lady of the Lake* and they were married in Durban. She was Mary Ann (Polly) Ford (7 Sep. 1834, ?Hampshire – 13 Oct. 1911, Durban), daughter of Edward Ford of Warblington, near Emsworth, Hants. and his wife Elizabeth (born Funnell).

Until about the end of 1857 Andrews was employed in Durban as a clerk. In November he took over a store in West Street previously in the occupation of a Mr Williams. The stock advertised included buttons, wools, embroidery and 'trimmings'. It appears that Mrs Andrews ran the business, judging from an advertisement in the *Natal Mercury* in Jan. 1858 in which she offered ladies' and children's clothing. Also, certainly later in the year, in April, Andrews was employed as storekeeper by A. McArthur*.

In May 1859 the Andrews family moved to Pietermaritzburg where he opened a business, his Stone Store in Church Street carrying similar lines to their Durban store, viz. materials and clothing. By the end of 1862 his premises were on erf 19 Church Street, and groceries had been added to his stock-in-trade.

Andrews's business did not survive the depression of the 1860s. In Mar. 1863 he voluntarily surrendered his estate. In a statement made at one of the meetings of his creditors he detailed the history of his trading activities in Pietermaritzburg. He started without any capital. For the first two years the business was able to keep him, but for the last two it had been a losing concern. He ascribed this to bad debts and competition. From his balance sheet, drawn up *c.* Mar. 1864, his deficit appears to have been only £60.

Information on the Andrews's activities over the next few years is scanty. He was employed by James Ashton*

‡ This supposition has since been proved correct. While this volume was in the press an undated, unidentified newspaper cutting was discovered which gives an account of the golden wedding celebrations of Mr & Mrs Andrews. This report states that Andrews came to Natal on the *Princeza* in 1853.

(handwritten) Polly Ford born at Emsworth, Hants. Died 13 Oct 1917.

who, in July 1865, also went insolvent. The Andrews family appear to have still been in Pietermaritzburg by mid–1866 but by Aug. 1867 Andrews was working in Durban as a clerk, and by Dec. 1870 the family was in Greytown. Here Andrews once again was employed as a clerk. He worked for the Greytown merchant Thomas Handley* for a number of years. In the early 1880s he started a store on his own account. During his Greytown days Andrews was a churchwarden of St James's Anglican Church.

He later retired to Malvern, on medical grounds. His final home was in Durban.

According to a grand-daughter, Miss Myrtle Andrews, he at one time tried farming at Tongaat, but could not make a living there. It is not clear when this was.

His wife's parents and most of their children emigrated to Natal on the *Phantom*. They arrived in July 1858 under the government-sponsored scheme then in operation, Andrews standing surety for the repayment of their passage money. Ford, in his turn, stood surety for his wife's sisters, Ann, her husband William Dawes and their family, and Lucy, her husband George Salmon and their children. The Dawes family arrived in Apr. 1860 on the *Lady of the Lake*, and the Salmons in Mar. 1861 on the *Leila*.

One John Andrews (born *c.* 1837, Farringdon, Hants.), possibly George's brother, was married in Pietermaritzburg in Nov. 1864. George witnessed the marriage. John's grand-father was William Penton of Farringdon and his parents were Andrew and Elizabeth Andrews (presumably born Penton), both of whom were deceased by Jan. 1866. Andrew Andrews had formerly lived in Winchester. John Andrews in 1866 executed a power of attorney in connexion with his mother's estate. One of the executors of the will was William Penton Andrews of Farringdon.

CHILDREN

George Edward (born 13 Sep. 1856, Dbn, died Escombe near Dbn) m. 3 Feb. 1879, Ficksburg, O.F.S., Emily Lees Mitchley (*c.* 1859, Imparane, Ficksburg – 5 Dec. 1925, Escombe, near Dbn), d. of F. Mitchley of Ficksburg.

Henry (17 Apr. 1858, Dbn – 22 Oct. 1860, Pmb.) died in childhood.

Charles William (born 29 Jan. 1860, Pmb.) m. 20 July, 1891, Newcastle, Emily Florence Meek (born 17 Aug. 1869, ?Greytown, died Jhb.), d. of Walter Edward Meek, and great-granddaughter of John Meek*.

Gertrude (born Oct. 1861, Pmb., died Greytown) m. 27 Dec. 1887, Greytown, Ernest Edward Tomlinson, son of Edward Tomlinson*.

daughter (21–22 Mar. 1863, Pmb.) died in infancy.

Arthur Penton (Apr. 1864, Pmb. – 29 Aug. 1936, Greytown) m. 13 July, 1897, Greytown, Sara Ann Wilson (*c.* 1868, Natal – 11 Feb. 1948, Greytown).

Percy (born *c.* 26 July 1866, Pmb.).

Frank (8 Dec. 1867, Dbn – 18 July 1939, Fort Nottingham) m. 25 June 1895, Greytown, Mary Rose McQueen (*c.* 1872 – 30 Sep. 1940, ?Nottingham Road), d. of A.G.K. McQueen and his wife Mary Jane Gordon, and granddaughter of Capt. A. Gordon*.

Constance Mary (22 Dec. 1870, Greytown – 7 Apr. 1932, Greytown) m. 4 June 1895, Greytown, Alexander Hay McLean, son of Alexander McLean*.

Ernest Frederick (born 8 Feb. 1873, Greytown).

Henrietta Selina (14 Nov. 1874, Greytown – Sep. 1951, Greytown) m. 22 Apr. 1897, Greytown, Charles West Handley, son of Thomas Handley*.

John Shirley (28 Aug. 1876, Greytown – 1 May 1942, Moseley, near Dbn) m. 27 Dec. 1913, Nina Muriel Symonds (born 30 Mar. 1894).

According to the unidentified newspaper cutting mentioned above, George jnr. was living at Ingagane (near Newcastle?) in 1905, Charles in Pietermaritzburg, Percy in Ladysmith and John in Durban. Gertrude and Henrietta were of Greytown and Constance lived in the Dargle.

SOURCES

Private source material
48; 56; 58; 67; 74; 86; 92; 94

Unpublished official papers
125 2282, 2284; **126** 63, 65; **127** 1584 p.80; **129** 42/244; **130** 1/26 no.36, 1/30 no.13, 1/31 no.25; **131** IV/3/68 no.47, IV/23/2 no.11/1868, IV/7/17 no.462; **137; 138; 139; 141; 144**

Official printed sources
168 15.8.1854, 6.8.1867, 20.8.1872, 22.9.1874, 8.8.1876

Newspapers, periodicals, etc.
180 5.1.1855; **181** 29.2.1860, 31.10.1860, 16.10.1861; **185** 26.11.1857, Jan. 1858, 29.4.1858, 8.11.1860, Mar. 1863, Aug. 1866, Dec. 1867, 17.1.1871, 20.2.1873, 20.2.1879; **187** 24.10.1855, 24.9.1856, 21.11.1857, 11.2.1860; **189** 10.6.1859, 3.2.1860, 5.9.1876, 22.2.1879, 29.12.1887, 6.6.1895; **197** 1863, 1879, 1882, 1884, 1888, 1895

Later sources
321

Personal communication
339; 349

Portraits, photographs, etc.
296 p.45, no. D51; **362** (also Mary Ann Andrews)

ANDREWS, John

Very little is known about this person. A son was baptised in Durban in June 1857, and a second was baptised in Pietermaritzburg in June 1862. His wife's name was Ann.

Presumably he was the John Andrews who (*c.* 1857–1860) was farming at *Valsch River* near the Umlaas river. He was also a trader. In 1859 he purchased William Slatter's* property in Pinetown. While living in Pinetown Andrews ran a butchery. This A.K. Murray* purchased in June 1861.

Possibly, too, he was the John Andrews who in the late 1860s and early 1870s was listed in the Pietermaritzburg County jury lists as a farmer of *Boschfontein*. He was renting this property.

He may have been the John of Bethlehem, O.F.S. formerly of Natal, who in 1865 was attacked by Africans and died as a result of his injuries. He died on 24 Aug. 1865.

CHILDREN

John William (May 1857, Dbn – 1906, ?Vryheid) m. 29 May 1890, Vryheid, Elizabeth Alice Amelia Sarah Emmett (born *c.* 1872, near Smithfield, O.F.S.), d. of John George Emmett of *Riet Vallei*, Vryheid.

Joseph Hobson (born Apr. 1862, ?Pmb.).

SOURCES

Private source material
  53; **77**

Unpublished official papers
  131 IV/12/13 dated 2 Apr. 1859; **155**;
  156 124/1906

Official printed sources
  168 10.8.1858, 14.8.1860

Newspapers, periodicals, etc.
  185 12.2.1857, 11.3.1958; **187** 29.6.1861

ANDREWS, John

Born *c.* May 1820, Kent. Died 21 Jan. 1900, Lower Umgeni, near Durban.

Blacksmith and boilermaker. Andrews, his wife Maria Henrietta (*c.* 1818 – 6 Dec. 1870, Durban) and four children sailed to Natal on the *Emily*. They emigrated under W.J. Irons's* Christian Emigration and Colonization Society. As an Irons settler his land was situated in the Verulam area. By Dec. 1850 the Andrews family were living in that vicinity. They suffered a setback in June 1853 when their home was burnt down, and they lost all their possessions. In reporting the incident the *D'Urban Advocate* described him as a 'hardworking and industrious man'.

The Andrewses were still farming near Verulam in July 1854, but sometime between then and Sep. 1857 they moved to the *Tongaat Estate* (see J.R. Saunders). In about Sep. 1857 Andrews started business in Durban as a boilermaker and machinist. Over the next number of years, in the various references found, his occupation is given as either blacksmith (1858, 1860, 1870), or boilermaker (1868, 1874, 1876, 1878). His addresses in the Durban area vary, eg. Umgeni (1863), Umgeni Road (1868), Victoria Street (1870), and St George's Street (1874, 1876, 1878).

CHILDREN

Maria Elizabeth (*c.* 1840, Kent – 15 or 16 Jan. 1905, Pmb.) m. 28 Sep. 1859, Dbn, George Goodwin (*c.* 1836–30 Oct. 1870, Pmb.), a confectioner.

Mary Ann (born *c.* 1843, ?Kent) m. 10 Dec. 1863, Dbn, William Kirk (Sep. 1836, Yorks. – 14 Aug. 1900, Dbn), formerly of Hutton Sessay, Yorks, brother of Joseph Kirk*. William had emigrated on the *Priscilla* in Mar. 1859. He was Foreman of Town Works, Durban, at the time of their marriage.

Sarah Agnes (born *c.* 1845, Kent) m. 22 Apr. 1868, Stamford Hill, near Dbn. William Chick, son of John Chick*.

Jane Henrietta (or Jeanette) (*c.* 1848, Bexley, Kent – 19 Sep. 1912, Dbn) m. 25 Sep. 1873, Dbn 1873, Dbn, George Wilkinson Turner (born Gravesend, Kent).

Martha (born *c.* 1853, Verulam) m. 27 June 1878, Dbn, Richard John Chick, son of John Chick, above.

Thomas William (1856, Verulam – 1928, ?Barberton) m. Aug. 1879, Pinetown, Louisa Maud Emily Horton, d. of Edward Horton*.

George Frederick (*c.* 1858, Dbn – 8 Feb. 1903, Hlabisa district) m. 4 July 1894, Liverpool, Isabel Gertrude Canty, d. of Dr Henry E. Canty, M.R.C.S.L., of Liverpool.

Thomas and George were pioneers of the de Kaap goldfields in the Eastern Transvaal where George discovered the Ulundi mine.

SOURCES

Private source material
  29 Chick papers; **34** Box 4. *Emily* lists; **36** W.J. Irons to Theophilus Irons July 1850; **48**; **53**; **78**; **92**

Unpublished official papers
  125 2239 no.B544, 2283, 2286; **126** 65;
  129 10/64, 11/334, 16/146, 22/132, 47/40;
  131 IV/19/37 no.100; **137**; **147**; **154**;
  156 62/1903, 15/1905

Killie Campbell Africana Library

William Henry Ablett

Killie Campbell Africana Library

Sarah Ablett

Local History Museum

William Henry Addison

Local History Museum

Juliana Addison

Ablett, W.H. 153
Abraham, Rev. A. 45
Acutt, R. 171
Acutt, W.H. 98
Anderson, J. (b. 1812) 115
Anderson, J. (b. 1816) 18
Arbuckle, W. 112
Armstrong, F. 22
Bale, W.E. 51
Baseley, J. 100
Baynes, J. 146
Baynes, R. 145
Baxter, J. 77
Behrens, C. 8
Bell, F. 167
Beningfield, F.S. 12
Beningfield, S. 11
Berning, F.S. 39
Blakey, H. 143
Blamey, J.C. 69
Bottomley, G. 40
Brander, A. 26
Brickhill, Jas. 13
Brown, Jno. 144
Browne, R. 99
Buchanan, D.D. 25
Burne, J. 31
Buttery, T. 139
Campbell, W. 113
Cass, T. 140
Cass, W. 141
Challinor, E.J. 127
Chapman, J.J. 117
Chapman, T. 156
Chick, J. 78
Churchill, J.F. 147
Clarence, A.F. 43
Clarence, R. 24
Clark, J. 79
Clark, W. 80
Compton, G. 68
Cooper, W. 118
Cowey, H. 102
Cowey, W. 116
Crowder, B. 168
Cubitt, J. 104
Cullingworth, J. 70
Dacomb, C. 103
Davenport, T. 119
Davidson, P.P.J. 34
Doig, J.D. 148
Dove, J. 38
Drew, G. 35
Duff, T. 83
Eastwood, G.F. 157
Elliott R. 53
Ellis, W.F. 135
Evans, A.W. 149

Fearnsides, D. 81
Ferreira, P. 7
Finnemore, I.P. 121
Forrest, J. 16
Fuller, F. 71
Fynn, H.F. 1
Garland, T.W. 72
Gavin, J. 130
George, W. 57
Giles, J. 41
Grant, J.H. 128
Grant, W. 129
Green, T. 19
Griffin, C.C. 28
Groom, T. 82
Grout, Rev. A. 3
Grout, Rev. L. 33
Haigh, G. 64
Handley, T. 86
Hartley, W. 87
Harvey, F. 131
Harvey, J. 134
Harvey, J.H. 132
Harvey, T.M. 133
Hathorn, J.P. 122
Hawkins, A.C. 170
Henwood, P. 54
Heys, T. 73
Hillary, G. 85
Hodgson, W. 106
Holding, W. 124
Holliday, J.D. 105
Humphrey, R. 59
Hunt, G. 174
Hunt, J. 142
Ireland, Rev. W. 42
James, J. 107
Jones, R. 84
King, G. 50
King, R.P. 2
Kinsman, G.W. 165
Kirkman, J. 4
Knox, H.J. 88
Lester, J. 89
Lindley, Rev. D. 5
Lister, W. 166
Lloyd, Rev. W.H.C. 44
London, E. 108
McArthur, A. 164
McDonald, C. 14
McGill, E.F. 27
McKen, M.J. 160
McKenzie, J.T. 10
McKenzie, W. 114
McKnight, J. 17
McLaren, J. 159
Mason, J. 49
Matterson, J.K. 74

Methley, J.E. 23
Middleton, W.H. 56
Morrison, R. 65
Muirhead, A. 29
Murray, A.K. 158
Nicholson, J.D. 91
Osborn, A. 32
Palmer, W. 61
Pay, G. 101
Pike, W. 15
Pinsent, S. 52
Plowes, G. 161
Polkinghorne, J.T. 136
Povall, C. 109
Poynton, T. 62
Reynolds, L. 151
Reynolds, T. 150
Rich, J.A. 60
Roberts, A.B. 173
Robinson, J. 152
Rood, Rev. D. 37
Russell, G. 123
Saker, G. 76
Saker, G.W. 75
Sanderson, J. 93
Savory, W.H. 66
Shaw, J.W. 48
Shepstone, T. 8
Shuter, J.D. 137
Simpson, H.G. 30
Smerdon, W. 172
Spearman, G. 92
Spradbrow, C. 63
Stanton, J. 125
Symons, J.P. 67
Tarboton, D.H. 95
Tatham, E. 90
Taylor, Jno. 94
Taylor, Dr W.G. 58
Thurston, H.L. 126
Towning, F.T. 154
Tunmer, W. 169
Turton, J. 111
Tyler, Rev. J. 155
Tyzack, R.W. 110
Vanderplank J. 9
Wade, J. 138
Walker, A. 21
Ward, J. 36
Warwick, F. 162
West, J.E. 47
Wheeler, J.N. 20
Whipp, J. 97
Wilder, Rev. H.A. 46
Wirsing, G.H. 55
Witherspoon, J.D. 120
Wright, W. 96

Group of Natal pioneers who arrived before 1852

A composite portrait group prepared in 1872 and signed by Jas. Brickhill. It includes children of settlers and also non-British colonists.

Photo: *Natal Museum*

The portraits within the oval are those of residents prior to the proclamation of peace with the emigrant farmers in 1842.

Hilton College

Thomas Allan

Natal Archives

Philip Allen

Macrorie House Museum

John Anderson (1816–1889)

Local History Museum

George and Mary Ann Andrews

Local History Museum

William Arbuckle

Local History Museum

Margaret Arbuckle

Local History Museum

Mary Arbuckle

Killie Campbell Africana Library

Jane Arbuthnot

EMIGRATION TO NATAL,

Under the Sanction of Her Majesty's Government.

This district (Natal) embraces a most beautiful country, strongly undulating and intersected by many streams, whose waters never fail. It possesses every advantage of climate; the land is most extensive and fertile, capable of producing cotton, indigo, and tobacco, wonderfully well watered, and possessing rich coal mines.—*Governor* SIR H. SMITH *to* EARL GREY, *February*, 1848.

ARRANGEMENTS having been made with HER MAJESTY'S GOVERNMENT for the encouragement of EMIGRATION to NATAL, parties are invited to avail themselves of the advantageous terms here offered, by which they may proceed to, and settle in, that salubrious and fertile colony.

Each adult will be provided with an Intermediate Passage, including provisions on a liberal dietary scale, for the sum of £19, or a Steerage Passage for £10; and on arrival in Natal have secured to him Twenty Acres of Freehold Land. Children above one year, and under the age of fourteen, will be charged £9 10s. for an intermediate, and £5 for a Steerage Passage, and in either case be entitled to Five Acres of Land; second class Intermediate (small sized cabin) and 50 acres of land £22 10s. Such is the locality of the land allotted and quality of the land itself that some emigrants by the "Washington" who sold their land, obtained £1 per acre for it. Each distinct holder of a land order under 100 acres, will have a further grant of a quarter of an acre of village or town allotment; if a holder of 100 acres or more, half an acre. Intending Settlers can purchase any additional quantity of Land, with a large extent of choice, at very moderate prices.

An Agent is appointed to receive Emigrants upon arrival at Port Natal, who will afford every assistance, and apportion land to each; priority of choice being given in the order in which passages are engaged. A deposit of one half the amount of Passage-money will be required on the Certificate as to Character, &c., being approved of, and the remainder to be paid two days previous to embarkation.

Each passenger, excepting those in the Chief Cabin, must be provided with a knife and fork, a table and tea-spoon, a metal plate, a hook-pot, and a drinking mug; all find their own bedding:—these will be supplied, if required, at a cost of £1. Each Steerage Passenger is particularly requested to provide himself with a bag to contain sufficient linen and other articles for 14 days' use on the voyage. Intermediate Passengers have the attendance of a Steward and the privilege of the poop deck.

Cabin Passengers will be allowed forty cubic feet of luggage, and Intermediate and Steerage Passengers twenty cubic feet; any excess is chargeable at the rate of 1s. per cubic foot. All packages of baggage to be distinctly marked with the name of the Passenger, and also with the words "Wanted on the Voyage," *and must be at the dock ready for shipment at least* THREE *days prior to the appointed day of sailing, and those marked* "Not Wanted on the Voyage," *must be at the dock ready for shipment at least* FIVE *days prior to the appointed day for sailing.*

J. C. Byrne & Co. have already despatched 1300 Emigrants to settle on their lands, and First-class Ships, of large size, will sail monthly from London, Liverpool, and Glasgow, adapted to effect speedy voyages, the duration of which is from nine to ten weeks. They will be fitted out under the inspection of Her Majesty's Emigration Agent, and sail punctually on the days appointed.

A Clergyman will proceed in each vessel, together with a Surgeon of undoubted qualifications and character, and temporary accommodation for the emigrants will, on arrival, be provided without charge.

*** To save freight, all ploughs, carts, &c., and other baggage, should be packed into as small a space as possible.

TO SAIL PUNCTUALLY ON THE APPOINTED DAYS.

Where from.	Ship's name.	Tonnage.	Commander.	To Sail.
From LONDON.	Lady Bruce	800	John Burns	February 10th, calling at Portsmouth.
	Diamond	800	Alexander Stewart	March 10th, calling at Plymouth.
From LIVERPOOL.	A Ship	1000		First Week in March.
From GLASGOW.	A Ship	700		First Week in March.

SCALE OF PROVISIONS FOR EACH ADULT STEERAGE PASSENGER.

DAYS.	Biscuits.	Beef.	Pork.	Preserved Meat or Soup and Bouilli.	Flour.	Raisins.	Suet.	Peas.	Rice.	Fresh or Preserved Potatoes.		Tea.	Coffee weight when roasted.	Sugar.	Butter.	Water.	Vinegar.	Mustard.	Salt.	Oatmeal.
	lb.	lb.	lb.	lb.	lb.	oz.	oz.	pint.	lb.	lb.		oz.	oz.	lb.	oz.	qts.	WEEKLY.			
SUNDAY	⅔	...	...	½	¼	2	1½	...	...	1	¼	¼	...	...	...	3	Half-a-pint.	Half-an-ounce.	Two Ounces.	OnePint-and-half.
MONDAY	⅔	...	½	...	¼	...	...	⅓	...	...	...	...	½	¼	3	3				
TUESDAY	⅔	½	...	...	¼	2	1½	...	¼	...	...	¼	...	...	...	3				
WEDNESDAY . .	⅔	...	½	...	¼	...	...	⅓	...	...	...	...	½	¼	...	3				
THURSDAY . . .	⅔	...	...	½	¼	2	1½	...	...	1	¼	¼	...	...	...	3				
FRIDAY	⅔	...	½	...	¼	...	...	⅓	...	...	...	...	½	¼	3	3				
SATURDAY . . .	⅔	½	...	...	¼	2	1½	...	¼	...	...	¼	...	...	...	3				

When fresh Beef and fresh Bread is issued, One Pound to each Adult per day will be allowed. There will be no Flour, Rice, Raisins, Peas, Suet, or Vinegar, during the issue of Fresh Meat.

WEEKLY SCALE OF PROVISIONS FOR EACH ADULT INTERMEDIATE PASSENGER,

For whom a separate portion of the Ship will be expressly fitted up.

1 lb. Preserved Meat.	4 lbs. bread.	¼ lb. Coffee.	⅛ oz. Mustard.
1 lb. Soup and Bouilli.	3 lbs. Flour.	½ lb. Butter.	½ oz. Pepper.
1 pint Assorted Soup.	½ pint Peas.	½ lb. Cheese.	1 oz. Salt.
1 lb. Tripe.	1½ pints Oatmeal.	1 lb. Raisins.	7 lbs. Potatoes. or 1 lb. Preserved ditto.
1 lb. Ham.	1 lb. Sugar.	¾ lb. Suet.	21 quarts of Water.
1 lb. Salt Beef or Pork.	⅛ lb. Tea.	½ pint Pickles or Vinegar.	
1 lb. Rice.	1 pint Preserved Milk.		

The charge for Cabin Passage will be £35 for Adults; £17 10s. for Children.

WEEKLY LIST OF PROVISIONS FOR EACH ADULT CABIN PASSENGER.

½ lb. preserved Salmon.	½ lb. Salt Beef.	½ pint Oatmeal.	¼ lb. Cheese.	½ pint Vinegar.
¾ lb. ditto Meat.	½ lb. do. Pork.	1 pint Preserved Milk.	½ lb. Currants.	⅛ oz. Mustard.
½ lb. ditto Fish.	½ lb. do. Fish.	½ lb. Sugar Refined.	½ lb. Raisins, Valentias.	½ oz. Pepper.
½ lb. Soup and Bouilli.	4 lbs. White Bread.	½ lb. do. Unrefined.	½ lb. Raisins, Muscatels.	2 oz. Salt.
½ lb. Assorted Soups.	4 lbs. Flour.	⅛ lb. Tea.	¾ lb. Suet.	7 lbs. Potatoes, Fresh, or
½ lb. Tripe.	1 lb. Rice.	¼ lb. Coffee.	½ pint Pickles.	1 lb. ditto, Preserved.
1 lb. Ham.	½ pint Peas.	½ lb. Butter.		

IN ADDITION to which a supply of LIVE STOCK, &c., for the Cabin Table will be put on board in the following proportion for every six Adult Cabin Passengers, viz—

3 Sheep and 3 Pigs.	3 pints Currie Powder.	24 lbs. Barcelona Nuts.	6 lbs. Sago.	2 Bottles Olive Oil.	6 lbs. Maccaroni.
3 doz. Fowls or Ducks.	½ lb Celery Seed.	12 lbs. Shell Almonds.	2 Jars Jams and Jellies.	1 ,, Cayenne.	3 Bottles Capers.
9 Bottles of Sauces.	3 doz. botls. Preservd. Fruits	6 lbs. Arrowroot.	2 Tins Herrings.	1 Canister Patent Yeast.	A quantity of Spice.

Each Cabin Passenger allowed one pint of Wine per day, or one bottle of Ale or Porter, and other Spirits and Wine may be had at reasonable rates on board.

Forms of Application to be had of MESSRS. J. C. BYRNE & COMPANY, Natal Emigration and Colonization Company, No. 12, Pall Mall East, and Sun Court, Cornhill, London, *who will afford any further information.*

Don Africana Library

Reproduced from: Byrne's Emigrant's Journal and Natal News. No.1. – Feb., 1850

Official printed sources
168 11.7.1854, 6.10.1874, 3.10.1876

Newspapers, periodicals, etc.
177 16.6.1853; 185 16.6.1853, 17.9.1857,
24.9.1857, 9.8.1858, 6.10.1859, Aug. 1860,
Jan. 1864, Apr. 1868, 26.11.1870, 15.12.1870,
2.7.1878; 189 18.10.1850, 24.6.1853, 4.7.1878,
31.7.1894; 197 1863, 1879, 1881

Later sources
287 pp.27–8; 300 pp.60, 325; 321

ANDREWS, John E.

Born c. 1828.

An 'agriculturalist' who arrived on the *Bernard*, leaving again on the same ship a month later. In Aug. 1851 an unclaimed letter awaited him at the Durban Post Office — he was supposedly at the Cape.

He did not claim his allotments in the Richmond area, viz. 43 *Little Harmony* (20 acres) and 9 Block O within circle in Richmond. These were finally forfeited in Sep. 1873 under Law 4, 1872.

SOURCES

Private source material
34 Box 4. *Bernard* list

Unpublished official sources
125 2263 no.H287; 126 73; 160

Official printed sources
168 24.6.1851

Newspapers, periodicals, etc.
189 18.7.1851

ANSELL, Henry

Born c. 1828.

He was an *Aliwal* emigrant who was allotted land at *Uys Doorns*.

In June 1854 he and fellow *Aliwal* passenger M.B. Smart* each entered into leases with R.P.(Dick) King* for 75 acre lots on King's *Isipingo* farm. It would appear that they did not at first reside on *Isipingo*. There is a reference to their being at *Clairmont* in Feb. 1855. When John Dove's * house there caught fire, Ansell, Smart and Robert Babbs*,

who were in the vicinity, attempted to rescue one of Dove's children trapped in the flames.

The *Natal Advertiser* which reported the above is also the source of the next piece of information on Ansell. In Apr. 1855 it carried a list of landed property in Durban County, giving owners and occupiers. Here Ansell and Smart were entered as occupiers, with William Kuhr (see R.N. Dunn), of Kuhr's farm *Sea View*. There is a possibility that this was out of date, but on the other hand, as late as Aug. 1855, when one of Smart's children was baptised, Smart's place of residence as entered in the register was *Sea View*.

Towards the end of 1855 Ansell decided to visit England. Being uncertain as to his future plans, on 1 Dec. 1855 he made an agreement with Smart whereby in the event of his deciding not to return, Smart could take over his *Isipingo* lease.

He sailed as an intermediate passenger on the *Lady of the Lake* later in December. Within weeks of departing he had the misfortune to lose much of his property and baggage in a fire at Smart's home.

As events developed Ansell decided not to come back to the colony and in June 1857 Smart formally took over his lease.

SOURCES

Private source material
34 Box 4. *Aliwal* lists; 53

Unpublished official papers
125 2242 no.C351; 126 73; 131 IV/12/13 no.122

Official printed sources
168 15.8.1854

Newspapers, periodicals, etc.
180 23.2.1855, 20.4.1855; 187 28.11.1855

Personal communication
342

ANSTEE, Alfred

Born 15 May 1827.

Anstee came to Natal on the *Nile* with the Singer family, as he was related to Mrs Singer*.

He did not take title to his allotments, viz. Lot 38 of the farm *Riet Vallei* (30 acres) and 11 Block G in Lidgetton. In 1854 when E. Parkinson*, as agent of John Lidgett, had negotiated with the Government for the transfer of the majority of unclaimed immigrants' allotments to Lidgett, he had excepted those of Anstee and a few others, considering there was a possibility they would claim their land. In May 1873 Parkinson petitioned the Lt.-Governor that the land of the five remaining immigrants who had not claimed their allotments be forfeited and transferred to Lidgett. Anstee was one of the five.

On 14 Nov. 1851 he married in Durban Amelia Elizabeth Snelus, both of them being resident in Durban at the time. He later lived in Pietermaritzburg. No further information has been found about his career.

Possibly he was the Anstey [sic] or Hanstey [sic] who left Durban for Port Elizabeth in the *Sarah Bell* in June 1852.

SOURCES

Private source material
29 *Nile* list; **120**

Unpublished official papers
125 2282; **126** 73

Newspapers, periodicals, etc.
188 14.11.1851

Later sources
296 p.43

ANSTIE, John

Born *c.* 1821. Died June 1851, Pietermaritzburg.

Most of what is known about this colonist, whose career in Natal was very brief, comes from the diary written on board the *Washington* by a fellow passenger, John Moreland*. Anstie appears in a rather unfavourable light. The passenger lists give his family as his wife, Sarah, aged 28, and four children, viz. Emma aged 4, Ann Maria aged 3, Sarah aged 2 and Mary Ann aged 1. Moreland states that the family, who were intermediate passengers, consisted of five small children under six years. The discrepancy may be explained by the fact that an infant of 4 months died at sea in June 1849, and may not have been born at the time Anstie applied to emigrate.

Moreland's description of Anstie runs thus ' . . . he had been following the business of a butcher — was well fed and in as good condition as any ox brought to the market, had laid in considerable ammunition for the inner man in the shape of extra provisions, half a dozen hams, extra cask of flour — a few dozen beer and spirituous liquors — had married well — that is of a good family — with a respectable sum for her dowry — his own father had done more than his duty by him — had after having squandered his all — assisted in defraying expenses of passages in the hope that he might reform — He was greatly suspected of abusing his poor submissive and evidently heart-broken

wife — those occupying neighbouring berths heard his blows and her subdued moans — but never did she open her mouth to make a complaint. His own account was somewhat different — some difficulties respecting money matters was the cause of his leaving home and when these were decided he should either have remittance of a few hundreds or return — in the meantime he intended following no particular calling but should (being an inveterate sportsman) amuse himself by hunting and shooting some of the wild Game which was said to be so abundant in the Colony — this, however, I have good reasons for taking as mere bombast — very few will assign the true reasons. . .'

Moreland's observations about his difficult personality are further borne out by the fact that in Mar. 1851, Anstie was fined £1.10s. for attacking two police constables in the course of their duty.

At this time he was a journeyman butcher in the employ of one of the Boshofs in Pietermaritzburg, and so presumably had abandoned his Little Bushman's River allotment.

He died in Pietermaritzburg, and in the following January his widow with three daughters (presumably one child had died since their arrival in the Colony) left Natal. They sailed for Cape Town in Jan. 1852 on the *Gem*.

SOURCES

Private source material
29 vol.2, pp.89–90; **34** Box 2. Moreland's *Washington* diary 20.6.1849 and Moreland's rewritten *Washington* diary 13.5.1849, 20.6.1849

Unpublished official papers
126 73; **157**

Newspapers, periodicals, etc.
184 13.3.1851; **189** 27.7.1849, 1.2.1850, 13.6.1851

ANSTIE, Paul

Snuff merchant and mill-owner. He was the son of Paul Anstie of Devizes, Wiltshire, and his wife Jane Kingdon, and grandson of Benjamin Webb Anstie. A younger brother was Francis Edmund Anstie (1833–1874), M.D., who for some years was on the editorial staff of *The Lancet* and in 1874 became the first Dean of the Medical School for Women. Anstie and his wife Mary Ann (born Cox) sailed for the Cape in the *Enchantress* and from there to Natal on the *Lalla Rookh*.

It appears that Anstie's first venture in the Colony was in the sphere of transport — an ambitious one for the undeveloped state of the countryside at that time. In July 1850 there appeared in the *Natal Government Gazette* a prospectus for the Natal Conveyance and Agricultural Company. Its objects were the 'speedy and punctual conveyance' of passengers and goods between Pietermaritzburg and Durban, and other towns which might be established. Another immediate aim was assistance with hiring of agricultural implements and draught oxen to 'facilitate the agriculture of small homesteads'. A long-term aim was the provision of horse-drawn spring vehicles 'as soon as road conditions would permit'. The capital was to be £1 000 and £2 shares were to be obtained from Anstie. His position is not defined in the prospectus, but by Nov. 1850 he was Secretary to the Company. No other name has been found as being connected with this enterprise, so he possibly was the initiator.

The first wagon trip to Durban took place on 6 Jan. 1851, and thereafter the timetable was — departure from Pietermaritzburg on a Monday and return from Durban on a Thursday. The service did not last six months. By June it was out of business and in July, the wagon, gear and 13 oxen were sold. It is interesting to note that the other pioneer attempt at organized public transport in Pietermaritzburg, albeit, solely around the town, seems to have had an even shorter life. James Pitcher* advertised an omnibus service in Dec. 1850, and in Jan. 1851 announced its discontinuance.

Shortly after the Natal Conveyance and Agricultural Company was mooted, Anstie purchased the snuff 'manufactory' of one Adriaan Smuts. He would have had experience in this line as his father was the principal in a firm of tobacco manufacturers in Devizes. He retained this business until about July 1854 when he sold it to Jeannot Bloch.

A few months after buying Smuts's business, Anstie applied, in Dec. 1850, for a vacancy that was about to occur in the office of the Secretary to Government. He backed up his application by stating that he had in his possession a letter of introduction from Earl Grey, the Secretary of State, to Lt.-Governor Martin West. Admiral Dundas, M.P., had recommended him to Grey's attention. In answer he was informed that there were many other applicants.

It would appear that sometime during 1851 he did for a short time hold a civil service position. At the beginning of Nov. 1851, the *Natal Witness* referred to Mr Anstie 'the Finance clerk in Government' who was 'dispensed with'. Later in November Lt.-Governor Pine reported to the Cape Governor that D. Moodie*, the Secretary to Government, had wanted to appoint Anstie as an extra clerk, but Pine had refused, partly because he 'was suspected to be in the confidence of, if not in the employment of, the editor of a newspaper [D.D. Buchanan*] which is teeming with the grossest abuse of myself'. This remark refers to Anstie's connexion with the Natal Political Association, of which more anon.

After his brief experience of the civil service, Anstie,

for the next year or so, appears to have confined his business activities to his snuff 'manufactory'. In Apr. 1853, from the *Natal Independent*, the general public got the first inkling of his next project. He advertised for tenders for the erection of the Belvidere flour mills.

As early as Sep. 1851 he had acquired, on a 50 year lease, five acres of Crown land on the Umsindusi river downstream from the Durban-Pietermaritzburg road. Here he eventually erected an impressive collection of buildings. Besides the mill there was a dwelling house, a labourer's cottage, piggeries, various other outbuildings, including a granary and a drying kiln. The piggeries were for the 'prime mill-fed bacons and hams' that he later produced as a sideline. To this end he had in Dec. 1852 gone into partnership with William Wilkinson* whereby the two of them would farm the 21 acres on the Little Bushman's (Umsindusi) river that Anstie leased from the Pietermaritzburg municipality. Anstie was to provide the implements, etc. and Wilkinson was to do the actual farming.

The Ansties appear to have been living on the premises as early as Sep. 1853. The opening ceremony took place in May 1854, a few hours after the Review to celebrate the Queen's birthday. The mill was one of the earliest of the undershot type in Natal, consisting of three storeys including a basement. It was also the largest. It has survived to the present, and is now a furniture warehouse.

For a number of years a large proportion of Natal's milling was carried out at this mill. In the 1850s most of the grain grown in the O.F.S. was ground in Natal, a considerable amount being processed at Belvidere.

Anstie's mill was too ambitious an undertaking for the Natal of the 1850s. The machinery and apparatus alone had cost him nearly £5 000. Natal was too poor at that time for him to recoup his capital outlay and within 18 months of the opening of the mill he was insolvent. In Nov. 1855 he left Natal for Cape Town, ostensibly to buy wheat. Prior to sailing he had given his power of attorney to his clerk, N.J. McKechnie*, and announced in the press that he intended being absent from the Colony for five to six weeks.

By the end of Jan. 1856 it was evident that he was not returning. According to an entry in the diary of John Fleming* the realisation 'created a complete panic throughout town, the creditors are very numerous and the liabilities about £9 000'. In February Anstie's estate was declared insolvent. The *Natal Chronicle* reported in March that he had proceeded to India. A week later the *Natal Guardian* came up with the information that he had embarked for Moulmein (Burma) under the name of Johnson. From enquiries made c. Jan. 1857 by the Cape Town Shipping Master it appears that Anstie had sailed from Simon's Bay on the *Star of Empire* under the alias Johnson. He left the ship at Moulmein and returned to the Cape under a different name, arriving either at the end of June or early July 1856. On about 9 July he sailed for England under yet another name on the *Swiftsure*. To digress somewhat — the Shipping Master stated that in the course of his enquiries, he had received the impression that Anstie was either under 'some aberration of mind', or was feigning such. Anstie's mental state was linked with his insolvency from the first. The entry in Fleming's diary already quoted mentions rumours that Anstie had 'become deranged in his mind'. The *Natal Chronicle* in Mar. 1856 euphemistically referred to his 'trip to the moon', while the *Natal Guardian*, on the other hand, rejected the rumours that he was insane. It seems that Professor Hattersley's summing up of him as an 'adventurer' albeit a 'gentleman adventurer' is a more likely explanation

To return to events in Natal — in May 1856 Anstie's wife and children took passage for Cape Town and London on the *Admiral*. In the same month the first meeting of creditors took place. At a subsequent meeting debts totalling £1 561 due to Anstie's father were proved. An unusual asset in the estate was a one-fifth portion of four closes of freehold property in the hamlet of Dunkirk (unverified) in the parish of Rowde, Wilts. This property Anstie was to inherit on the death of a gentleman 'now aged sixty years' (i.e. his father). One of the larger creditors was D. B. Scott*. Anstie's debts to him amounted to more than £4 000. Scott had been associated with Anstie in the milling business and there was a move to have him declared a partner. The trustees investigated the situation fully and concluded that he had been employed by Anstie as a miller and was not in partnership.

Another sufferer through Anstie's bankruptcy was N. J. McKechnie. Anstie had persuaded him to give up his government employment and become his clerk. As late as Feb. 1857 McKechnie was still unsettled and in a temporary post.

The auction of the Belvidere mills took place in Nov. 1856. The sale had been advertised as far afield as Cape Town, Grahamstown and Bloemfontein. D. B. Scott was the purchaser, the price being £1 800. The firm Henderson & Scott ran the Belvidere mills until their partnership was dissolved in 1872.

Of Anstie's later movements not much is known. He eventually landed up in the United States and died fighting for the North in the Civil War. His family settled in Vancouver, Canada.

Before he became involved in the Belvidere mills Anstie had taken an unofficial role in Natal's political affairs. When D. D. Buchanan had founded the Natal Political Association in Oct. 1851, Anstie became one of the seven original members, and the secretary. The Association was a radical body advocating self-government for Natal.

Anstie was a founder member of the Pietermaritzburg Congregational Church. He appears also to have had a sense of social commitment in his early days in the Colony. One of the committees he served on was one which tried (c. Nov. 1852) to establish a school in Pietermaritzburg for 'coloured' children (the term 'coloured' at that time embraced Africans).

CHILDREN

The Ansties had four children by the time they left Natal. Their names are unknown. Three were sons, born June 1850, Jan. 1852, and Sep. 1853.

SOURCES

Private source material
9 Frank Churchill to Isabella Churchill 8.6.1854, and 9 May 1856; **31** 26.1.1856; **34** Box 2. Surveyors' and Immigrants' correspondence book — Anstie to Moreland 4.11.1850; **116**

Unpublished official papers
125 16(1) nos.3 and 15, 51(3) nos.226 and 249, 56 nos.22, 221 and 252; **126** 73; **127** 783 no.86 p.158, 1299 dated 1.11.1851 quoted in **326** p.81; **130** 1/30 no.2; **131** IV/2/64 no.82, IV/18/12 nos.4, 239 and 263, IV/18/13 nos.142, 170, 197, 218, 225 and 227

Official printed sources
168 30.7.1850, 31.12.1850, 10.8.1852, 8.8.1854

Newspapers, periodicals, etc.
177 29.12.1853; **179** 19.3.1856; **183** 25.3.1856; **184** 26.12.1850, 16.1.1851; **189** 28.6.1850, 14.11.1851, 9.1.1852, 1.4.1853, 9.9.1853, 14.7.1854, 9.11.1855, 8.2.1856, 25.7.1856, 24.10.1856

Journals, biographies, autobiographies, letters
203 p.94

Later sources
247 p.26; **266** pp.82–8; **267** pp.168–9 287; **273** p.11; **274** pp.21–2

Personal communication
347

ARBUCKLE, William

Born 23 Mar. 1812, Ecclesmachan, Linlithgowshire. Died 30 Apr. 1886, Durban.

Farmer. He was the son of Alexander Arbuckle (1785–1867) and his wife Margaret Dickson/Dixon (1788–1855), who both died in Bathgate, Linlithgowshire.

William and his family lived in Stirlingshire in the 1830s and 1840s. In about 1835 they were on the farm *Langdale* near Falkirk, while in about 1839 they were living near Larbert. Bathgate was another of their places of residence. It would appear that they had also lived at or near Greenloaning, Perthshire, at some stage. When they emigrated they were members of the Presbyterian Church of this town.

The family sailed for Natal on the *Conquering Hero*. According to the ship's passenger list Arbuckle was a brick-maker and labourer.

Arbuckle's 85 acre allotment was in the Richmond district. The family did not settle there, however, but remained on the coast. This land plus his Richmond village erf was sold to William Newlands*.

After landing the Arbuckles first lived at the Point. In Mar. 1852 they were in Victoria Division, near the Umgeni river. They were still in Victoria early in 1856 when they suffered a great setback. Arbuckle was employed on Capt. Smerdon's* farm at the time. Smerdon's house, in which the Arbuckles and four other employees and their families were living, was struck by lightning and razed to the ground. It appears that the Arbuckles moved back to Durban shortly afterwards.

By 1857 Arbuckle was employed by A. McArthur* on his estate at Wentworth near Durban. He was still at Wentworth in Aug. 1859. Possibly through McArthur he became acquainted with John Gray*, McArthur's employee and agent. From Feb. 1860 to Jan. 1861 Arbuckle, his son William and Gray were in partnership as Arbuckle, Gray & Co., sugar planters and manufacturers. Their estate was *Springbank* (300 acres), part of the farm *Zee Koe Vallei*, ten miles north of the Umgeni. The division of labour was thus — William jnr. was to keep the books, Arbuckle was to run the growing and manufacturing department, and Gray was to attend to the selling and general business side. The *Natal Star* reported in May 1860 that 20 acres of sugar cane on the estate had been destroyed by fire. As it would seem the first cane had been planted only the previous year, this would have been a serious loss.

Less than a year later Arbuckle was back in Durban. He was appointed Foreman of Town Works in Mar. 1861. He still had this post in 1867, but by 1869 was managing *The Delta* sugar estate at Isipingo.

From at least the early 1870s this estate was owned by the Glasgow and Natal Sugar Co. Ltd., represented in Natal by Couper, Arbuckle & Co., his son William's firm. In Nov. 1874, while Arbuckle was managing *The Delta* for the firm, the estate was awarded two first prizes at a grand exhibition of Natal sugars held in Durban.

Some time in the first half of 1875 Arbuckle retired to Durban. Here he resided on what was called the Durban Flat, near Queen Street.

Before moving to Isipingo Arbuckle had been active in the affairs of the Durban Presbyterian Church. He was on the Church's general committee in 1862 and 1863, and in Mar. 1863 was put on the committee organizing the drawing up of plans for the new church. In Oct. 1863 he was elected to the Committee of Management of the new church. He was one of the deacons from 1863 to 1868.

Arbuckle was twice married. His first wife, Margaret, (born Marshall) died at *The Delta* estate on 21 Jan. 1875, aged 62. On 19 Aug. 1875 he married Mary Baxter (*c*. 1831, Farnell, Angus — July 1911, Pmb.). They were married in Durban.

CHILDREN

Janet Hind (19 Mar. 1835, near Falkirk, Stirling — Apr. 1901, Dbn) m. June 1856, Dbn, William Wright*.

William (25 July 1839, near Larbert, Stirling — 4 Aug. 1915, Dbn) m. 18 Nov. 1865, Verulam, Henrietta Shire, d. of Henry Shire*. William went into business in Dbn. He was four times Mayor of the town, 1877, 1878, 1881 and 1882. He was a member of the Legislative Council, and from 1897–1902 was Treasurer for Natal. He was knighted in 1902. He then became President of the Legislative Council (Upper House). From 1904 to 1909 he was Natal's Agent-General in London. (see *D.S.A.B.* vol. 3)

Helen Oswald (4 Apr. 1844, ?Larbert — 17 Mar. 1883, Ladysmith) m. 25 Oct. 1861, Dbn, David Gamley (16 Dec. 1836, Montrose, Angus — 24 Mar. 1893, Burnside, Phoenix, Victoria County), son of William and Elizabeth Gamley. David was a blacksmith.

Margaret (*c*. 1846, Larbert — Feb. 1940 ?Pmb) m. 21 June 1872, Isipingo, Charles Isaac Inman (*c*. 1835, Lincoln — 29 June 1881, Pmb.), son of Richard and Sarah Inman. Charles was a storekeeper in Ladysmith.

Alexander (*c*. 1849 — 19 Feb. 1900, Ladysmith) m. 25 Mar. 1881, Ladysmith, Mary Louisa Wetherill (born Mar. 1863, ?Pmb.), d. of Frederick and Sarah Wetherill. Alexander was a storekeeper of Stanger in 1874. Later he lived in Ladysmith. He died of enteric during the Siege.

Elizabeth (born Mar. 1852, Victoria Division) m. 21 June 1872, Isipingo, Richard Hatch (*c*. 1844, Peel, Isle of Man — 15 Mar. 1913, Dbn), son of Richard and Ann Hatch who came to Natal in Dec. 1858 on the *Jane Morice*. Richard jnr. and Elizabeth lived at one time at Springs, Tvl.

Robert (Mar. 1856, Dbn — Oct. 1928, Pmb.)
  m. (1) July 1883, *Cleveland Hill*, Sarah Fell (1862, Eaglescliffe, Durham — 30 Jan. 1886, Ladysmith), d. of Henry and Sarah Fell of *Cleveland Hill*, Beaumont, near present Eston.
  m. (2) 21 Dec. 1887, Dbn, Eliza Amelia Peddie, d. of W.H. Peddie*.

SOURCES

Private source material
  20; 41; 44; 49; 50; 51; 60; 66; 71; 72; 76; 85; 90; 92; 97; 100; 102

Unpublished official papers
125 41 nos.61 and 74, 55 no.145,
56 nos.200 and 309, 72 no.2317, 2282, 2283,
2285–2287; **126** 64, 72, 73; **127** 1584 p.80;
129 6/240, 8/73, 10/408, 41/75, 48/168, 49/13;
131 IV/12/13 nos.109 and 157, IV/16/4 dated 25 Oct.
1861, IV/18/17 dated 17 June 1872, IV/19/36 dated
18 June 1872, IV/19/40 dated 15 Nov. 1865; **137**;
143; **147**; **156** 35/1881, 45/1885, 79/1893,
62/1900; **161** 1867, 1877, 1878, 1881, 1882

Official printed sources
168 6.8.1867, 13.8.1867, 10.8.1869, 6.8.1872,
8.9.1874, 15.9.1874, 6.10.1874, 3.10.1876

Newspapers, periodicals, etc.
185 18.1.1856, 11.8.1859, Nov. 1865, 20.7.1872,
26.1.1875, 1.7.1881, 3.8.1883, 21.3.1884,
9.4.1901; **187** 5.5.1860; **189** 29.1.1875,
22.3.1883, 20.3.1913; **197** 1870, 1876, 1881

Journals, biographies, autobiographies, letters
205 19.2.1900; **212** p.16

Later sources
257; **278** pp.47, 95, 97, 112; **296** pp.76–7;
297 pp.85, 221, 291

Personal communication
351

Portraits, photographs, etc.
358; **362**

ARBUTHNOT, David Carnegy

Born *c.* 1825, Scotland. Died *c.* 12 Mar. 1852, near Umhlatuzi river, Zululand.

Trader and hunter. He was the son of James Carnegy Arbuthnot, a gentleman of Balnamoon, Angus, in Scotland.

Arbuthnot came to Natal in Dec. 1851 on the *Devonian.* Soon after arriving he became the proprietor of the Mauritius Store in Durban.

Early in 1852 he joined a hunting and trading expedition into the Zulu country led by John A. (Elephant) White*. Within two months of leaving for Zululand, Arbuthnot died of fever. Other victims of this ill-fated expedition included J. H. Monies*, E. R. Price* and Frederick Hammond*. One of the few survivors was W.C. Baldwin, the famous hunter, who had been a fellow-passenger of Arbuthnot's on the *Devonian.*

SOURCES

Unpublished official papers
126 73; **129** 3/10 no.37, 3/14 no.A4

Newspapers, periodicals, etc.
189 9.4.1852

Journals, biographies, autobiographies, letters
202 pp.6, 21

ARBUTHNOT, George

Born *c.* 1836. Died Aug. 1856, *Berryden* near Richmond.

Son of William Arbuthnot of Dens, Aberdeenshire, and his wife Susan (born Marshall), and brother of James Arbuthnot*.

He was presumably the Mr Arbuthnot who landed in Durban in Dec. 1854 from the *Lady of the Lake.* Nothing is known of his career in Natal. Mrs James Arbuthnot in her *Autobiographical sketch* mentions him only indirectly. She writes of the great kindness of Archdeacon Fearne* of Richmond 'especially on two occasions of domestic bereavements'. As the Arbuthnots lost one child while at Richmond, the other bereavement she refers to was presumably George's death.

SOURCES

Private source material
80

Unpublished official papers
126 73

Newspapers, periodicals, etc.
189 8.8.1856

Later sources
230 p.10

ARBUTHNOT, James

Born *c.* 1817, Peterhead, Aberdeenshire. Died 4 May 1861, *Umzinto Lodge.*

Farmer and M.L.C. A fair amount is known about him and his family through the *Autobiographical sketch* written in 1897 by his widow, Jane. He was the brother of George Arbuthnot* and the eldest son of William Arbuthnot, a landowner of Dens, Aberdeenshire, and his wife Susan (born Marshall). James was educated at Aberdeen College and started life farming in Buchan. He successfully drained and cultivated the swamps and peat-bogs on his leased farm, but found the work unprofitable. In 1842 he married Jane Cordiner (1819, Peterhead – 2 July 1907, *Arborville*, Equeefa). She was the daughter of Macduff Cordiner, a surgeon in the East India Company's service, and his wife Elizabeth (born Arbuthnot). At the age of five months she was left with two of her mother's unmarried sisters at Kinmundy (unverified), while her parents went to India. Her mother died of cholera three weeks after landing, and her father died within a year.

After their marriage the Arbuthnots settled on a large farm called *Downie Hills* just outside Peterhead. There were clay deposits on *Downie Hills* and Arbuthnot eventually formed a company to manufacture water-pipes, tiles, bricks, etc. This project fulfilled a need in the district, but when all expenses and salaries had been paid it was found there was no money over for Arbuthnot's own salary as manager. For the second time Arbuthnot had the experience of hard work not bringing in sufficient returns. He and his wife then decided to emigrate.

He had difficulty in finding servants to accompany the family. At length he made arrangements with Peter McKay* and his wife, and Jane Smith*, the latter to act as children's nurse. The party sailed on the *Unicorn*. Byrne & Co.'s list of *Unicorn* passengers states that Robert Fowler* was also brought out by Arbuthnot, but Mrs Arbuthnot does not mention him. Before leaving England, the Arbuthnots had, at Byrne's suggestion, handed him £200 for safety, there being no banking facilities in Natal. Byrne informed them that his agent, J.S. Moreland*, would pay them out on arrival. In a letter dated 14 June 1850, Byrne instructed Moreland to pay Arbuthnot his £200. By the time the Arbuthnots arrived in the colony, however, Byrne was insolvent and Moreland did not have the cash to pay them. The Arbuthnots were delayed three months in Durban while trying to get some redress from Byrne & Co. When they had sold all the possessions they could dispense with, and were reduced to 1/6d in cash, they turned to G.C. Cato*, to whom they had a letter of introduction, and who had already aided them, albeit unsuccessfully, in their dealings with Moreland. He lent them money, two wagons complete with oxen, drivers and *voorloopers*, plus provisions for six months. He also told Arbuthnot to buy whatever cattle he needed. All the security he had for his generous help was the few goods the Arbuthnots could spare, and his trust in their friends and relatives in Scotland. It was over a year before he could be refunded because the Arbuthnots' letter home, by mistake had gone via India.

The Arbuthnots settled on their allotment, which they named *Berryden*. It was about four miles east of Richmond. Arbuthnot was an enterprising and hard-working person, and within a few years had built up *Berryden* into a flourishing farm. He was particularly successful with his cattle. His sheep-farming, although carried out on a smaller scale, also showed promise.

Their success at the Illovo was only temporary. The lung-sickness which ravaged the country in the mid–1850s decimated their cattle and out of a herd of between 300–400 a mere 24 survived. Mainly for this reason the Arbuthnots decided to give up stock-farming in favour of sugar-farming.

By the Proclamation dated 29 Apr. 1857 the Government was offering grants of land, 1 000 acre lots inland and 600 acre lots on the coast. Arbuthnot applied for and received 598 acres near the Umzinto river mouth. This property the Arbuthnots named *Umzinto Lodge*. The family moved thither in 1858. Arbuthnot employed a large gang of Africans and soon had many acres under cultivation. He ordered a sugar mill from James Abernethy and Co. of Aberdeen. It started crushing in Dec. 1860. He also let out land for cane cultivation to small farmers and thus ensured the supply to his mill. Between 1858 and 1861 Arbuthnot built up a thriving sugar estate. Two sons were of an age to assist him, and a sugar boiler with previous experience in Demarara was employed. He acted as manager during Arbuthnot's absences. Towards the end of 1860 Arbuthnot purchased from James Ely* the grant farm *Bushy Park* on the south bank of the Umzinto river. John Robinson (later Sir John, son of George Eyre Robinson*) made a fact-finding tour of sugar estates on the south coast in early 1861. Of Arbuthnot's property he had this to say, 'There is no sugar estate in the colony more likely to attract the stranger's eye than *Umzinto Lodge* sugar estate . . . there are about 130 acres bearing fine cane, and eighty acres ready for the year's manufacture'. He then went on to describe the mill in detail and concluded that ' . . . it seems to comprise every expedient that is necessary . . .' Robinson's observations on *Umzinto Lodge* were published in the *Natal Mercury* six weeks after his visit. By this time Arbuthnot had died. His health had been deteriorating in the latter part of 1860, but it was dysentery that hastened his end. In reporting his death the *Natal Star* remarked, 'No public man in Natal will be more thoroughly missed than the quiet, gentlemanly and sensible Member of the Legislative Council who is the subject of our present notice'.

Arbuthnot had been one of Natal's foremost colonists. With his superior education and his relative wealth, in comparison with most of the surrounding settlers, plus his progressive outlook and his drive, he naturally became one of the leaders in the community at the Illovo. Early in 1857 he had been requested to stand as a candidate for Pietermaritzburg County in the elections for the Colony's first Legislative Council and he and Moreland were returned. Soon after his election he had moved to the coast but had continued representing Pietermaritzburg County. Before the elections for the second Council in Mar. 1859, a large number of Richmond voters had petitioned him to stand again. He and Moreland were once more elected.

Arbuthnot also became the leader of the Lower Umzinto

district. Not only were the Arbuthnots among the earliest arrivals there, but, as mentioned before, Arbuthnot had encouraged small farmers to lease part of his lands. With these tenants and neighbouring grantees of government land a small community developed and the need for a church and school was felt. At his own expense Arbuthnot obtained the services of Rev. J. Barker* and had a parsonage built for him on the estate. A large schoolroom which doubled up as a church was also erected. The Barkers arrived at *Umzinto Lodge* in Jan. 1861. The first burial recorded in the Umzinto parish registers is dated 1860 with Arbuthnot as the officiant. The second, and the first burial service performed there by Barker, is that of Arbuthnot himself.

Arbuthnot took his part in the volunteer movement. He had joined the Richmond branch of the Natal Carbineers when it was first formed. Later he took a prominent role in raising a troop of the unit in the Umzinto district and was chosen its captain. Their first muster was held in Aug. 1859. That there should be an Umzinto troop of the Carbineers is not surprising considering the number of Pietermaritzburg County people, and particularly from the Richmond district, settled in that area.

A memento of Arbuthnot is Dr R.J. Mann's* *The colony of Natal: (1859)*. Arbuthnot and the John Robinson aforementioned were the joint winners of a competition organized by the Natal government for essays 'on practical matters relating to the characters of the colony as a field for Emigrants'. Mann was requested by the Lt.-Governor to prepare a book chiefly from the subject material in these two essays. Arbuthnot's essay appeared in Scotland in 1862 under the title *Emigrant's guide-book to Port Natal*. The publishers were Geo. and Robt. King in Aberdeen and Oliver & Boyd in Edinburgh.

To return to the position of Mrs Arbuthnot and her family after her husband's death, her last child was born posthumously, and in Jan. 1862 her husband's estate was declared insolvent. For the second time since arriving in Natal she was to see the fruits of their labours set at nought.

The largest debts proved in the insolvent estate were for the sugar machinery supplied by Abernethy & Co. At a meeting of creditors in Sep. 1862 it was resolved to sell the estate and all movable property belonging thereto. The estate was not sold, however, and *Umzinto Lodge*, until at least 1870, was owned by its creditors and managed by James Bell*. Mrs Arbuthnot states in her *Autobiographical sketch* that, years later when her eldest son visited Scotland, it was discovered that when Arbuthnot had purchased the machinery, five years was the time arranged in which payment was to be made. This fact had been concealed when Arbuthnot's estate was sequestrated.

Mrs Arbuthnot was allowed to remain in the homestead and to cultivate five acres. With the money brought in by the two wagons she had, which were used in transporting sugar to Durban, she was able to provide for her family.

In about 1865 the Arbuthnots left *Umzinto Lodge* and moved inland. They bought a few hundred acres of A. Brander's* farm *Rosemond's Bower* near present Equeefa. In the 1870s Mrs Arbuthnot and her son, St George, purchased the farm *Arborville* in the same district. In 1878 she had Holy Trinity Church built at Equeefa in memory of her husband. She died in 1907 and with other members of the Arbuthnot family is buried in the Equeefa churchyard. The church was demolished in 1919 because of 'structural decay'.

An album of pencil sketches by Mrs Arbuthnot is still in the possession of the family.

CHILDREN

William Thomas (*c.* 1844, *Downie Hills* – 10 May 1881, Umzinto) m. 24 June 1869, Umzinto, Constance Leigh, d. of James Leigh*. William was employed as interpreter and Clerk to the Resident Magistrate of Lower Umkomanzi Division, later Alexandra County from 1862–1874. He then became a sugar planter at *Greenwood*, near Equeefa. When he died he was the Captain of the Alexandra Mounted Rifles.

Macduff (*c.* 1845, ?*Downie Hills* – 22 Jan. 1927, Dbn) m. 17 Dec. 1877, Umzinto, Jean Ogilvie Will Bruce (*c.* 1858, Peterhead – 16 Dec. 1906, Equeefa), d. of John and Jessie Will Bruce. Macduff was a sugar planter of *The Dens*, Equeefa.

Eva (8 Feb. 1847, ?*Downie Hills* – 20 June 1934) m. 17 Jan. 1872, Umzinto, Edward William Hawksworth (4 May 1849, ?Scotland – 23 Mar. 1923, Dbn), son of William Hawksworth (1824–1910) and his wife Louisa Emma (born Batty). E.W. Hawksworth arrived in Natal in May 1867 and became a successful sugar planter at *Beneva Estate* near Equeefa. His father, who followed him to Natal two years later, had been of the Galgness Iron & Steel Works, Lanarkshire.

Hubert (*c.* 1849, ?*Downie Hills* – Apr. 1915, ?Pmb.) m. 20 July 1875, Umzinto, Rosa Evangeline Barker, d. of Rev. J. Barker aforementioned. Hubert was a sugar planter of *Kinmundy* near Equeefa.

Susan Frances Rubina (Aug. 1850, at sea – 11 Sep. 1923, Dbn) m. 12 Nov. 1873, Umzinto, Norris Edward Davey (*c.* 1848 – 30 July 1889, Pmb.), son of Norris Falsham Davey, M.R.C.S. of Romford, Essex. N.E. Davey was the Captain and Staff Officer of Natal volunteers at the time of his death.

Fitz James (*c.* 1853, *Berryden* – 28 Feb. 1936, Fawnleas) m. 15 Nov. 1876, Umzinto, Eliza Sarah Crocker, d. of John Crocker*. Fitz James was a sugar planter of *Rydal Mount*, Equeefa.

Carmina Corinna (bapt. Apr. 1856 at Richmond – 4 Dec. 1857, *Berryden*) died in childhood.

St George (7 Feb. 1859, *Umzinto Lodge* – 8 Nov. 1911, Pmb.) m. 18 June 1890, Ladysmith, Blanche Florence Barker, d. of Rev. J. Barker. St George was a sugar planter first at *Arborville*, then at *Rydal Mount*. A locust infestation in the 1890s forced him to leave *Rydal Mount*.

Crofton (9 Oct. 1861, *Umzinto Lodge* – Oct. 1953 ?Pmb.) m. 29 Dec. 1896, Umzinto, Maria Emilie Maby (*c*. 1875, Lytes Cary, Somerset – Jan. 1947, ?Pmb.), d. of J. Maby of Lytes Cary. Initially Crofton was a sugar planer at *Arborville*. He later purchased A. Brander's farm *Bellemonte*. He also had to leave his property because of locust infestation.

In the 1870s and 1880s one of Arbuthnot's relatives, possibly a nephew, Norman George Arbuthnot, was living on the farm *Rydal Mount*, at Equeefa. He was the son of James Arbuthnot of Invernettie (unverified), Peterhead, and his wife Jane Ogilvie (born Will). He died unmarried at the age of 37 on 25 Nov. 1885 at Mrs Arbuthnot's farm, *Arborville*. Fitz James Arbuthnot had farmed with him at *Rydal Mount*.

SOURCES

Private source material
   21; 33 10.12.1860; 34 Box 1. J.C. Byrne to Moreland 14.6.1850. Box 4. *Unicorn* lists; 44; 64; 68; 80; 83; 93; 102; 103; 110; 113

Unpublished official sources
   125 2253 no.F234, 2260 no.G623; 129 3/14 no.A10, 5/239, 6/227, 28/163, 38/113, 48/230, 130 1/30 no.11; 132 III/5/24 no.85, III/12/1 p.89; 137; 145; 147; 152; 156 51/1889, 63/1907, 148/1907

Official printed sources
   166; 168 25.7.1854, 29.7.1856

Newspapers, periodicals, etc.
   181 2.1.1861; 185 Jan. 1858, 10.3.1859, 9.5.1861, 16.5.1861, Oct. 1861, 25.2.1862, July 1869, 23.1.1872, 18.11.1873, 27.7.1875, 14.5.1881, 28.11.1885; 187 5.2.1859, 26.3.1859, 19.1.1861, 11.5.1861, 5.2.1863; 189 15.1.1858, 21.1.1859, 4.2.1859, 18.3.1859, 30.7.1875, 22.12.1876, 14.5.1881, 6.7.1907, 10.11.1911, 2.4.1915; 197 1879, 1881, 1882, 1884, 1888, 1895

Miscellaneous unofficial contemporary printed sources
   223 pp.iii–iv

Later sources
   230; 267 p.191, 292 vol.1 p.50; 297 pp.298–301, 316–8; 300 p.11; 306 p.3; 324 v.3 p.24

Personal communication
   341

Portraits, photographs, etc.
   361 (Mrs Arbuthnot only)

ARCHBELL, Rev. James

Born Jan. 1798, Tadcaster, Yorkshire. Died 30 Mar. 1866, Pietermaritzburg.

Wesleyan minister, businessman, newspaper proprietor and editor, politician. Little is known of Archbell's antecedents. One ancestor, however, was an Admiral Archbell.

1818 Oct.25 — he married Elizabeth Haigh (19 Oct. 1797, Leeds – 15 June 1854, Pmb.), daughter of William Haigh of Leeds. They were married at Leeds.

1819 early — he arrived at the Cape as a Wesleyan missionary.

The following brief sketch of his career prior to his arrival in Natal is taken mainly from evidence he gave before the Natal Native Affairs Commission in 1852.

— he landed at the Cape in 1818 [*sic*], was first stationed ... 'in Little Namaqualand and subsequently in Great Namaqualand on the borders of the Demararas Country. I then spent two years in Cape Town and afterwards in 1824 I went to the Bechuana country on the borders of the [Orange River] Sovereignty. In 1833 I removed to the Sovereignty and occupied a locality within two hours' ride of the present Bloemfontein. I continued in that position until 1838 when after spending one year in England I returned again to the Cape Colony, and shortly after in 1841 received an appointment as Wesleyan Minister in Natal. . .'

1841 — Archbell was sent to Natal by Rev. William Shaw to investigate the possibility of establishing a mission there. He travelled thither through Pondoland. Archbell's contact with the Voortrekkers at Thaba Nchu was one of the reasons for Shaw's choice.

Sep. — having recently returned to the Cape Archbell wrote a letter to the *Grahamstown Journal* describing Natal, its inhabitants, climate, vegetation and settlements. This is reprinted in J.C. Chase's *Natal papers*, v.2.

1842 Apr.1 — Capt. T.C. Smith and his force of British troops left the post on the Umgazi river to take possession of Natal. Archbell and his family took the opportunity of travelling to Natal with them, Archbell having been sent to form a mission in Natal.

1842 May 4 — Smith's force arrived at Port Natal.

May — the first two baptisms to appear in the Durban Wesleyan Church register date from this month. They were performed by Archbell on board the brig *Pilot*.

May 24 — British attack on the Boer camp at Congella repulsed.

June 1 — Archbell was sent by the Boers to the British camp under a flag of truce to get the women and children from there to the safety of the schooner *Mazeppa*.

June 10 — *Mazeppa*, under the command of C.J. Cato*, escaped from Port Natal harbour and sailed to Delagoa Bay in an attempt to find a British warship to render assistance to the besieged British troops. On board were the Archbell family and other civilians, mainly women and children.

June 26 — British troops relieved on arrival of reinforcements on H.M.S. *Southampton* and the *Conch* from Algoa Bay.

June 27 — *Mazeppa* returned to Port Natal.

Aug. — Archbell received permission from Capt. Smith to erect in Durban a Wesleyan Chapel and a residence for himself — these were the only buildings Smith would allow to be erected at that stage.

1842 Sep. — Archbell performed his first baptisms in his new Wesleyan Chapel. This was the second church to be built in Natal.

1844 Apr. — by this time Archbell had recently taken over the temporary American Board mission station at a drift on the Umgeni, six or seven miles from Durban. On this spot, formerly known as Landman's Laager, there were some disused wattle and daub buildings erected by Voortrekkers. Rev. A. Grout had occupied them in Oct. 1842 with permission of Capt. Smith. On taking over the site Archbell paid Grout £20.

1845 Apr.– June — Archbell visited Cape Town. While there he endeavoured by personal interview and correspondence with the Cape Secretary to Government to gain land in Pmb. for the Wesleyan Church and to establish the Church's right to the Umgeni Mission Station. He was unsuccessful in the latter. Henry Cloete, the Commissioner investigating land claims, had as early as July 1843 expressed the opinion that this site was too near the town of Durban to be suitable for a mission station.

June 25 — Archbell was informed by Major T.C. Smith that erf 15 Longmarket Street, Pmb. would be granted to the Wesleyan Church.

1846 Apr. — two more Wesleyan missionaries, viz. Revs. W.J. Davis* and J. Richards*, arrived in Natal.

— for health and other reasons Archbell retired from active work, but retained his clerical status and continued to receive a small stipend from the Wesleyan Church's Annuitant Fund, largely from contributions he had made over the years. He was now classed as a supernumerary — i.e. a minister with no regular pastoral charge.

June — Archbell was already resident in Pmb., (for many years he owned land on erfs 30 and 31 Loop Street facing on to the Market Square — Archbell Street is a reminder of this).

1847 Apr. to 1848 June — at the instance of Rev. Richards, the Wesleyan minister in Pmb., Archbell was placed under suspension.

1848 Apr. — Archbell stated to the Government his willingness to relinquish his claim to a piece of ground, formerly intended for part of a village, on the Umgeni river near the waterfall, in favour of the resuscitation of the idea of a village there, on condition he be allowed to select an erf when the village was laid out. In answer he was informed that the village would be laid out as soon as possible. (This village is present Howick.)

June — a Special Committee of the Albany and Kaffraria District of the Wesleyan Mission (of which Natal was then a part), met in Pmb. to investigate complaints against one another by several brethren in the Natal Section. One of the cases dealt with was the Revs. Richards's, W.C. Holden's* and James Allison's* charge against Archbell for 'devotion' to temporal things.

Archbell's complete retirement from the ministry appears to have been a result of this meeting. He entered secular life and began a varied career as agent, printer, publisher, newspaper proprietor, banker and money-lender. For the next 17 years he was in the forefront of matters political, municipal and cultural, and was a by no means insignificant member of the Wesleyan laity.

1849 Feb. — by this time Archbell was Chairman of the Board of Municipal Commissioners for Pmb. As he was not chosen in Mar. 1848 when the Board was first elected, he was presumably, therefore, one of the two additional Commissioners elected in Dec. 1848.

Apr.2 — Archbell was issued with title to *Stocklands* and *Oatlands* (11 992 acres) on the north bank of the upper Umgeni river. He had purchased in 1843 from D.B. Snyman and P.J. Joubert these farms, originally named *Cypher Fontein* and *Waai Hoek*.

1850 Jan.3 — the first number of his *Natal Independent and General Advertiser* issued.

Apr. — a meeting held to establish a bank in Natal. Archbell was elected chairman of the board of 12 directors. Nothing eventuated from this move.

June 13 — Archbell explained in the *Natal Independent* the circumstances leading to his retirement as a missionary. He stated that his stipend (about £50 p.a.) had been insufficient to support his family. At the time a verbal vendetta was in progress between himself and the *Natal Witness*. Archbell's antagonism towards Rev. Allison had entered the columns of his newspaper, and D.D. Buchanan*, editor of the *Witness* joined the affray on Allison's side.

1851 Mar. — Archbell was appointed a Municipal Commissioner. He resigned in the following month.

June — appointed Treasurer at the election of the first committee of the Natal and East Africa Society (Natal Society).

Dec. — Archbell was appointed to the foundation committee of the Pmb. Agricultural Society (later the Royal Agricultural Society).

1852 Jan. — his son, John Philip, joined him on the *Natal Independent*.

Apr. — Archbell, his son-in-law R. Lawton*, and T. Puckering* started issuing £1 notes.

Aug. — by this time Archbell was back on the Board of Commissioners.

1853 Apr. & May — duration of the *Natal en Zuid Oost Afrikaan* which he edited. It was printed and published by J. Archbell & Son.

June — Archbell resigned as Chairman of the Board of Commissioners and as Commissioner after a disagreement about the Board's protest against the suspension from office of the Recorder, Henry Cloete.

Nov. — his son and partner, John Philip, died.

1854 Feb. — the Prospectus for the Bank of Natal published in the *Independent*. Among the provisional officers listed was Archbell as chairman.

Mar.23 — he purchased *Woodlands* (6 318 acres, formerly *Leeuw Spruit*) from Jan Abraham Landman.

June — his wife Elizabeth died.

Nov.4 — Bank of Natal general meeting. A majority of the subscribers for shares decided to throw in their lot with the rival Natal Bank (established 1 May 1854).

1855 — the Bank of Natal provisional directors periodically announced their intentions to open a bank when sufficient capital was subscribed. This stage was never reached and the Bank of Natal faded out of the scene.

Feb.22 — last issue of the *Natal Independent*.

May31 — he married Sarah Anne Strickland (born Haigh) (c. 1808, Little Woodhouse [unverified] near Leeds, dead by Oct. 1868), widow of William Strickland (died 1844) of Leeds, and sister of his first wife. They were married in Pmb.

Nov.8 — his *Times, Natal and South East Africa* first appeared. In this issue he stated his intention to resuscitate the *Natal Independent* under this new name.

1856 Jan.3 — announced in the *Times* that he had entered into arrangements with C. Barter* and the editorship and 'future conduct' of the *Times* had been transferred to him. One of the reasons for his retirement was his health. Barter decided to change the title to the *Natal Guardian*.

Jan.8 — first number of the *Natal Guardian* issued with Barter as editor and Archbell as printer and publisher. Barter announced it as the 'voice of the Church of England in the Colonial press'.

Apr.29 — last issue of the *Natal Guardian*.

May14 — *Times, Natal and South East Africa* reappeared with Archbell, his health restored, as editor.

Aug. — he was elected to the Pmb. Town Council. From then until 1864 his service on the Council was unbroken.

Oct. — his son, Tempest Edmonson, took over his printing establishment.

1857 c. Feb. — Archbell stood as a candidate for Victoria County in the first Legislative Council elections — unsuccessful.

Apr.1 — the *Times* expanded in order to give full coverage to the proceedings of the first session of the Legislative Council.

Oct.28 — last (?) issue of the *Times*, the object for which it had been enlarged (the Legislative Council session) having been completed. Archbell announced that for the sake of his health he was compelled to reduce it to little more than an advertising sheet. This issue is the last filed in the Natal Archives.

1858 Aug. — elected Mayor of Pmb. for the year 1858–59.

1859 May — the Natal Bank received its Charter of Incorporation by Natal Law 21, 1859. Archbell by this time was a shareholder.

1860 Aug. — elected Mayor, a position he held until 1864.

1861 May — returned unopposed as a member for Pmb. County in the Legislative Council, a vacancy having been caused by the death of J. Arbuthnot*.

1862 July — Archbell retired from farming. His stud of about 159 horses was auctioned.

end — by this time he was a director of the Colonial Bank of Natal. He resigned from the Board in 1865.

1863–1864 — Chairman of the Pmb. Agricultural Society.

1864 Apr. — Archbell resigned as Mayor and Councillor for reasons of health.

Nov. — his son, Tempest, was swept over the Howick Falls.

1865 Jan. — at this juncture his immovable property consisted of the farms *Spitz Kop* (1 068 acres) in the Karkloof, *Stocklands*, *Oatlands* and *Woodlands* all four in Pmb. County. In addition he owned part of a Durban erf, the remainder of erf 30, and portion of erf 31 Loop Street, Pmb., plus 40 acres of the Pmb. Townlands.

— later in the year Archbell went insolvent.

May 12 — official announcement of his resignation as a member of the Legislative Council (gazetted 18 May).

May 16 — Master of the Supreme Court announced the dates of meetings of his creditors (gazetted 30 May).

1866 Mar.30 — Archbell died in Pmb.

June — a special meeting of creditors held. A resolution was passed that family portraits be handed over to his son, James William, that all the movable property be auctioned, and that all the landed property in Pmb. and Dbn and the lots on the Pmb. Townlands be sold.

Archbell's nickname was 'Old Shixhty' because he lent money on short loan at 60% interest. With the scarcity of cash existing in Natal in the 1860s such rates were possible. 'Shixhty' suggests he lisped. A likely explanation for this could be the ill-fitting dentures of the day.

CHILDREN

Sarah Ann (20 Dec. 1819, Reed Fountain, near Kamiesberg — 10 Feb. 1902, Pmb.) m. 13 Apr. 1841, Salem, Cape, Rev. John Whittle Appleyard (15 June 1814, Cirencester, Glos. — 4 Apr. 1874, King William's Town, Cape), son of Rev. John Appleyard. Rev. J.W. Appleyard was a Wesleyan missionary and Xhosa linguist. (See *D.S.A.B.* vol.1)

Elizabeth (c. 1821 ?Namaqualand — 1 Mar. 1863, Congella, Dbn) m. 1840s, ?Dbn, Charles McDonald*.

James William (Apr. 1823 — 19 Jan. 1891, Pmb.) m. Apr. 1850, ?Pmb., Catherine Holgate, d. of George Holgate*. James was Field Cornet for Ward 3, Pmb. County from 1854 to 1860.

John Philip (9 June 1825, Modder river, near junction with the Vaal river — 22 Nov. 1853, Pmb.) unmarried. John was in partnership with his father from 1852.

Eliza Jane (?Mar. 1826, ?Platberg — 23 Dec. 1905, *Knollebank*, near Howick) m. Jan. 1851, Pmb., Richard Lawton*.

Joseph Haigh (born c. 1832, died ?O.F.S.) m. by 1863, Jane Hiscock, d. of John Hiscock*. Joseph farmed in the Howick district, at *Stocklands* (1856) and *Woodlands* (1860). By 1861 he was in the O.F.S.

Jabez Samuel (c. 1832, Thaba Nchu — 30 Aug. 1900, *Overdale*, near Dundee) m. Feb. 1856, *Stocklands*, Sarah Jane Turton, d. of Josiah Turton*. Jabez was ferryman and postmaster at Howick in 1861. In 1862 he had the Spring Grove Hotel at Howick. He later farmed near Dundee.

Emily Mary (c. 1834, Thaba Nchu — 8 or 9 Aug. 1903, Pmb.) m. 15 Jan. 1857, Pmb., James Thomas Button, son of J.C. Button*.

Tempest Edmonson (Oct. 1836, Thaba Nchu — Nov. 1864, Howick) unmarried. Tempest had taken over his father's printing business in 1856. He was swept over the Howick Falls in attempting to cross the swollen Umgeni. He was buried at *Stocklands House* [sic].

Walter (c. 1838 — Oct. 1897, Pmb.) Walter was farming at *Stocklands* in 1867. He was still there in 1870.

son (born 7 Feb. 1842, ?Cape) died in infancy.

SOURCES

Private source material

13 J.E. Methley to his father Dec. 1854 and 8.10.1855;

29 Fannin papers;   **34** Box 2. Tour through the upper districts of Natal 1853;   **38** Box 336;   **53**;   **58**;   **77**; **102**

Unpublished official papers
 125 1 nos.8, 10, 11, 13 and 15, 8 no.10, 12(2) no.116, 38(1) no.9, 2282;   **129** 3/7 no.92, 3/14 no.A13, 4/298, 12/160, 13/137, 18/230, 25/17;   **130** 1/30 no.19;   **131** IV/2/70 no.663, IV/18/12 no.272;   **132** III/12/1 p.70; **133** II/1/3 no.50;   **141**;   **147**;   **156** 40/1902, 217/1903, 2/1906;   **164** pp.794–9

Official printed sources
 166;   **168** 10.8.1852, 5.6.1855, 29.7.1856, 1.5.1860, 14.8.1860, 16.5.1865, 23.5.1865, 30.5.1865, 6.8.1867, 16.8.1870, 29.9.1874, 22.8.1876;   **171**;   **172** pp.85–7;   **174** p.273

Printed documents
 175 vol.1 pp.709–11, vol.2 pp.18, 71; **176** vol.2 pp.184–9, 207–8, 212, 222, 224, 241

Newspapers, periodicals, etc.
 181 2.8.1861, 17.1.1862, 9.7.1862;   **182**; **183** 8.1.1856, 11.3.1856;   **184** 13.6.1850, 16.1.1851, 15.1.1852, 24.11.1853, 1.12.1853, 22.6.1854;   **185** Supp. 30.5.1861, 6.6.1861, 13.4.1864, 22.11.1864, 1.12.1864, Apr. 1866; **187** 11.8.1860;   **188** 28.11.1851, 23.7.1852; **189** 1.12.1848, 2.3.1849, 26.4.1850, 11.4.1851, 4.11.1851, 13.5.1853, 10.6.1853, 9.6.1854, 8.8.1856, 7.8.1857, 6.8.1858, 15.10.1858, 22.10.1858, 5.8.1859, 24.1.1891, 11.8.1903, 4.1.1906, 5.4.1967;   **190** 18.4.1845, 13.6.1845; **191** 8.11.1855, 3.1.1856, 14.5.1856, 8.10.1856, 12.11.1856, 21.1.1857, 25.3.1857, 28.10.1857; **197** 1863–65, 1881

Journals, biographies, autobiographies, letters
 215 pp.3, 35, 108

Miscellaneous unofficial contemporary printed sources
 219 Book 2, Chapters 15 and 17;   **220**

Later sources
 231 pp.85–9, **234** pp.31, 33, 50, 90, 188, **249**; **253**;   **266** pp.91, 98–100, 105–6, 109, 120 n., 192–3, **267** pp.89, 140–1, 309;   **273** p.33; **274** pp.141–2;   **275** p.32;   **312** pp.3, 10;   **316**; **317**;   **331** p.167;   **333** *passim*, especially pp.31, 37

Personal communciation
 342;   **347**;   **355**

Portraits, photographs, etc.
 359 p.42

ARCHER, George

Born *c.* 1810. Died 9 Dec. 1857, Durban.

Pilot and coxswain of the Port Boat in Durban. He had gone to sea at the age of about 14, and for his last five years at sea had commanded three different vessels. He had been on the Cape coast run and in 1841 had been master of the London-registered schooner, the *Sovereign*. In July 1843 the schooner of which he then was master, the Cape Town registered *Hero*, struck the Durban Bar and was later condemned and sold. Archer then appears to have settled in Natal. At times he acted as sub-pilot at the port. In June 1847 he was appointed coxswain, a position held until his death. During this period, as his obituary in the *Natal Mercury* noted, he did not lose a single vessel.

Capt. Archer's name was for many years remembered in Durban through 'Archer's Duck Pond' or 'Archer's Hen Coop', a bathing enclosure. He got the scheme off the ground, petitioning the Government in Apr. 1854 for permission to erect this 'so long-felt public convenience' near the Channel at the upper part of the Bay between Field and Grey (now Broad) Streets. He already had, at this time, 52 subscribers. Although obtaining the sanction of the Government, and advertising in Oct. 1854 his intention of building swimming baths, sufficient support was not forthcoming for the building to be started. Archer then enlisted the support of Mark Foggitt* and it was he who eventually erected the 'bathing house' in June 1857.

Archer died in Dec. 1857 of dysentery: 'a man of strict integrity but his generous disposition involved him, lately, in pecuniary embarrassments', according to the *Natal Mercury* obituary.

He was twice married. His first wife's name was Maria, but nothing further has been discovered about her. He next married Susara Johanna Saunders, (*c.* 1830 – 22 May 1867). This was in Feb. 1849, in Durban, and was the first marriage performed in Natal by Dean James Green*.

On 21 Dec. 1862 in Durban his widow married George Hewson or Henison Watson, eldest son of William Watson of Campbeltown Argyllshire. Watson was farming at *Clifton Farm* near Pinetown at the time of their marriage.

CHILDREN

Sarah (born Sep. 1846, ?Dbn).

John William Walter (born 26 July 1852, Dbn, died Taungs, Cape).

Cornelius (born 4 July 1853, ?Dbn, died Standerton, Tvl) m. 25 July 1878, Llanwarne (unverified) Tvl, Annie Eleanor Meek (born *c.* 1854), youngest d. of J.J. Meek of Cowie's Hill and grand-daughter of John Meek*.

Edward Silvester (26 July 1855, Dbn – 4 Jan. 1925, Pinetown) m. Elizabeth Randle.

Thomas William (born 26 Aug. 1856, ?Dbn) Possibly he was the William Thomas [sic] Archer who married Mahalia Flood Cutbush Ward, d. of Josiah Ward* and his wife Clarissa (widow of J.J. Meek). This marriage ended in divorce in 1879 in the Transvaal.

Georgianna (born 26 Mar. 1860 [sic]).

SOURCES

Private source material
29 S.W.B. Griffin papers; 44; 53

Unpublished official papers
125 7 no.44, 38 no.105, 2243 no.C740, 2282, 2287; 127 33 no.47 p.104; 129 3/14 no.A3, 4/52, 7/227; 131 IV/16/4 no.150; 132 III/5/3 no.15; 148

Official printed sources
166 1850–1856

Newspapers, periodicals, etc.
185 26.10.1855, 10.12.1857, 17.12.1857, Dec. 1862, May 1867; 189 11.9.1846, 27.11.1846, 30.8.1850, 15.2.1856, 18.12.1857, 3.8.1878; 198 1852 p.10

Miscellaneous unofficial contemporary printed sources
220

Later sources
234 p.309, 241 p.24; 323 pp.12, 26

Personal communication
338

ARCHER, James William

Born c. 1828.

A farmer from Tullibardine near Auchterarder in Perthshire, who emigrated on the *Unicorn*.

He was probably the Mr Archer whom James Ellis*, a colonist who originated from near Tullibardine, requested to call at Moreland's* Durban office in Nov. 1850 for an answer to a letter Ellis had written to Moreland. Ellis at this time was living at Sterk Spruit on the Durban-Pietermaritzburg road, superintending road works.

The only other reference found to Archer's presence in Natal is his signature on a petition of Pinetown residents dated Dec. 1851.

SOURCES

Private source material
34 Box 2. Surveyors' and Immigrants' correspondence book — J. Ellis to Moreland 16.11.1850. Box 4. *Unicorn* lists

Unpublished official papers
125 2240 no.B787; 126 73, 74

Official printed sources
168 24.6.1851

Newspapers, periodicals, etc.
189 27.9.1850

ARCHIBALD, Walter James

Born c. 1823, Fifeshire. Died 26 Oct. 1861, Durban.

He came on the *Conquering Hero* with his wife Agnes (born Hutton) (c. 1827 – 24 May 1895, Clairmont, Durban). His occupation is given as a ship's carpenter, but by the end of 1852 he appears in the *Directory of Durban and Pietermaritzburg* as Capt. Walter Archibald of erf 3 Block D Durban. By Aug. 1855 he was in Australia, but his name appeared on the list of those eligible to serve on juries in Durban County — here he is described as a seaman. He was back in Durban by Jan. 1860 when two children were christened. He died at the Point, Durban. The *Mercury* in Nov. 1861 in reporting his death stated that he had been a churchwarden of Christ Church, (Addington) and 'long connected with the Port Establishment'. He could not, however, have had a government appointment as his name does not appear in any of the Blue Books.

His death notice states that he was a mariner of Kincardine, but on the occasion of his daughter's wedding in 1883 he was described as 'Capt. Archibald of Kirkcaldy, Fifeshire'.

Shortly after his death his widow acted as housekeeper to the young men on the *Bankhead* sugar estate owned by James Bell* and Robert Morrison*. She was still at *Bankhead* in 1869 but was again living in Durban in 1870.

CHILDREN

James (Aug. 1852, Dbn — Mar. 1934, buried Dbn) m. 4 Aug. 1885, Dbn, Ellen Isabel Forrest, d. of John Forrest*.

Margaret Ann (born Nov. 1859, Addington, Dbn) m. 24 Apr. 1883, Dbn, Richard John Albert Matthews (born c. 1861, Calcutta), son of R.H.G. Matthews (c. 1831–1912) and his wife Zelia Caroline (born Cockerell) (c. 1830–1912), sister of A.S. Cockerell*.

SOURCES

Private source material
7; 22; 44; 48; 49; 50; 92; 113

Unpublished official papers
125 2287; 126 64; 129 3/14 no.A7, 48/2, 48/37;
131 IV/16/6 no.20, IV/19/34 no.102; 137;
156 106/1898

Newspapers, periodicals, etc.
185 8.8.1855, Nov. 1861, 25.4.1883, 6.8.1885;
187 6.4.1861; 189 19.3.1896

Miscellaneous unofficial contemporary printed sources
220

ARMSTRONG, Francis

Born May 1815, Gowland (unverified) Co. Longford, Ireland. Died 11 Mar. 1902, Pietermaritzburg.

Boot and shoemaker and farmer. His father, whose Christian name is not known, was a shoemaker. His mother's maiden name was Waters.

Armstrong senior brought his family to the Cape in 1835 on the *Maria*, two of his brothers having already emigrated to that colony. The Armstrongs settled in Port Elizabeth, and it was here in Jan. 1839 that Francis married. His wife was Mary Crooks (*c.* 1823, Port Elizabeth – 9 Dec. 1902, Pmb.) sister of the wife of J.T. McKenzie*.

In Jan. 1841 Armstrong and his family disembarked at Port Natal from the *Conch*. The McKenzies arrived in the same month. Both families were in Durban in 1842 and inevitably were involved in the Boer-British confrontation. The Armstrong's second child was born on the very day hostilities began.

Years later when trying to obtain a land grant, Armstrong claimed that he and James Gregory (son of J.D. Gregory*) had captured the Boer colours and had delivered them to Capt. Smith. Confirmation of this has not been found. Armstrong does not mention it in his statement on the 1842 events in J. Bird's* *Annals of Natal*, nor does he refer to it in his reminiscences in the Kit Bird papers.

The English civilians took refuge on the *Mazeppa*. Two days after the Battle of Congella the Boers attacked the Point and ordered all civilians off the *Mazeppa* under threat of sinking. The men, with the exception of C.J. Cato* and J.T. McKenzie who managed to stow themselves away, were made 'close prisoners', as Armstrong later put it, and marched to the Congella laager. After eight or nine days they were sent to Pietermaritzburg and eventually were imprisoned for about six weeks. Meanwhile the womenfolk remained on the *Mazeppa*. On the 10th June the *Mazeppa*, under the guidance of C.J. Cato, managed to brave the Boer guns and put out to sea in an endeavour to get assistance for Capt. Smith and his troops. When Armstrong was released he went to Durban to

rejoin his wife who had returned on the *Mazeppa* a few days previously. They found their home had been looted and they were left with nothing. As his shoemaker's tools had been taken he had to find other work. He took a job cutting reeds for the thatching of the barracks being erected for the troops. As soon as he could get fresh tools from England he set up once more as a shoemaker.

Armstrong is next heard of in July 1845 when two of his children were baptised. These entries can be found in the Pietermaritzburg Dutch Reformed Church register.

From the record in the Surveyor General's papers of title deeds issued, it appears that on 1 Jan. 1852 Armstrong was given title to 3 218 acres between the Umhloti and Tongaat rivers. Nothing further has been discovered of this phase of his life. According to the *Directory of Durban and Pietermaritzburg* published at the end of 1852 he was a shoemaker in Durban, in Aliwal Street (erf 1 M Smith Street). By May 1856 the family was living in Pietermaritzburg where Armstrong opened a shop selling boots and shoes he imported. By at least July he was renting property on erf 14 Loop Street.

In Aug. 1859 Armstrong first petitioned the Lt.-Governor for a land grant in view of the losses he had suffered in the 1842 disturbances. He based his claim on the cases of G.C. Cato*, C.J. Cato and R.P. King*. He was informed that the Lt.-Governor had no power to make such grants and that the Catos and King were special cases. His petition was however forwarded to the Secretary of State, Lord Newcastle. In his reply to the Lt.-Governor, Newcastle stated that King and the Catos were given grants 'for important services rendered to the troops' and this formed no precedent for Armstrong. To make a grant to Armstrong might result in a 'precedent of great inconvenience'.

Armstrong went bankrupt in Nov. 1861, (he attributed this in later life to having given too much credit). Sometime thereafter he left Pietermaritzburg and went to the Mooi River district. Here he rented the farm *Sutherland Vale* and went in for mixed farming from which he was just able to make a living.

In Jan. 1867 he renewed his plea for a land grant, setting forth the active service he had rendered in 1842 (i.e. capturing the Dutch flag), and stating that the Legislative Council had twice recommended that he be given such a grant. In Jan. 1871 he once more petitioned the Lt.-Governor on this question. This had no more success than his earlier memorials.

Eight years later Armstrong left Mooi River for Pietermaritzburg. In his reminiscences he dated this move as 'after the Isandhlwana scare'. Possibly, therefore, that event influenced his decision to return to Pietermaritzburg. Back in the capital he was able to live comfortably on the earnings from the transport work of his two wagons.

By the end of 1880 he was living on erf 3 Loop Street, facing on to Fleming Street. It was here in 1902 that both he and his wife died.

CHILDREN

Eliza (12 Dec. 1839, P.E. – 16 Aug. 1904, Pmb.) m. Dec. 1858, Pmb., Alexander Gibson, son of George W. Gibson*.

Mary Elizabeth (23 May 1842, Dbn – 15 Oct. 1913, Highlands, near Mooi River) m. Mar. 1869, Pmb., John Button, son of J.C. Button*.

Amelia (5 Sep. 1846, Dbn – Apr. 1886, Pmb.) m. 30 Aug. 1869, ?Mooi River, William Young, son of Edwin Young*.

William (27 Aug. 1848, Dbn – 12 Sep. 1894, Jhb.) m. 30 Aug. 1877, Dbn, Jane Fanny Arnold, d. of Thomas Arnold*. William was a storekeeper in Bethlehem and Harrismith in the O.F.S.

Sarah (born Aug. 1850, Dbn) m. Mar. 1869, Pmb., David Fraser (born c. 1844), a farmer of *Sutherland Vale*, Weenen County at the time of their marriage, afterwards of Bethlehem, O.F.S.

Annie (Mar. 1856, Pmb. – July 1933, Pmb.) unmarried

SOURCES

Private source material
   23; 29 Armstrong papers, S.W.B. Griffin papers; 53; 58; 71; 75; 76; 96; 102

Unpublished official papers
   125 2249 no.E278 (plus F564 and G385 filed with E278), 2283, 2285; 127 35 no.45 p.94; 129 12/238, 15/219, 21/242; 130 1/30 no.10; 131 IV/23/2 nos.2–3/1869; 132 III/12/1 p.74; 147; 156 3/1903, 183/1904

Official printed sources
   168 29.7.1856, 10.8.1858, 14.8.1860, 1.9.1874, 22.9.1874

Printed documents
   175 vol. 1 pp.729–30

Newspapers, periodicals, etc.
   185 1.9.1877; 189 4.9.1877, 22.9.1894, 22.10.1913; 197 1881, 1882, 1884, 1888, 1895

Miscellaneous unofficial contemporary printed sources
   220; 222 p.121

Later sources
   231 p.53; 234 p.62; 245 p.10

Portraits, photographs, etc.
   358 no.L160

ARMSTRONG, John

Born c. 1816, Pleasley, Nottinghamshire. Died 20 Oct. 1895, ?Durban.

Ex-soldier and blacksmith. In Dec. 1836, in Nottinghamshire, Armstrong joined the 45th Regiment. His regimental number was 1047. At the time of enlisting he was a toolmaker.

Armstrong arrived in Natal in July 1843 with the first two companies of the 45th to come to the Colony. In Mar. 1848 he purchased his discharge from the army. He was a private at the time. By May of that year he appears to have been working in the blacksmithy of J.T. McKenzie*. At that time he applied, as a discharged soldier, for an erf in West Street, Durban. He was granted erf 7L, which was not in the 'front street', as Dr Stanger*, the Surveyor General, put it. He considered soldiers should not get the best erfs.

In June 1848 Armstrong took over McKenzie's business in Pietermaritzburg. In May 1849 he and M.E. Williams* went into partnership as blacksmiths on the premises of Williams's brother, Abraham Williams*, in Pietermaritzburg.

Armstrong is described in the 1854–55 and 1856–57 jury lists for Pietermaritzburg County as a sawyer of the farm *Buffel's Hoek*. In Dec. 1857 he was on S.W. van der Merwe's farm *Vlak Hoek* in the Karkloof. According to the *Natal Witness* he was still there in May 1859. By August of that year, however, he was the owner of the farm *Rats [sic] Spruit*, Weenen County. In 1858 he had applied for a government farm, and had been granted one. This presumably was *Rats Spruit*, which he appears to have renamed *Mount Pleasant*, a 2 632 acre farm on the Weston-Weenen road.

In Oct. 1862 he married Margaret Ross (born Southell), the widow of Edward Ross*. He was a widower at the time. No information has been found about his first wife. When he married he was doing blacksmith's work at *Mount Pleasant*. From records in the Surveyor General's papers it appears that in Aug. 1862 one James Howard had taken over the farm. Armstrong had had to sell it because he was pressed for money. One of the reasons for his embarrassment was that he had spent about £300 on buildings on *Mount Pleasant*. To further complicate matters he owned a 2 203 acre farm, *Karkloof*, for which he had not paid, and which he had mortgaged for its full value to J.W. Winter*. After disposing of *Mount Pleasant* he had difficulty in finding employment, and was out of work for a long period. By June 1863 he was back in Pietermaritzburg. In this month the chaotic state of his finances resulted in the surrender of his estate. The balance sheet finalized in Jan. 1866 showed that in the three years before his insolvency his capital had consisted of, besides the farms, which were not included in the reckoning, livestock to the value of £1 173, and debts due to him worth £803. On paper the deficiency between his assets and liabilities was £159, but when his property was liquidated only £36–odd was available for distribution. This went to the preferent creditors, two employees, in partial payment of wages.

When Armstrong applied for rehabilitation in Feb. 1866, one of the creditors objected on several grounds, one of which being, that since Mar. 1864, Armstrong had been carrying on a blacksmithy business in his wife's name, and that her estate had also recently been surrendered. Mrs Armstrong had gone insolvent c. Mar. 1865. Her assets included a mortgaged property in Raven Street, Pietermaritzburg, and a bond on the farm *Krantzfontein* in the Bethulie district, O.F.S. The Pietermaritzburg property had come to her through her husband, E. Ross, while at the time of his death, Ross had owned *Krantzfontein.* Mrs Armstrong's trustee did not hold out much hope that the creditors would collect on the *Krantzfontein* mortgage as the bondholder, A.G. van Abo, was also insolvent.

The 1867–68 and 1870–71 Pietermaritzburg County jury lists have an entry for John Armstrong, a sawyer of *Buffel's Hoek*, and an occupier as distinct from an owner of property. However the former list also has John Armstrong, farmer and occupier of property at New England, and the latter has John Armstrong, farmer and occupier of erf 11, Church Street. As Armstrong's wife Margaret had owned property at New England and in Raven Street (erf 11 Church Street), it seems likely that the *Buffel's Hoek* address was out of date.

Armstrong and his wife Margaret were later divorced and he married again. His third wife was Jane (born Johnson), the widow of Edward Westley*. They were married on 10 Apr. 1875 at Isipingo. Armstrong by this time was living at Isipingo, and was working once more as a smith. Jane died at Isipingo in 1892, and he died three years later. His death certificate gave his occupation as blacksmith and wagonmaker.

In 1858 Armstrong had applied to the government for an assisted passage to Natal for a relation, William Armstrong, a miner of Heath, Derbyshire. It has not been ascertained whether William came to the colony or not.

SOURCES

Private source material
61; 76

Unpublished official papers
125 104 no.R401, 2283; 130 1/30 nos.15 and 18, 1/33 no.42; 131 IV/19/35 no.112; 132 III/5/13 undated, received 29.5.1848, III/5/32 no.40, III/11/11 p.41, III/12/1 p.93; 137; 158 12/5751 July–Sep. 1843, 12/5756 Jan.–Mar. 1848

Official printed sources
168 22.5.1849, 8.8.1854, 29.7.1856, 10.8.1858, 6.9.1867, 16.8.1870, 22.8.1876, 3.10.1876

Newspapers, periodicals, etc.
181 20.4.1864; 186 30.6.1848; 189 18.5.1849, 25.12.1857, 27.5.1859, 5.8.1859; 197 1879, 1881, 1882, 1884, 1888, 1895

Later sources
234 p.64

ARMSTRONG, Dr William

Born c. 1817, Rodborough, Glos. Died 10 Aug. 1872, Greytown.

M.R.C.S. (England). Doctor and farmer. Armstrong and his family left Liverpool for Natal on the *Zulu*, arriving in Oct. 1857. Also on board, but in the steerage was William Armstrong*. The Armstrongs came from Stroud, Gloucestershire, where Armstrong had been in practice from at least 1843. However he owned property in Ireland, viz. a farm, *Curraughamulkim*, near Omagh, County Tyrone. This was still in his possession as late as 1866.

In Nov. 1857 Armstrong was licensed to practise in Natal as a physician and surgeon. By mid–1858 the Armstrongs had settled in the Karkloof. J.E. Methley* of *Shafton*, in a letter to his father in June of that year, writes of them as comparatively new neighbours, very nice people, and 'well off for this world's goods'. The Armstrongs had settled on the farm *Roode Spruit*. William Armstrong was with them on *Roode Spruit* at this time although the connexion between this young man and the Armstrongs has not been established. Armstrong gave his property the name *Rodborough*. In Oct. 1860 a grass fire destroyed the Armstrongs' house, together with valuable furniture and their library. The last reference found to Armstrong being at *Rodborough* dates to June 1866.

By Feb. 1868 Armstrong was acting as the District Surgeon Umvoti County, in place of Dr F.D. Kan, and was living in Greytown. Kan resigned a year later and Armstrong took on the post on a permanent basis. In May 1870 Armstrong was temporarily appointed as Acting Resident Magistrate Umvoti County, during the absence on leave of J.W. Shepstone*. At the time of his death Armstrong was still the Umvoti District Surgeon.

His memory was perpetuated by the entrance archway and two windows in the first Greytown Anglican church. These have been incorporated in the present St James's Church.

Armstrong's wife was Mary Ann Stevens (c. 1822 – 2 Nov. 1901, Pmb.), daughter of the Rev. John Stevens, a Wesleyan minister of Stroud. Armstrong's father was also a Wesleyan minister. The Armstrongs were married in Stroud – the marriage settlement entered into shortly before their union being dated 11 Mar. 1843. For some years after her husband's death Mrs Armstrong remained in Greytown and she was still there in 1888. She died at her son Ernest's residence, *Monte Cristo*, on the Town Hill. *Monte Cristo* is still (1981) standing. Armstrong Drive nearby takes its name from this family.

Dr Armstrong and one of his daughters are numbered among the early collectors of Natal plants.

Professor Hattersley states that Armstrong took over the farm *Amberley* and renamed it *Rodborough*. No reference has been found during Armstrong's lifetime to the name *Amberley*. His address in the Karkloof was either *Roode Spruit* or *Rodborough*. When his daughter Olivia was married in 1872 her husband, J.T. Ball, was of *Rodborough*. By the end of 1878 the Balls, according to the *Natal Almanac*, were still of *Rodborough*, Woodside (i.e. Karkloof). By the end of 1881, however, their address in the *Almanac* is given as *Amberley*, Woodside. From the 1:50 000 Trigonometrical Survey series it is evident that *Amberley* is part of the farm *Roode Spruit*. It seems likely therefore that *Rodborough* was renamed *Amberley*, and not *vice versa*. Amberley is the name of a village in Gloucestershire very close to both Stroud and Minchinhampton, Ball's birthplace.

CHILDREN

Mary Jane (27 Nov. 1843, ?Stroud – 29 Apr. 1856, ?Stroud) died in childhood.

Olivia Wolfenden (born *c.* 1845, Stroud) m. 9 Sep. 1872, Greytown, James Thomas Ball (*c.* 1831, Minchinhampton, Glos. – 13 May 1906, Pmb.), son of John Garlic and Mary Ball of Stroud. James had been in the East India Company's Bengal Artillery, and had served in the Indian Mutiny. The Balls later lived at Kimberley.

William (*c.* 1847, ?Stroud – 21 Sep. 1878, *Fordoun*, near Harding) m. Oct. 1873, Pmb., Mary Louisa Prentice (*c.* 1851 U.K. – Oct. 1931, ?Pmb.). William was farming at *Landsberg*, near Greytown at the time of his marriage. In *c.* June 1880 his widow married a Mr Kinsman, possibly a son of G.W. Kinsman*.

Mary Kathleen (born ?Stroud) unmarried. Still alive 1934.

Charles St John (*c.* 1853, ?Stroud – 5 June 1883, Pmb.) unmarried

Amy Kathleen (31 July 1854, ?Stroud – 8 July 1856, ?Stroud), died in childhood.

Ernest Victor (9 Sep. 1855, ?Stroud – 3 June 1915, Pmb.) unmarried. Ernest taught in East London for a time, then farmed in East Griqualand and Pmb. County. Ended his days at *Monte Cristo*.

Amy Jane (born Jan. 1859, ?*Rodborough*) unmarried. Still alive 1902.

Edith (born Mar. 1862, ?*Rodborough*, died ?England) m. Dec. 1887, Greytown, Christopher John (Kit) Bird, son of John Bird*.

Arthur Sidney (Aug. 1863, ?*Rodborough* – Apr. 1918, Pmb.) unmarried

Henry Eustace (1 July 1870, Greytown – 3 July 1870, Greytown), died in infancy.

SOURCES

Private source material
11 E.P. Lamport to his wife, 4 July 1880;
13 J.E. Methley to his father, July 1858;
35 11.8.1872; 39; 56; 72; 73; 77; 94; 95;
102; 115 no.226; 117 Nov. 1873

Unpublished official papers
125 2285; 126 73; 127 48 no.90 p.145;
129 3/22 no.3, 5/12, 11/390, 11/400, 12/57,
26/122; 131 IV/23/2 no.A187 dated 29 June 1866;
132 III/5/27 no.413; 139; 140; 147;
156 387/1878, 47/1897, 226/1901

Official printed sources
168 2.2.1869, 29.6.1869, 7.6.1870

Newspapers, periodicals, etc.
181 5.9.1860, 10.10.1860, 185 19.11.1857,
7.7.1870, 189 28.9.1878, 28.12.1887, 5.11.1901,
17.5.1906, 5.6.1915; 197 1869–1872, 1879,
1881, 1882, 1884, 1888, 1895; 199 1910 p.37

Journals, biographies, autobiographies, letters
207 p.21; 212 p.26

Later sources
313

ARMSTRONG, William

A steerage passenger aboard the *Zulu*, which arrived in Oct. 1857 from Liverpool. Also on board, but travelling cabin class, were Dr William Armstrong*, his wife, son William, aged about 10, and 4 other children.

In June 1858 Armstrong applied to the Government for a land grant. He stated that he had been in Natal nine months, and was residing with Mr [*sic*] (i.e. Dr) Armstrong at *Roode Spruit*.

Could he be the William Armstrong, mechanic, who died 17 Apr. 1896 in Greyville aged 62?

SOURCES

Unpublished official papers
126 73; 132 III/5/27 no.413; 137

ARNOLD, Henery ‡

Born c. 1813, Lincoln. Died Jan. 1883, *Slang Spruit*, near Pietermaritzburg.

Carpenter, joiner and farmer. Arnold, although born in Lincolnshire, had been living in Yorkshire before he emigrated to Natal. He, his wife Hannah (c. 1809 — Oct. 1872, Illovo, Pmb. County), and family arrived on the *Emily*.

Although he claimed his 80 acre emigrant's allotment near Richmond, the Arnolds do not appear to have lived on it, and c. 1855 Henery sold it to his son Charles.

The Arnolds' first years were spent in Pietermaritzburg where Henery carried on his trade of carpenter and joiner. By the end of 1852 his address was erf 33 Pietermaritz Street. In Jan. 1854 he purchased 20 acres on the *Vaalkop* estate, but as late as Aug. 1858 was still resident in Pietermaritzburg, his address then being given as 12 Behrens Street (now St Andrew's Street).

In this year Arnold applied for a government quit-rent farm in Ward 6, Pietermaritzburg County, adjoining the farm *Illovodale*. He was granted this piece of land (1 138 acres), and he gave it the name *Lincoln*. Title was issued to him on 1 Mar. 1858.

Arnold went insolvent in 1867, and the only other immovable asset in his estate, besides *Lincoln*, was a portion of 33 Pietermaritz Street (presumably his Behrens Street property). His liquidation and distribution account dated May 1869 shows that *Lincoln* was sold for £232 odd. Arnold applied for rehabilitation in July 1872. At this time he was still living at *Lincoln*, but as a renter. He was still there in 1876, but by the end of 1880 was farming at *Slang Spruit* near Pietermaritzburg.

Arnold married again in Oct. 1881. His second wife was Mrs Sarah Redman, widow of Henry Redman*. They were married in Pietermaritzburg.

Arnold and some members of his family are buried in the Commercial Road cemetery, Pietermaritzburg.

The railway siding on the Pietermaritzburg-Richmond line, Arnold's Hill, takes its name from this family.

CHILDREN

Charles Henry (c. 1835 — 22 June 1888, Pmb.) m. 16 Feb. 1860, Pmb., Emma Jane Amelia Catherine Mallandain, d. of Robert Mallandain*. Charles farmed at *Blackwood Grove* in the area now known as Arnold's Hill.

William (c. 1838, Yorks. — 21 Jan. 1916, Pmb.) m. 1 Jan. 1867, Pmb., Mary Tennant (c. 1849, Scotland — 7 June 1906, Pmb.), d. of John and Christina Tennant. Mary and her family had come to Natal on the *Priscilla*, Sep. 1860. William was a farmer.

John (c. 1839 — June 1915, Pmb.) m. 8 Jan. 1862, Richmond, Louisa Beaurain (c. 1840, Cape — 25 Mar.

‡ Arnold's own spelling.

1910, Pmb.), d. of Charles John Beaurain of near Salt River, Cape. John was a farmer.

Sarah Ann (c. 1841, York, Yorks. — 28 Aug. 1908, Deepdale) m. June 1859, Pmb., John Samuel Root*.

Mariah (c. 1845, York, Yorks. — Aug. 1922, Pmb.) m. Aug. 1865, ?Pmb., Frederick Joseph Leadley*.

infant (born c. 1850, England) died young?

Emma (c. 1853, ?Pmb. — Oct. 1874, Pmb.) m. Oct. 1870, Pmb., William Language, son of William Language*.

Hannah (born c. 1855, ?Pmb.) m. Sep. 1872, Pmb., Andrew Tennant (born c. 1847), son of John and Christina Tennant above.

SOURCES

Private source material
34 Box 4. *Emily* lists; **69**; **71**; **72**; **77**; **80**; **102**

Unpublished official papers
125 2244 nos.D113 and D161, 2247 no.D826, 2283, 2284, 2287; **129** 26/187, 33/198, 38/17; **130** 1/31 no.35, 1/87 no.59; **131** IV/23/1 no.55; **132** III/5/26 no.287, III/12/1 p.89, **147**; **156** 10/1883, 75/1888, 80/1910

Official printed sources
168 30.5.1854, 8.8.1854, 10.8.1858, 14.8.1860, 6.8.1867, 16.8.1870, 20.8.1872, 25.8.1874, 29.9.1874, 19.9.1876

Newspapers, periodicals, etc.
189 18.10.1850, 26.1.1916; **197** 1879, 1881, 1882, 1884

Miscellaneous contemporary printed sources
220

Later sources
321

ARNOLD, Thomas

Born c. 1824. Died 24 Jan. 1875, Durban.

Hairdresser and innkeeper. Arnold originally came from Poole in Dorset, but had lived in London. He emigrated to Natal on the *Ballengeich* with his wife and infant daughter. As a Murdoch settler (see E. Morewood) he was entitled to 40 acres on the coast between the Tongaat and Umhlali rivers. His lot was Subdivision 7 of Lot 69, but by June 1856 he had not claimed it and it had reverted to the Government.

To gain the approval of Her Majesty's Emigration Commissioners, Arnold and his wife were described in the *Ballengeich* passenger lists as a 'gardener' and an 'agricultural labourer'. In fact Arnold was a hairdresser and perfumer. By Oct. 1850 he was advertising his services as such in Durban, and by the end of the year was, in addition, running the London Coffee and Dining Rooms. He kept on with these two avocations for the next few years. In Sep. 1852, when one of his children was baptised, his occupation was given as 'innkeeper', and in the *Directory of Durban and Pietermaritzburg* for 1853, published at the end of 1852, he is described as a hairdresser of West Street, Durban.

Arnold moved from West Street to Pine Terrace (Street) *c.* Oct. 1853 to take over the Trafalgar Hotel, previously in the ownership of William Platts*. It is with the Trafalgar that his name is most commonly associated. In Aug. 1854, when advertising the hotel, he stated that he was continuing with hairdressing. This is the last reference found to the latter trade.

Arnold tried sugar planting as a sideline. In May and June 1855 he took out nine-year leases on two ten acre lots on the Milner* brothers' farm *Springfield*. Under the terms of these one third of the land had to be put under cane, which was to be sent to the Milners' and J.B. Miller's* mill for processing. In October he and seven other lessees entered into a lease for the entire *Springfield* farm, forming themselves into the Springfield Sugar Company. Arnold's sugar venture did not last and in July 1856 he sold the lease of one of the plots to Robert Browne*. In May 1857 Browne also took over the other one.

The Trafalgar continued in Arnold's hands until about June 1859 when Edwin Vale* began leasing it. At the end of this year Arnold was living at *Rose Mount*, part of the farm *Sea View*, near Durban.

From the baptismal register entries of two of his children, dated Nov. 1860 and Nov. 1861, it appears that Arnold was the innkeeper at Sterk Spruit on the Durban-Pietermaritzburg road. The later entry is more specific, viz. Assegai Kraal, near Sterk Spruit. He was still mine host at Assegai Kraal in Apr. 1863, but by Feb. 1864 was back in Durban. In this month and in July 1866 when children were baptized his calling was given as 'gentleman'.

In May 1865, according to English's *The Story of the Royal D'Urban Rangers*, Arnold took over the licence granted to Mary, the wife of one Richard Baynes, (not to be confused with Richard Baynes (1811–1881))*. The Bayneses had had the hotel from about Sep. 1863. However, it seems that Arnold did not take possession at this juncture as T. Barker* was running it *c.* Aug. 1866. In this month Barker assigned his estate and one of the terms of the assignment was that he would discontinue the business of the Trafalgar Hotel and allow the landlord to take it over.

During Arnold's absence the Trafalgar had had a varied career. In Sep. 1859 Vale's lease had been assigned to one Thomas Morton. It seems as though the hotel and the billiard room were later run as two separate entities as in

Dec. 1860 Vale advertised his intention of operating the billiard room. In Apr. 1861 G.E. Walker* announced he had taken over the 'Billiard and Refreshment Rooms' at Mr Morton's Trafalgar Hotel, 'lately' managed by Mr Vale. Morton continued with the lease until Apr. 1863 when he and Arnold reached agreement that Arnold would resume possession of his hotel. It appears that instead of doing so, Arnold got Baynes and his wife to run it.

After the Natal Supreme Court had decided that the existing English Church properties were to remain in Bishop Colenso's* hands, the Durban anti-Colensos used the Trafalgar billiard room as their temporary place of worship. It was here in Feb. 1869 that the newly-arrived Bishop Macrorie first worshipped in Natal. By June 1870 'the Arnoldites', as they were dubbed locally, had moved into a temporary school/chapel to which was given the name St Cyprian's.

For many years the Trafalgar Hotel, which had a large room, had been used for concerts and meetings. In 1869 Arnold had it rebuilt for a two-fold purpose — as a concert hall, seating 600, and as a bar. In 1873 he rented the Trafalgar Hall to the Durban Town Council. He appears to have kept on with the bar, for when he died two years later, his death certificate described him as a canteen-keeper.

One of his daughters, Emily, carried on the family tradition. She and her husband, John Arnold, and her brother George, had the Trafalgar Theatre and Bar in the 1880s, and when she died in 1911 she was of the Clarendon Hotel in Durban, while her husband was of the Lincoln Hotel, also in Durban.

Arnold was a fairly prominent citizen of Durban. He was initiated into the Port Natal Lodge of Freemasons in 1858. It would seem that he was the Arnold who was a Steward for the Durban Races in May 1859.

His wife was Jane Tinlen (*c.* 1825 – 16 Aug. 1892, Greytown). They were married on 3 Mar. 1849 in St Mary's Church, parish of Marylebone, Middlesex. His sister, Sarah Oxford Arnold, married George Willson* in 1859. She had come to Natal in the previous year.

CHILDREN

Jane Fanny (1850, ?London – July 1926) m. 30 Aug. 1877, Dbn, William Armstrong, son of Francis Armstrong*.

George Thomas (born Aug. 1852, ?Dbn).

Elizabeth Mary (born June 1854, ?Dbn).

Emily Jane (4 Apr. 1856, Dbn – 16 June 1911, Jhb.) m. 17 Oct. 1878, Dbn, John Arnold, soda water manufacturer.

Julia Anne (born Mar. 1858, ?Dbn) m. 14 June 1888, Pmb., Gustav Albert Lutkens (*c.* 1862, Hamburg, Germany – 2 Apr. 1903, Dundee), son of Julius George Lutkens. Julia in 1882 had been a teacher at the Pmb. Girls' Model Primary School.

Helen Elizabeth (born Mar. 1860, Dbn County) m. June 1882, ?Dbn, George Kitchen Henderson (born *c.* 1845, Carlisle, Cumberland), son of Christopher Woodall Henderson and his wife Elizabeth Kitchen, and nephew of Joseph Henderson*. G.K. Henderson was in Johannesburg in the 1890s.

William Marshall (born Oct. 1861, ?Dbn County) m. May 1884, Dbn, Julia Elizabeth Jessie Irwin (born *c.* 1865). William was a mineral water manufacturer.

Alice Ross or Rose (Sep. 1863 – Oct. 1895, Pmb.) m. Apr. 1889, Pmb., Laurence Henry James Walker, son of Dennis Walker*. Alice had been a teacher at the Pmb. Girls' Model Primary School, 1884–1887.

Sarah died in infancy.

Kate (born Feb. 1866, ?Dbn) m. 27 Dec. 1888, Pmb., Archibald Fisher.

Edith Oxford (13 Mar. 1868, Dbn – 24 Aug. 1873, Dbn) died in childhood.

SOURCES

Private source material
23; 41; 44; 48; 71; 72; 92

Unpublished official papers
125 2245 no.D405, 2287; **126** 73; **129** 7/85, 42/140; **131** IV/7/17 nos. 385 and 396, IV/19/33 nos.19, 20, 61 and 62, IV/19/35 no.90, IV/19/37 no.194; **136; 139; 147; 156** 182/1875; **157; 161** 1873

Official printed sources
166

Newspapers, periodicals, etc.
181 19.2.1862; **184** 13.10.1853, 24.11.1853; **185** 23.8.1854, Jan. 1858, 15.4.1858, 9.8.1858, 27.1.1859, 12.5.1859, 9.6.1859, 11.8.1859, Aug. 1860, 28.8.1873, 28.1.1875, 11.9.1877, 22.10.1878, Supp. 22.5.1934; **187** 1.10.1859, 8.10.1859, 22.12.1860, 13.4.1861, 27.4.1861, 8.2.1862; **189** 4.10.1850, 2.2.1875, 4.9.1877, 24.10.1878, 29.10.1888, 17.8.1892; **197** 1881; **198** 1851

Miscellaneous unofficial contemporary printed sources
220; 225

Later sources
241 pp.81, 83; **265** pp.402, 444; **283** p.21; **324** vol.3 pp.65, 142

ASHFORD, Frederick

Born *c.* 1819. Died 9 Mar. 1900, *Langefontein*, Durban County.

Hotelkeeper and farmer. Ashford emigrated to Natal on the *Dreadnought* with his wife Maria (*c.* 1819 – Jan. 1857, Greytown). It appears that they were friends of Henry Goodwin* and his wife as they brought out the Goodwins' land order. The Goodwins arrived later on the *Aliwal*.

Four weeks after landing Ashford and another *Dreadnought* passenger F.W. Good (see James Good), leased part of the farm *Wentworth* from R.B. Willy*. A month later, at the end of Dec. 1849, Good pulled out of this partnership. In Jan. 1851 Ashford agreed to Willy's taking back 100 of the 200 acres involved in the lease. This land had a 50 yard frontage on the Bay.

Ashford appears to have left *Wentworth* by the end of 1851. In about December he opened a hotel on the Isipingo Flat, which he named the Isipingo Inn. In Dec. 1853 he signed a petition of residents of Sterk Spruit and district on the Pietermaritzburg-Durban road. By August of the following year he was renting the Botha's (Hill) Half-way House on the same route. As Botha's and Sterk Spruit are not far from each other it is possible he was already running the hotel at the end of 1853.

By the time Mrs Ashford died in Greytown in 1857 they had already left Botha's. By July of that year he was running a board and lodging house in Loop Street, Pietermaritzburg. From then until the end of 1878 his career is a blank but in the latter year he was farming at Field's Hill, Pinetown. During the 1880s his address is given in the *Natal Almanac* as 'Botha's, Pinetown', or just 'Botha's'. By the end of 1894 he was farming at Gillitts. This may have been at *Langefontein* where he later died.

His second wife Hannah (born Smith) died at *Langefontein* on 23 Aug. 1907, aged 75. She may have been related to William Hart Smith* who for 20 years lived at *Langefontein*.

SOURCES

Private source material
34 Box 4. *Dreadnought* lists; **78; 113**

Unpublished official papers
125 2242 no.C612; **129** 30/150, **131** IV/7/16 nos.34, 47, 196; **137; 156** 80/1900; **157**

Official printed sources
168 15.8.1854

Newspapers, periodicals, etc.
178 2.1.1852; **185** 5.2.1857; **189** 31.7.1857; **197** 1879, 1881, 1882, 1884, 1888, 1895

ASHLEY, Thomas

Born c. 1822. Died June 1870, Pietermaritzburg.

Ex-sailor and carrier. Ashley began his career in the merchant navy but about the beginning of 1840 he entered the Royal Navy and in Jan. 1841 signed on as an A.B. on the brigantine *HMS Fawn*. He was later drafted from the *Fawn* to man a prize she had captured that was being sent to Africa. In the Cape he was ordered to proceed on *HMS Cleopatra* to Durban to rejoin the *Fawn*. He arrived in Durban in early June 1843 and remained with the *Fawn* until she was scrapped after being damaged in crossing the Bar.

Ashley has two versions of how he came to settle in Natal. Both appear in memorials he wrote in connexion with government land grants. In the first, dated 1848, he stated that when the *Fawn* was condemned he was induced to remain in Natal by Major T.C. Smith by a promise of a land grant. In the other, ten years later, he averred that such crew of the *Cleopatra* [sic] as would consent to remain and assist the small military force at Port Natal, were offered their discharge and were promised grants of land by Admiral King, the Commander of the Cape Station. Ashley accordingly received his discharge from Captain Nourse of the *Fawn*, and in his own words, 'faithfully fulfilled' these conditions. As Nourse and those of his crew not wishing to remain in Natal left for Cape Town on the *Pilot* in June 1844, Ashley's discharge presumably dates from about that time.

At first Ashley lived in Durban. Here he gained experience of the peculiarities of the Bay and was intermittently employed at sounding. In Sep. 1846, having heard that the Government intended appointing a licensed pilot for Port Natal, he applied for the job. He detailed his past experience, both at sea and in the Durban harbour. Besides his four and a half years in the Royal Navy, he claimed he had 14 years' service in the merchant navy. Judging from his age, this could not be possible. As there was at that time no intention of appointing a pilot, Ashley's memorial was of no avail.

By Dec. 1848 Ashley was living in Pietermaritzburg. This was when he first applied for a grant, which he did under the scheme then in operation for discharged soldiers and sailors. According to an annotation on his memorial he was given erf 4F in Durban, the grant being dated 30 Oct. 1849. Ashley later owned an erf in Umgeni village near Durban (erf 16), but had sold it by the end of 1850.

Ashley, by mid-1853, was making his living as a butcher in Pietermaritzburg. For the rest of his working life he appears to have been a carrier, or transport rider. He may have been doing this as a sideline as early as 1851, because in June of that year he hired a wagon to Captain R.J. Garden of the 45th Regiment when the latter went to Pondoland.

In Sep. 1857 Ashley applied for a government farm in Victoria County. On 1 Oct. 1858 he received a grant of 620 acres, which he named *The Fawn*. In the same month he petitioned the Lt.-Governor that it be not subject to quitrent and the various other conditions under which he had received it. He stated that he had never been given a free grant of land, despite his service to Her Majesty, which he detailed in full. The granting of such a request was outside the powers of the Lt.-Governor, and Ashley was informed accordingly.

By Aug. 1860 Ashley was renting property on erf 39 Loop Street. In 1862 he was living in Church Street. He died in 1870.

Ashley's wife was Mary Peacock, the daughter of Joseph Peacock*. They were married in Pietermaritzburg on 4 July 1853. Mrs Ashley remarried in Aug. 1870. Her second husband was a farmer, Johnson Pollard. At the time of their marriage they were both of the farm *Aasvogels Krans* on the Umgeni river, east of Pietermaritzburg. This marriage is recorded in the Pietermaritzburg Wesleyan register. In Dec. 1872, once again a widow, she and one Alexander Munroe took out a special marriage licence in Pietermaritzburg. She appears to have died soon afterwards. This one surmises from the fact that when one of her daughters, a minor, was granted a special marriage licence in Feb. 1876, she had no parents or guardians and had to obtain a court order for her marriage.

CHILDREN

Martha Ann (born May 1854, ?Pmb.) m. Henry John Watson, who was possibly the son of John Watson*. Henry and Martha Ann were in Kimberley in 1875, and at Sand River, O.F.S. in 1877.

Elizabeth Mary (Nov. 1855, Pmb. – 27 June 1922, Bergville) m. Dec. 1875‡, Malton near Pmb., James Day, son of John Day*.

George Peacock (born Nov. 1858, ?Pmb) m. Mar. 1886, Richmond, Ellen Jane Walsh. George was a saddler.

‡ **Alfred Ernest** (born c. 1862, ?Pmb.).

‡ **Joseph Leo** (born Sep. 1864, ?Pmb.).

SOURCES

Private source material
32 p.46; **74**; **77**; **80**; **121**

Unpublished official papers
125 13 no.56, 38 no.104, 2238 no.B78, 2248 no.E124, 2282, 2286; **129** 3/14 no.A16,

---

‡ This date is as it appears in the Pietermaritzburg Wesleyan marriage register. The special licence was issued only in Feb. 1876.

‡ These two were at Sand River, O.F.S. in 1877.

4/34, 4/100; **131** IV/2/69 no.598,
IV/23/2 no.19/1870; **132** III/5/13 no.51,
III/5/19 no.590, III/5/26 no.329, III/12/1 p.92;
134; **147**; **150**

Official printed sources
168 14.8.1860

Printed documents
175 vol.2, p.176

Newspapers, periodicals, etc.
181 4.10.1862; **189** 26.4.1846; **190** June 1844;
197 1884

Later sources
231 p.103

ASHMORE, Felix George

Born c. 1812. Died Feb. 1875, Pietermaritzburg.

Farmer. Ashmore and his wife Elizabeth (c. 1800 –
6 Nov. 1870, Richmond) emigrated to Natal on the *Lady
Bruce*. Accompanying them were Joseph George Ashmore*
and his daughter. Presumably Felix and Joseph were
brothers. The Ashmores came from either Dover in Kent,
or from Devon. Most sources found give the former place.
During the voyage one of the Ashmore men acted as
ship's constable, for which service he was paid £1.

By Nov. 1850 all the Ashmores were resident in Richmond. Felix and his wife appear to have lived there for
the rest of their days. At first Felix farmed but by the end
of 1851 he was supplementing his income with some
unofficial liquor dealing. In Jan. 1852 he and Charles
Dacomb* unsuccessfully petitioned the Lt.-Governor
to remit the fines they had incurred for supplying wine
and spirits without a licence. They maintained that they
had been supplying travellers for a considerable time,
and had done so under the impression that as they were
not in town a licence was not necessary.

Felix was still farming in Richmond in mid–1854.
He appears in the Pietermaritzburg property valuation
lists, published in the *Natal Witness* in Oct. 1855, as the
renter of J. O'Brien's* property in Burger Street, but it
seems that it was Joseph who actually occupied these
premises. From Jan. 1858 to the end of 1861 he was
poundmaster at Richmond.

Up until c. 1870 Ashmore appears in the jury lists for
Pietermaritzburg County as a farmer of Richmond, and
an owner of property. The entries for him in the 1872–73
jury list and the 1874–75 voters' roll describe him as an
apothecary. His occupation as given on his death certificate is chemist. Although there is evidence dating back

to 1854 that he had some medical knowledge, his name
does not appear in the lists of licensed chemists and drug-
gists that appeared in the *Natal Almanac* from 1871.
From these lists it is evident that in the early 1870s there
was no chemist in Richmond. Possibly therefore, Ashmore
was fulfilling a need, albeit unofficially.

He died in Pietermaritzburg and was buried in Richmond.

SOURCES

Private source material
34 Box 4. *Lady Bruce* lists; **80**

Unpublished official papers
125 56(2) no.113, 2241 nos.C11 and C252; **147**

Official printed sources
168 25.7.1854, 19.1.1858, 10.8.1858, 14.8.1860,
31.12.1861, 6.8.1867, 16.8.1870, 21.8.1872,
25.8.1874, 29.9.1874

Newspapers, periodicals, etc.
185 16.12.1858, 22.11.1870; **189** 27.2.1852,
26.10.1855, 17.12.1858, 22.7.1859

ASHMORE, Joseph George

Born c. 1813, Dover, Kent. Died 25 Nov. 1871, De Beer's
(later Kimberley).

Carter and miller. He was the son of Joseph and Louisa
Ashmore. He emigrated to Natal on the *Lady Bruce* with
his daughter Mary Ann. His wife Ann's name appeared on
Byrne & Co.'s list of *Lady Bruce* passengers, but was later
crossed out. On this list Ashmore's occupation is given as
'grazier and butcher'. Also on board was Felix George
Ashmore*, presumably his brother. Either Joseph or
Felix acted as ship's constable during the voyage, for which
he was paid £1.

By Nov. 1850 all the Ashmores were living in Richmond,
and Joseph was working as a butcher and grazier. Some
time between Apr. 1851 and May 1854 he moved to
Pietermaritzburg and began business as a carrier. He was
renting erf 5 Burger Street at this juncture. It would seem
that in 1855 he was occupying J. O'Brien's* premises in
Burger Street, which were rented in Felix's name.

By Sep. 1855 his wife Ann (born Hanson) (Oct. 1821,
?Dover, Kent – 6 July 1879, Pmb.) and their other
children had joined him in Natal.

According to the 1858–59 Pietermaritzburg County
jury list Ashmore was renting premises on erf 22 Burger
Street, and was working as a labourer. The 1860–61
jury list gives him a similar entry. By 1867 he was renting
property on erf 74 Burger Street and was a miller.

In 1871, Ashmore was described on his death notice as a miller 'formerly of Burger Street'. He died at the diamond fields.

CHILDREN

Mary Ann (*c.* 1840, ?Dover — 5 July 1883, Pmb.) m. Apr. 1869, Pmb., George Thomas Holliday (born *c.* 1844, ?London), who came on the *Phantom*, July 1858 with his parents Thomas and Ann. He was a nephew of J.D. Holliday*.

Joseph George (*c.* 1841, Dover — 31 Dec. 1905, Dbn) m. 26 Dec. 1870, Pmb., Mary Ellen Boocock, d. of William Boocock*. Joseph was a storeman.

Caroline Ann (*c.* 1847, Dover — 10 Oct. 1906, Pmb.) m. 27 Oct. 1867, Pmb., John Kean, formerly of the 20th Regiment.

Emily Ann (born 5 July 1858, ?Pmb.) m. July, 1879, Pmb., William Holliday (*c.* 1852, ?London — 4 May 1885, Pmb.), son of Thomas and Ann Holliday above.

Henry Thomas William (born Jan. 1860, ?Pmb.). Died before 1871.

SOURCES

Private source material
34 Box 4. *Lady Bruce* lists; **71**; **73**; **76**; **92**

Unpublished official papers
125 2240 no.B625; **126** 64; **129** 3/12 no.80, 4/3, 25/78, 27/251; **137**; **147**; **156** 131/1900, 263/1906

Official printed sources
168 30.5.1854, 8.8.1854, 29.7.1856, 10.8.1858, 14.8.1860, 6.8.1867, 16.8.1870

Newspapers, periodicals, etc.
185 17.1.1871, 19.12.1871; **189** 27.2.1852, 8.7.1879, 5.7.1883; **197** 1872, 1873, 1879, 1881, 1882, 1884, 1888, 1895

Later sources
321

ASHTON, Charles

Born *c.* 1829.

He was a cabin or intermediate passenger on the *Edward*. He did not take title to his allotments in the Richmond district viz. 70 *Beaulieu*, Illovo (20 acres) and 6 Block R within circle, Richmond village. In Sep. 1873 this land, under Law 4, 1872, was liable to forfeiture to the Government.

SOURCES

Unpublished official papers
125 2263 no.H287; **126** 64

Newspapers, periodicals, etc.
189 10.5.1850

ASHTON, Charles John

Born *c.* 1818, Liverpool. Died 1 Jan. 1861, Wentworth, Durban.

Agricultural implement maker and farmer. He was the son of Michael Ashton of Liverpool and brother of H.P. Ashton*, Sarah Hannah Ashton*, and R.B. Ashton*. He and his brother-in-law Henry Joseph Barrett* were in partnership as agricultural implement makers at the Ceres iron works in Hull. Advertisements for the products of the firm Barrett & Ashton appear in *Byrne's Emigrants' Journal*, offering intending emigrants all kinds of farming implements, delivered free in London.

Ashton and others including Barrett chartered the *Pallas* in Hull, and, with their families 'and adherents', as the *Natal Independent* put it, set sail for Natal. Ashton's sister, Sarah Hannah, accompanied them. Barrett & Ashton brought with them a large quantity of agricultural machinery. The *Pallas* was the vessel that had been chartered by Henry Boast* and his associates to bring out the emigrants who eventually settled at York. It had been condemned as unseaworthy by the Emigration Commissioners, and after a long delay these emigrants sailed on the *Haidee*.

By Nov. 1851 the Ashtons were living near the 'German House' i.e. H.H. Lange's inn at Westville. This was probably on the farm *Attercliffe* about two miles from Pinetown, where it is known they had settled by Aug. 1852. By Feb. 1856, when Eliza and John Leyland Feilden* visited them they had a 'very nice house', beautifully situated. Later in the same year, in December, *Attercliffe* was advertised for sale. The Ashtons retained the property until 1860, however. It was sold in December of that year. The auction notice in the *Natal Star* stated it was 'one of the most complete and perfectly gentlemanly residences in Natal' in a 'park-like estate, containing 108 acres'. A large portion of the 'elegant furniture' was also advertised. Ashton died ten days after the sale.

Attercliffe Road in Westville takes its name from Ashton's estate.

Ashton had been fairly prominent in the life of Durban. In 1852 he was a member of the committee of the Natal Agricultural and Horticultural Society. In Nov. 1854 he and W.H. Middleton* were appointed auditors for the County of Durban. He was one of the original shareholders in the Natal Railway Company in 1859.

Ashton was married to Mary Ellen Barrett (c. 1818, ?Hull, Yorks. – 5 Oct. 1904, Virginia Water, Surrey), the daughter of John Dickinson Barrett and Margaret Youle of Hull, and sister of Eliza Mary Barrett* and Henry Joseph Barrett. In Feb. 1861, a month after her husband's death, Mrs Ashton left for England on the *Oak*, accompanied by her sister and brother-in-law, Eliza Mary and John Sanderson*. The three of them returned to Natal in Mar. 1862 on the *L'Imperatrice Eugenie*. Mrs Ashton remained in Durban until about 1889, when she went to Harrismith, presumably to join members of the Barrett family. Before she died she had been living at Upper Clapton, Berkshire.

SOURCES

Private source material
27 14.11.1851; 53; 92

Unpublished official sources
126 73, 74; 129 3/14 no.A2, 6/268;
131 IV/16/4 nos.36, 72

Official printed sources
168 15.8.1854; 174 p.221

Newspapers, periodicals, etc.
180 24.11.1854; 184 21.11.1850;
185 17.5.1854, 11.8.1859, Jan. 1861, Feb. 1861;
187 22.12.1860; 188 20.8.1852; 189 25.2.1851,
19.12.1856; 192 Mar. 1850

Journals, biographies, autobiographies, letters
208 pp.276–7

Later sources
267 p.148

ASHTON, Henry Prior (born c. 1814) and Richard Bury or Berry

These two were the sons of Michael Ashton of Liverpool and brothers of Charles John Ashton* and Sarah Hannah Ashton*.

Henry and Richard sailed as cabin passengers on the *Haidee*. From a diary written on board by Martha (Patty) Lofthouse, wife of Benjamin Lofthouse*, it is known that 'Mr Ashton' and 'Mr Bell' conducted the religious services on board. As there were two Ashtons and two Bells on the ship, further identification is not possible.

In Feb. 1853 Henry, described as an English merchant on the passenger list, left on the *Wee Tottie* for Melbourne. He was back in May 1854, having come on the *Golden Age*. He then advertised that he wanted to purchase as much Natal produce as possible for the Australian market.

He also offered passages for Melbourne on the *Golden Age*. Presumably he left with that ship on its return voyage to Melbourne in July 1854.

From the will executed by their sister, Sarah Hannah, in 1859, it emerges that both Henry and Richard were then in Australia, as was their father. This will was superseded by one dated 1862 in which Sarah makes no mention of her brothers, but states that Michael Ashton was in Melbourne. The will of Charles John Ashton's widow, made in 1861, is more specific. Michael Ashton was described as being of Collingwood, Victoria, Australia. Collingwood is now a suburb of Melbourne.

SOURCES

Unpublished official papers
126 73; 131 IV/16/4 nos.36, 72, 145

Newspapers, periodicals, etc.
180 20.5.1854, 27.5.1854; 184 17.10.1850

Additional sources
366 16.7.1850, 21.7.1850, 28.7.1850

ASHTON, James

Storekeeper and agent. He was possibly the Mr Ashton who came to Natal on the *Lady of the Lake* in Oct. 1855. According to the *Natal Chronicle* his wife and son accompanied him. The *Natal Mercury* on the other hand makes no mention of a son. The Ashtons were steerage passengers.

The Ashtons may have come from Kent as they were friends of the family of one of George Franklin's* daughters-in-law, Bethiah Millne. The Millnes lived at Faversham. Further evidence linking them with the south of England is their connexion with the Harding family of London, of which more anon.

The Ashtons settled in Pietermaritzburg. To begin with Ashton was employed in the store of Player & Grant (James Player* and Samuel Grant*). Then in Oct. 1856 he and a fellow employee, A.W. Goulden*, started their own business. They described themselves as family grocers and drapers, and called their store Sebastopol House. The firm Goulden & Ashton was dissolved on 18 Nov. 1856, and Ashton continued alone until Mar. 1860 when Samuel Button (son of J.C. Button*) took over the business. Sebastopol House stood on Sub J of erf 6 Loop St.

Six months previously, in Sep. 1859, Ashton and Joseph Wheeler* had been appointed Auditors for the Borough of Pietermaritzburg.

Ashton became insolvent in June 1861. In August, with the sanction of his trustees, he began business as an agent — land, estate and commercial. He made a success of his new enterprise and was rehabilitated in Jan. 1863.

For a short period Ashton carried out a profitable business. He also became a bill and sharebroker. According to E. Rosenthal's *On 'change* he was the first in this field in Pietermaritzburg.

About two years after rehabilitation Ashton was once more in financial difficulties and in July 1865 his estate was compulsorily sequestrated, the final balance sheet being drawn up in Feb. 1867. From the papers concerning his insolvent estate it is apparent that he was to apply for discharge from his insolvency in May 1868, but that this was to be opposed. The final outcome is not given.

Ashton and his wife, Mary Sarah or Sayer, married in England in about 1852. They had parted company by the time of his second insolvency, their separation being legalized by a deed dated Sep. 1864. At the same time Ashton had a second deed executed whereby Subdivision C of his erf 21 Loop Street, Pietermaritzburg was hypothecated to Mrs Ashton's trustee for due payment of £100 p.a. to her as his wife.

At the time these deeds were drawn up Ashton had taken as his mistress a young woman, Mary Ann Beard (1843–1887), daughter of James R. and Mary Ann Beard. In Feb. 1865, five months before his second insolvency, he caused a formal deed of gift to be drawn up whereby he gave Mary Ann a full complement of household furniture, two horses, a carriage and various other smaller items.

Ashton's career after his attempt at rehabilitation in May 1868 remains a blank. The 1869 *Natal Almanac* is the last in which his name appears in the advertisements. The 1870–71 Pietermaritzburg County jury list has an entry for Ashton as an agent, and as an occupier of property on erf 23 Church Street. Ashton owned land in Alexandra County. He appears on the 1867–68 jury list and on the voters' rolls for this county during the 1870s. In the voters' rolls his occupation and his place of residence are entered as 'Unknown'.

Charles Harding (born *c.* 1845) was living with the Ashtons by May 1860. Possibly he was the Mr Harding who arrived on the *Lady of the Lake* in May 1859. In 1861 Charles's father, a schoolmaster, his mother and the rest of the family came to Natal. Ashton stood surety for the repayment of their passage money but before the fares were paid Ashton had gone bankrupt.

Ashton's nicknames were 'Finnifin' or 'Little Jemmy'. This identifies him as 'Little Fine-fin, who stole the daughter of Whiskers' in Book 4 of the Prophet Ignoramus.

CHILD

A child born 12 Feb. 1865, Pmb. Presumably this was the Lewis Beard Ashton listed on Mary Ann's death notice as one of her children.

SOURCES

Private source material
112

Unpublished official papers
126 65, 74; **130** 1/31 no.25; **131** IV/2/69 no.648, IV/23/1 no.105A; **156** 49/1887

Official printed sources
168 10.8.1858, 14.8.1860, 6.8.1867, 20.8.1867, 16.8.1870, 15.9.1874, 8.8.1876

Newspapers, periodicals, etc.
179 17.10.1855; **181** 21.3.1860; **185** 19.10.1855, 12.3.1857, 11.8.1859, 4.3.1865, 8.3.1865 (the latter two the Pmb. edition with which was incorporated **181**); **189** 1.10.1856, 3.4.1858, 11.6.1858, 18.3.1859, 9.9.1859; **191** 26.11.1856; **197** 1863–1867, 1869

Miscellaneous unofficial contemporary printed sources
219 Book 4, Chapter 1

Later sources
235 p.18; **298** p.39; **321**; **327** Joseph Millne to his daughter Bethiah Millne Franklin 28.10.1857

ASHTON, Sarah Hannah

She was the youngest daughter of Michael Ashton of Liverpool, and the sister of C.J. Ashton*, H.P. Ashton* and R.B. Ashton*.

Sarah came to Natal with her brother Charles and his wife on the *Pallas*.

By Apr. 1855 she was living at *Cato's Manor* [sic], having purchased 373 acres of this farm. When she made her will in mid–1859, she was described as being of Durban and *Attercliffe* near Durban (her brother Charles's residence).

On 23 Feb. 1861 at Durban she married D.A.L. Buist*.

From the terms of her 1859 will and one made in 1862 it is evident that she was fairly wealthy. Also she owned the store in Durban from which her husband's business, Buist & Co., was run. Furthermore, in about 1863, at a time when cash was scarce in Natal, she handed James Ashton* about £2 000 to use in discounting for her. Ashton was her agent in this matter.

SOURCES

Unpublished official papers
125 2283; **126** 73; **130** 1/31 no.25; **131** IV/16/4 nos.35, 36, 73, 145

Newspapers, periodicals, etc.
180 20.4.1855; **185** Feb. 1861

ATHERTON, or ATHERTON—HOWSE, John

Born *c.* 1829.

Storekeeper. Atherton came from Hollingworth near Mottram in Longdendale, Cheshire. He came to Natal as a cabin passenger on the *Unicorn*. His allotments were in the Richmond district, viz. 41 *Harmony*, Illovo (20 acres), and 4 Block K within diamond, in Richmond. By as late as Sep. 1873 they were unclaimed and, under Law 4, 1872, were liable to forfeiture to the Government. Although he did not take title to his Richmond land, by Dec. 1850 he had bought the allotments at Mount Moreland of two *British Tar* emigrants, viz. J.A. Stirton* and C. Agar*. These totalled 90 acres.

Atherton did not settle at Mount Moreland, however. He set himself up as a general storekeeper in Durban. In May 1852 he advertised that he possessed a very powerful press and a cotton gin, and was prepared to clean, pack and store for shipping, wool, cotton and 'other fibrous substances'. At the end of 1852 his store was in St Andrews Street.

Natal and particularly Durban suffered from a surfeit of shopkeepers and Atherton was one who did not survive. In Dec. 1852 the *Natal Witness* carried a notice to the effect that, by order of his assignees, his stock-in-trade was being sold up.

Of Atherton's family very little is known. His wife's name was Matilda and he appears to have married her in Natal. A child Winifred Atherton, was baptised in St Paul's, Durban, in Oct. 1852, under the surname Atherton-Howse. She had been born in July 1852.

There is no sign of any Athertons leaving Natal in the 1850s. A Mrs Howse (alias Mrs Clarridge) [*sic*], with two children left for Cape Town in the steerage of the *Gem* in Jan. 1853[‡]. In Oct. 1859 a Mr and Mrs House [*sic*] and four children sailed on the *Waldensian*. They were steerage passengers.

SOURCES

Private source material
   29 Deane papers; **34** Box 1. General correspondence book — Moreland to E. Tatham 10.12.1850. Box 4. *Unicorn* lists; **44**

Unpublished official papers
   125 2263 no.H287; **126** 73, 74

Newspapers, periodicals, etc.
   184 13.1.1853; **188** 12.9.1851, 28.5.1852, 31.12.1852, 14.1.1853; **189** 31.12.1852, 14.1.1853

‡ The *Natal Times* 14.1.1853 lists her thus. The *Natal Witness* and the *Natal Independent* give her name as Mrs Clarridy, without an alias.

Miscellaneous unofficial contemporary printed sources
   220

ATHRELPHO, William

A passenger on the *John Bright* who was entitled to an allotment in the Lidgetton area. His career in Natal was short as he died in the Pietermaritzburg gaol-cum-hospital at the end of 1851, or beginning of 1852.

In Sep. 1855 the Vicar of Weston, near Bath, wrote on behalf of Athrelpho's brothers and sisters to claim any property Athrelpho might have had. However, all that had been realised from the sale of his effects was £6 odd.

J.J. Chapman* knew his friends in England.

SOURCES

Unpublished official papers
   129 3/8 no.108, 3/14 no.A1

Newspapers, periodicals, etc
   189 16.5.1851

ATKINSON, John

A bricklayer who came to Natal on the *Herald*.

Nothing whatever has been discovered of his activities in Natal, nor those of fellow passengers Alfred Herrington or Hewington* and Edwin Todd*. It is known that three *Herald* people, rather than remain in the Colony, signed up as crew. It is therefore assumed that these were the three.

The *Herald* with all hands was lost on the return voyage.

SOURCES

Newspapers, periodicals, etc.
   189 31.5.1850

Later sources
   267 p.117

ATKINSON, John

Born *c.* 1802, Yorkshire. Died 10 Dec. 1873, Yafforth, Yorks.

Farmer. Atkinson came to Natal on the *Haidee*. He bought the allotments at York of three other *Haidee* passengers Joseph and Thomas Kirk** and Thomas Cass*.

From a letter written by William Boast*, another *Haidee* emigrant, one learns that Atkinson returned to England as early as 1851. Before closing his letter, dated 5 Jan. 1851, Boast wrote that Mr Atkinson and Mr Tutin* were leaving for England 'this afternoon' and would take it. The Port Captain's passenger lists make no reference to their departure. The 1852–53 list of jurors for Pietermaritzburg Division has an entry for Atkinson as an agriculturalist of York, and describes him as an owner and occupier of property. Again the Port Captain's lists have no record of his return to the colony. One can only query the accuracy of both the shipping lists and the jury list.

By July 1854 he was certainly back in England and he appears not to have returned to the Colony. In Oct. 1854 his son William came to Natal on the *Rydal*. Four years later, in June 1858, another son, Henry, arrived on the *Princeza*. Both had embarked in Liverpool.

More Atkinsons arrived in the Colony in Aug. 1859 on the *Early Morn*, this time from London. One was George, John's nephew, while the other two were F. Atkinson and Miss M. Atkinson. The latter was probably the Miss Atkinson who left Durban in the *Lady of the Lake* in May 1860.

William settled in Natal and went sugar planting at Isipingo. He became well-known for his efficient and scientific farming. At the time of Henry's death, in 1859, he was also farming. The *Natal Witness* notice of his death describes him as the son of John Atkinson, Esq. of *Yafforth Lodge* near Northallerton, Yorkshire. When John Atkinson made his will in 1872 his property consisted of 'land, tenements and real estate at Yafforth and elsewhere in England and at Port Natal and elsewhere abroad'.

His wife's name was Mary.

CHILDREN

Francis
David
Mary
William Anthony (c. 1826, York, Yorks. – 6 Apr. 1874, Dbn) m. Elizabeth Buckley. By 1884 Elizabeth was living in Manchester.
Anne m. ?Calton
Roseanna
Robert – a farmer of Sowerby near Thirsk, Yorks.
Rachel ?m. ?George Ayre.
John Slater – a farmer of Toffirth (unverified) near Northallerton, Yorks.
Henry (c. 1833, Yafforth, Yorks. – 14 Oct. 1859, Pmb.) unmarried.

SOURCES

Private source material
  92; 102

Unpublished official papers
  125 2249 no.E272; **126** 73, 74; **129** 3/14 no.A8, 4/102; **136**; **137**; **156** 193/1873, 133/1874

Official printed sources
  168 10.8.1852, 25.7.1854, 8.8.1854, 29.7.1856, 10.8.1858, 14.8.1860, 6.8.1867, 10.8.1869, 6.8.1874, 29.9.1874

Newspapers, periodicals, etc.
  184 17.10.1850, 18.9.1851, **185** 23.9.1858, 11.8.1859, 9.4.1874, 26.6.1875, 29.6.1875; **189** 21.10.1859

Later sources
  297 pp.63, 129, 284

Additional sources
  365

ATTWOOD, Charles

Born *c.* 1807.

He emigrated on the *King William* with his wife Sarah Jane (born *c.* 1807) and two daughters. He is designated in the passenger list as a market gardener. By Sep. 1850 he was advertising that he intended starting a school for young gentlemen next to his wife's school for young ladies. A month later, however, he announced that 'owing to engagements which will occupy most of his time' he would be unable to open a school, but intended, twice a week, to give instruction in phototypy and phonography. During 1851 he worked as a draughtsman in the office of John Moreland*. By the end of 1852 he was living at *Redland*, Wentworth, near Durban. His son, George Dare, who had followed the family out in the *Justina*, died at *Redland* in 1853.

By July 1855 Attwood was working in Cape Town as a tradesman. Presumably he was the Attwood who left for Cape Town in Jan. 1854. He had travelled steerage on the *Elizabeth*.

A Miss Attwood left the Colony for Cape Town in Mar. 1856 on the *Gitana*.

Attwood was possibly no longer in Cape Town by 1865 as there is no entry for him in the *Cape Town Directory* published in that year.

CHILDREN

George Dare (c. 1831 – 20 June 1853, Wentworth, Dbn) unmarried.

Elizabeth Hannah (*c.* 1835 – July 1853, Dbn) m. Dec. 1852, ?Dbn, Alexander Jacques*. Elizabeth was buried at *Redland.*

Clara (born *c.* 1838).

SOURCES

Private source material
    34 Box 3. Voucher N 15. Box 4. *Conquering Hero* lists

Unpublished official papers
    125 2282; **126** 64, 73

Newspapers, periodicals, etc.
    180 13.7.1855; **184** 19.9.1850, 19.10.1850;
    185 23.6.1853, 7.7.1853, 15.8.1856, 27.8.1857,
    9.8.1858, Aug. 1860; **189** 15.11.1850; **196**

ATTWOOD, George

A passenger on the *John Line.* Possibly he was the Attwood who left for Cape Town on the *Douglas* in July 1851.

SOURCES

Unpublished official papers
    126 73

Newspapers, periodicals, etc.
    189 9.5.1851

AUSTEN, George William

He was living in Verulam by Mar. 1852.

Possibly he was the G.L. [*sic*] Austin [*sic*] whose infant son died in Apr. 1851, in Durban.

SOURCES

Unpublished official papers
    125 2241 no.C251

Newspapers, periodicals, etc.
    189 11.4.1851

AUSTEN, Mary Orpah

Born *c.* 1826.

Mary Austen emigrated to Natal on the *Minerva.* She travelled under arrangement with W.J. Irons's* Christian Emigration and Colonization Society. The passenger lists describe her as a bracemaker.

In Apr. 1851 she married John Irwin*. The wedding took place in Durban.

SOURCES

Private source material
    44

Newspapers, periodicals, etc.
    189 12.7.1850

AUSTIN, John Bird Sumner

Born *c.* 1829, England. Died 19 July 1862, Durban.

Farmer. Austin was living in Durban as early as Apr. 1851. Presumably he was the Austin who arrived on the *Tuscan* the previous October.

Possibly he was the Austin associated with Adolph Coqui in bringing a 5 000 lb consignment of ivory from 'Overberg' *c.* Feb. 1854. Edward Snell* bought the lot at 5/4½ d per lb. When a request to Coqui to stand for the Legislative Council was prepared in Jan. 1859 Austin was one of the signatories.

In Jan. 1856 Austin entered into the lease of 60 acres of R.P. (Dick) King's* farm *Isipingo.* This was due to run for 50 years but Austin sold it in Apr. 1862.

Austin died after taking a dose of five grains of 'strychnia'. In reporting this the *Natal Star* stated he was well known in Durban and was 'respectably connected' but had for some time been 'a victim of intemperate habits'. According to his death notice he did not have any land in Natal, but had a small property in the Barbadoes.

CHILD

Wiltshire Stanton (4 Dec. 1859, Isipingo – 10 Dec. 1886, *Walker's Lease*, Umgodi, Ixopo district) unmarried. Wiltshire was a farmer and storekeeper of *Walker's Lease.* His mother was Jane, daughter of James Calverley*.

SOURCES

Private source material
    61

Unpublished official papers
129 3/14 no.A9, 6/281; 131 IV/19/34 no.27

Official printed sources
168 24.6.1851

Newspapers, periodicals, etc.
184 10.4.1851; 185 20.1.1859; 187 26.7.1862;
189 3.2.1854

Personal communication
342

AUSTIN or AUSTEN, William

Born c. 1830.

An agricultural labourer who emigrated to Natal on the *Edward*. His wife Sarah (born c. 1830) accompanied him. They came out under the auspices of W.J. Irons's* Christian Emigration and Colonization Society. Byrne & Co's list has the word 'inft.' next to their names, but crossed out, while the *Natal Witness* list of *Edward* passengers mentions a Thomas Austin as accompanying them. Possibly Thomas was their child and he died before they sailed.

By Sep. 1850 Austin had sold his town allotment to R. Balderston*.

Nothing more has been discovered about this person. A fair number of references have come to light on a William Austin (c. 1840, London — 4 Sep. 1899, Dbn) who was the son of Job Austin and nephew of William Austin, the protegé of George IV's queen, Caroline. As there is a ten-year discrepancy in the ages of the two William Austins, and the earliest reference found to the second dates from 1864, it is assumed that they are two different people.

SOURCES

Private source material
34 Box 2. Surveyors' and Immigrants' correspondence book — R. Balderston to Moreland 17.9.1850. Box 4. *Edward* lists

Unpublished official papers
129 9/332

Newspapers, periodicals, etc.
185 Apr. 1865, 3.12.1870; 189 10.5.1850

AVISON, John

Born c. 1824.

A farmer or labourer who arrived on the *Henrietta*. He did not claim his allotments at Byrne, viz. 18 Block Q and 165 *Dunbar*. Under Law 4, 1872, this land became subject to forfeiture to the Government, not having been claimed by Sep. 1873.

Presumably he was the Mr Avison who left for England on the *Sandwich* in Mar. 1851.

SOURCES

Private source material
34 Box 4. *Minerva* lists

Unpublished official papers
125 2263 no.H287; 126 64, 73

AYRES, John

Born Oct. 1791. Died 6 July 1878, Durban.

Farmer. Before emigrating to Natal the Ayres's home had been *The Priory* in Hertford. Ayres was at one time the mayor of Hertford. He apparently did contracting for the Office of Ordnance, for among the Ayres papers in the Local History Museum is a letter from the Office enquiring if he could deliver at Woolwich a further 200 loads of oak timber hewn batts, measuring not less than 50 feet each.

Ayres and his family sailed for Natal on the *Tuscan*, which he had chartered for the purpose. Besides the Ayres family of eight, there were eleven other passengers. The *Natal Independent* list of passengers has Ayres entered as master of the vessel.

At first the Ayres lived in Durban, but by at least the end of 1854 they had settled at or near Pinetown. By Apr. 1855 they were on a property they had named *Glen Ayres*, the address of which is given in different sources as either Cowie's Hill or Pinetown.

In June 1859 Ayres was appointed a J.P. In November a notice appeared in the Government Gazette announcing that he and George Bishop* were to assist the Durban Resident Magistrate in the trial and decision of criminal cases at the branch courts to be held at Pinetown. In Sep. 1862 Ayres, together with the Collector of Customs, the Port Captain and the Resident Magistrate for Durban County, was appointed to a board established to consider applications by persons desirous of importing firearms into the Colony. A year later he was appointed Acting Resident Magistrate for Durban County during the short absence on leave of H.J. Meller*.

Ayres's farming operations received recognition in 1862 when he gained a medal at the International Exhibition in London for his long staple cotton and an honourable mention for his coffee. At the same exhibition his son Thomas received a medal for his specimens of natural history.

The Ayres's last years were spent in Durban. By at least Oct. 1874 they were living in St Andrews Street.

His wife was Martha Duchesne (c. 1808, France – 21 June 1883, Durban) who was related to General J.C.R.A Duchesne, the commander of the French force which conquered Madagascar. One source states she was his sister, but that seems unlikely as the conquest took place as late as 1895. The Ayres were married in 1829 in London.

CHILDREN

Thomas (July 1828, Hertford – 31 July 1913, Potchefstroom) m. Apr. 1855, ?Pinetown, Sarah Willes*. Thomas was a farmer and naturalist. In Oct. 1852 he sailed for Australia via Mauritius on the *Narcissus*, returning in Mar. 1855 on the *Gitana*. In 1865 he went to live in Potchefstroom. Dr P.A. Clancey of the Durban Museum has observed that Thomas's ornithological work was such that by the time he went to the Transvaal there were no new forms at species level left in Natal for later workers to describe. From 1859–1864 his 'List of a collection of birds in Natal in South Eastern Africa' appeared in the *Ibis*, while from 1869–1886, in the same journal, his 'Notes on the birds of the territory of the Transvaal Republic' were published. In 1868 he led a party to the Tati goldfields. (See *D.S.A.B.* v.3)

Ellen (Feb. 1833, ?Hertford – 2 Dec. 1902, Dbn) m. Aug. 1851, ?Dbn, John Millar*.

John (born ?Hertford) married. John was a clerk in the Durban Post Office in 1855 and 1856. He afterwards went trading. By 1865 he was in Potchefstroom.

Martha (c. 1838, ?Hertford – 18 Feb. 1860, Pmb.) m. 28 Apr. 1859, Pinetown, Charles Hammond Dickinson*.

Walter (born ?Hertford, died 1899, near the Waterberg, Tvl) m. 9 Jan. 1873, Potchefstroom, Maria Rutherford, d. of Dr ?E. Rutherford of Potchefstroom, who had been a member of the Cape Parliament. By 1860 Walter was working in Durban as a clerk, while by 1865 he was employed in a similar capacity by the Durban municipality. He was living at Potchefstroom by 1873. In 1878 he was clerk to the Landdrost of Rustenburg, and in 1879 was First Clerk to the Auditor of the Transvaal. He made several expeditions into the interior. When returning to Rustenburg after three years' wandering in Matabeleland, he was gored by a wounded buck. He died on the banks of the Mogalakwena river, near the Waterberg. Articles by Eugene Marais in the *Volkstem* in Nov. 1935 give prominence to Walter among the three Ayres brothers, as a naturalist. Marais stated that in papers in Europe the identity of the three brothers is often confused and animals and birds described by Walter are attributed to one or other of his brothers. He maintained that in 1862 Walter discovered a new South African eagle, *Spizoentus Ayrsii*, probably the rarest in Africa. However, later sources, viz. Dr Clancey and Dr V.F.M. Fitzsimons credit Thomas with the groundwork of ornithological knowledge in Natal and the Transvaal.

Alice Agnes (c. 1848, Hertford – 3 Nov. 1918, ?Dbn) m. 4 Oct. 1884, Dbn, George Henry Wirsing*.

SOURCES

Private source material
9 Marianne Churchill to Isabella Churchill 9.1.1859; **14**; **24**; **41**; **78**; **92**; **104**; **113**; **118**

Unpublished official papers
125 2245 no.D593, 2246 no.D684, 2247 no.D894, 2282, 2283, 2288; **126** 73; **129** 45/214; **131** IV/7/17 no.378, IV/12/13 no.9; **137**; **156** 5/1869, 49/1886, 90/1890

Official printed sources
166 1855; **168** 16.9.1862, 6.10.1874, 3.10.1876

Newspapers, periodicals, etc.
180 27.4.1855; **181** 29.5.1863, 25.9.1863; **183** 25.3.1856; **184** 17.10.1850, 14.8.1851, 28.12.1854; **185** 20.12.1854, 5.5.1859, 11.8.1859, 23.2.1860, 28.1.1873, 25.4.1874, 8.7.1878, 23.6.1883, 26.6.1883, 16.10.1884; **187** 12.11.1859; **189** 15.8.1851, 4.5.1855, 10.6.1859, 4.11.1859, 11.7.1878, 28.6.1886; **195** Nov. 1884 p.125; **197** 1879, 1880, 1882, 1884, 1888, 1895

Miscellaneous unofficial contemporary printed sources
222 p.258

Later sources
258; **260** vol.17 p.278; **304** p.4; **310**; **314**; **324** vol.3 pp.106, 141

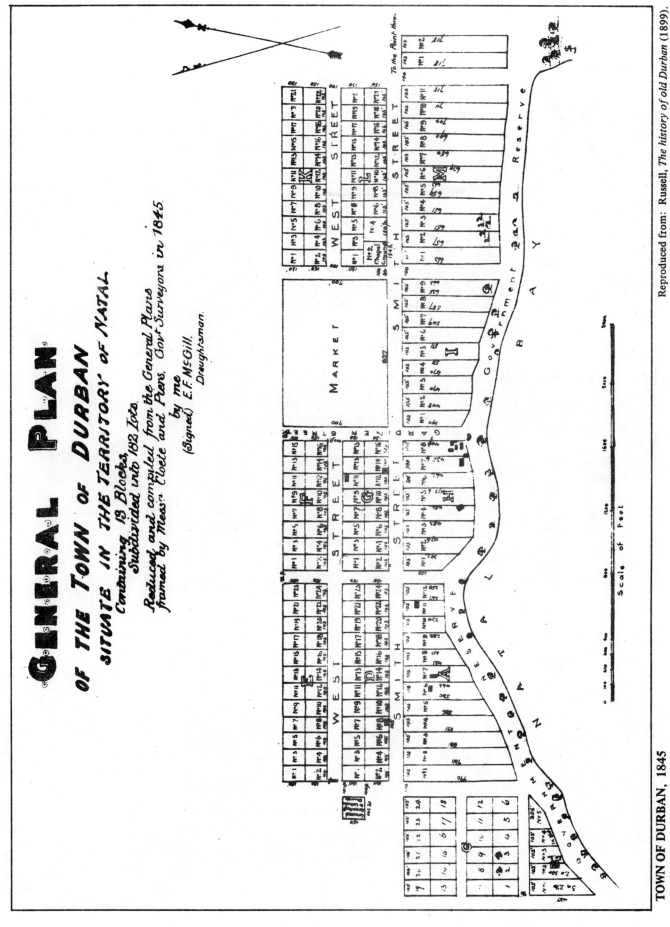

TOWN OF DURBAN, 1845

Reproduced from: Russell, *The history of old Durban* (1899).

PLAN of the City of PIETERMARITZBURG.

CITY OF PIETERMARITZBURG, 1868

88

Addenda

ACUTT, W.H.
For his ante-nuptial contract with Mary Caroline Gower see **131** IV/19/29 no.1030.

ADCOCK, Joseph
For the ante-nuptial contracts of his daughters Catherine Louisa (1865) and Mary Ann see **131** IV/19/15 no.55 and IV/19/16 no.103.

AITCHISON, J.C.
His father, Alexander Aitchison (born c. 1779), was in Cape Town as early as 1807. There, at various times, he made a living as a baker, a carrier and a storekeeper. His mother was Ann Hay (born c. 1802), from Dublin. Alexander and Ann were married in Cape Town on 21 Aug. 1819.
Source: Philip, Peter: *British residents at the Cape, 1795–1819: biographical records of 4800 pioneers.* Cape Town, David Philip, 1981. pp.2–3. This work does not appear in the Source List as it was published when this volume of this *Register* was at an advanced stage.

AITCHISON, J.M.
Baptized 17 Dec. 1820, Cape Town.   Source: As above.

AKERMAN, Sir J.W.
Akerman is mentioned frequently in the *Four books of the prophet Ignoramus*, his nickname being 'the Hakim'.
Source: **219**

ALDRIDGE, Dr C.M.
Before leaving for England in 1869 Aldridge sold the goodwill of his practice to Dr Charles Gordon for £500. In May 1871 after his return to the Colony and to Pietermaritzburg, he and Gordon made a new agreement, binding for five years, whereby he could once again practise in the city. This involved a payment to Gordon of £250 and the undertaking to make up any shortfall in Gordon's income should it amount to less than £800 p.a. From this deed it is evident that Aldridge's return to Grey's Hospital was not immediate as provision was made in case of Dr Otto leaving the city and either of them being appointed as Surgeon at Grey's. In this event the two of them were to go into partnership.
Source: **131** IV/19/21 no.304.

ALLERSTON, William
For the ante-nuptial contracts of his daughters Laura, Rosina and Harriet see **131** IV/19/20 nos.269, 285a and IV/19/29 no.1051.

ALLISON, Rev. James
His adopted daughter Elizabeth Warren was born in Grahamstown.
Source: **131** IV/3/67 no.61.

ALLISON, J.T.
In a protocol dated Apr. 1869 Allison is described as a farmer of *The Cedars*, near Pietermaritzburg.
Source: IV/19/19 no.235.
For the ante-nuptial contract of his daughter Alice and Charles Pitman see **131** IV/19/42 no.263. Pitman was a hotelkeeper of Pietermaritzburg.

ANDERSON, John (1816–1889)
Ignoramus's name for his is 'Jock, the shoemaker'.
Source: **219** Book 2, Chap. 17.

ANDERSON, W.P.
His second marriage took place in Durban in Mar. 1875.
Source: **53**.
For his daughter Frances's ante-nuptial contract see **131** IV/19/40 no.190.

ANDREWS, George
Two powers of attorney were executed by him in 1866 to recover his inheritance from the estate of his grandfather William Penton of Farringdon. The second, dated Oct. 1866, was given to William Penton Andrews, farmer, of Farringdon. Andrews was still in Pietermaritzburg at this time and was working as a clerk.
Source: **131** IV/19/16 nos.89 and 129.
John Andrews in Nov. 1866 signed a power of attorney for the same purpose. He was then living at Caversham.
Source: **131** IV/19/16 no.136.
George Andrews's daughter Gertrude died in Dec. 1927.
Source: **94.**

ANDREWS, John (1820–1900)
His second daughter's name is given as Marion Ann in the special licence issued for her marriage.
Source: **125** 2284.

ANDREWS, John of *Valsch River*
The supposition that he was the John Andrews who appeared in the Pietermaritzburg County jury lists as a farmer of *Boschfontein* is probably incorrect as it has since been discovered that George Andrews's relation, John, was living at Caversham near *Boschfontein* by 1866.
Source: **131** IV/19/16 no.136.

ARCHBELL, Rev. James
He and his wife arrived in South Africa on 29 May 1819 on the *Marianne* ex Portsmouth.
Source: Philip, Peter: *British residents at the Cape, 1795–1819* ... p.95, (See **J. C. Aitchison** above).

ARMSTRONG, Francis
For the ante-nuptial contract of his son William see **131** IV/19/25 no.514.

ARMSTRONG, John
The Armstrongs were living at New England in June 1867 and Oct. 1868 when Margaret signed notarial protocols in connexion with her first husband's property in the Orange Free State.
Source: **131** IV/19/17 no.166 and IV/19/18 no.212.

ARMSTRONG, Dr William
Mrs Armstrong's sister Sarah Stevens died on 27 Mar. 1854 at Stroud. Her brother was William Stevens who in 1868 was living at Woodford, London. She also had a half-sister Elizabeth Stevens.
Sources: **131** IV/19/18 nos.188, 189; **156** 47/1897.

ARNOLD, Thomas
For the ante-nuptial contract of his daughter Jane Fanny see **131** IV/19/25 no.514.

AYRES, John
He resigned from the Firearms Board *c.* Sep. 1874.
Source: **168** 22.9.1874.

Immigrant Vessels

This list is based on the one to be found in W.C. Holden's* *Colony of Natal*, pp.288–9, which in turn is derived from the 1851 and 1852 issues of Jeremiah Cullingworth's* *Port Natal Almanac*. Amendments in dates of arrival have been made from the European Immigration papers vols. 64 and 73 in the Natal Archives and passenger lists as they appeared in the *Natal Witness*.

Name	From	Arrival	Promoters
Beta	Bremen	Mar. 23, 1848	B & J
Sarah Bell	London	Oct. 18	
Gwalior	London	Dec. 24	
Elizabeth Jane	London	Mar. 9, 1849	
Lalla Rookh	London & Plymouth	May 13	
Wanderer	London & Portsmouth	May 16	B
Washington	London	July 18	B
Henry Tanner	London	Oct. 10	B
John Gibson	London	Oct. 23	G & J
Dreadnought	London	Nov. 2	B
Aliwal	London	Dec. 10	B
King William	London and Plymouth	Jan. 22, 1850	B
Ina	Glasgow	Mar. 8	B
Sovereign	London and Plymouth	Mar. 24	B (+ I)
Edward	London	May 2	B (+ I)
Lady Bruce	London and Portsmouth	May 9	B (+ I)
Hebrides	London and Plymouth	May 10	H
Herald	London	May 27	L
Conquering Hero	Glasgow	June 28	B
Minerva	London	July 3	B (+ I)
Henrietta	Liverpool	July 4	B
Ballengeich	London	July 26	M
Sandwich	London	July 27	B
Henry Warburton	Liverpool	Sep. 4	
Globe	London	Sep. 7	B
Unicorn	Liverpool	Sep. 17	B (+ I)
Nile	London	Sep. 25	H & L
British Tar	London and Plymouth	Sep. 28	B (+ I)
Haidee	Hull	Oct. 7	Boast & Lund
Tuscan	London	Oct. 8	

Name	From	Arrival	Promoters
Emily	London and Plymouth	Oct. 10	B (+ I)
Choice	London	Oct. 11	H & L
Devonian	Liverpool	Oct. 31	B (+ I)
Justina	London	Nov. 11	M
Pallas	Hull	Dec. 11	
Amazon	London	Dec. 31	
Wilhelmina	Liverpool	Jan. 7, 1851	
Dreadnought	London	Feb. 13	
Bernard	London	Feb. 16	B (+ I)
Vixen	London and Falmouth	Mar. 10	
Ceres	London	Mar. 22	
Albinia	Glasgow	Apr. 26	
John Line	London	May 3	(+ I)
Lady Sale	Glasgow	May 7	
John Bright	London	May 8	H & L
Harlequin	London	May 23	
Jane Morice	Liverpool	July 7	
Jane Greene	London and Plymouth	July 8	
Cheshire Witch	London	July 26	
Urania	Leith	Aug. 15	
Isle of Wight	Glasgow	Sep. 20	
Borneo	London	Sep. 24	
Bellona	Liverpool	Sep. 26	
Killermont	London	Nov. 28	
Devonian	Liverpool	Dec. 2	
Iris	London	Dec. 30	
Trent	London	Feb. 6, 1852	

ABBREVIATIONS

B	—	Byrne & Co.
B & J	—	Bergtheil & Jung
G & J	—	Garrod & Johnston
H	—	Hackett
L	—	Lidgett
M	—	Murdoch
(+ I)	—	plus Christian Emigration and Colonization Society settlers (Irons group)

Related Surnames

Acutt* *see* Anderson, Robert
(*c.* 1818–1878)
Adam *see* Alder, Charles
Aingworth *see* Anderson, W.P.
Aldwynckle *see* Allison, A.B.
Allen *see* Alison
Allison* *see* Anderson, William
(1790–1873)
Appleyard *see* Archbell
Ayre *see* Atkinson

Bagley *see* Adams, George
Ball *see* Armstong, Dr William
Barker* *see* Arbuthnot, James
Barrett* *see* Ashton, C.J.
Barry *see* Akerman
Bates *see* Aitken
Batty *see* Arbuthnot, James
Baxter *see* Arbuckle
Beard *see* Allerston, William
Beater* *see* Acutt and Anderson,
Robert (*c.* 1818–1878)
Beaurain *see* Arnold, Henery
Behrens *see* Acutt, Robert
Binns *see* Acutt, W.H.
Bird* *see* Armstrong, Dr William
Blaine* *see* Acutt, W.H.
Bland *see* Allison, A.B.
Bloy* *see* Alborough, and Anderson,
John (1812–1898)
Boden *see* Anderson, John
(1812–1898)
Boocock* *see* Ashmore, J.G.
Border *see* Allan, Thomas
Borland *see* Anderson, W.P.
Bowman *see* Allan, Thomas
Brandon (Brennan)* *see* Alder,
Charles
Brennan* *see* Adams, John
Brimelow *see* Adams, George

Brock *see* Akerman
Brook *see* Adcock
Brooks *see* Anderson, William
(1790–1873)
Bruce *see* Arbuthnot, James
Brumby *see* Akerman
Buckley *see* Atkinson
Buist* *see* Ashton, S.H.
Burniston *see* Allison, J.T.
Button* *see* Archbell and Armstrong,
Francis

Caldwell* *see* Anderson, William
(*c.* 1818–1898)
Callaway* *see* Acutt, Robert
Calton *see* Atkinson
Cameron *see* Allison, James
Campbell* *see* Anderson, Robert
(*c.* 1818–1878)
Canty *see* Andrews, John
(1820–1900)
Chambers *see* Allison, J.T.
Chaplin* *see* Alborough
Chatterton* *see* Akerman
Chick* *see* Andrews, John
(1820–1900)
Cockerell* *see* Archibald
Cocks *see* Allen, Philip
Colenbrander *see* Addison, W.H.
Cordiner *see* Arbuthnot, James
Cotter *see* Anderson, Robert
(*c.* 1818–1878)
Cotton *see* Acutt
Cox *see* Anstie, Paul
Cranswick *see* Allerston, William
Crocker* *see* Arbuthnot, James
Crooks *see* Armstrong, Francis
Crosby *see* Akerman

Dales* *see* Anderson, John
(1812–1898)

Davey *see* Arbuthnot, James
Davis *see* Agar
Dawes *see* Andrews, George
Day* *see* Ashley
Deegan *see* Agar
De Jager *see* Adams, William
(1820–1916)
De Kok *see* Allison, A.B.
Denby *see* Allerston, William
De Vries Robbé *see* Allison, A.B.
De Winnaar *see* Allen, James
Dickinson* *see* Ayres
Dickson/Dixon *see* Arbuckle
Dixon *see* Allen, James
Douglas *see* Allerston, William
Duchesne *see* Ayres
Duffy *see* Adlam
Dunlop *see* Adams, George
Dunn *see* Allison, James

East *see* Acutt, Robert
Ellis *see* Adams, William
(*c.* 1824–1894)
Emmett *see* Andrews, John, of
Valsch River.
Erridge *see* Agar
Essery *see* Adlam
Evans *see* Anderson, John
(1812–1898)

Fannin* *see* Allison, James
Fell *see* Aitken and Arbuckle
Field* *see* Adams, George,
Addison, W.H. and
Anderson, William (1790–1873)
Fisher *see* Arnold, Thomas
Foley* *see* Allison, A.B.
Foord *see* Adcock
Ford *see* Andrews, George
Forrest* *see* Archibald

Foster* see Anderson, James
Franklin see Adams, William
    (c. 1824–1894)
Fraser see Armstrong, Francis
Friday* see Allan, Thomas
Funnell see Andrews, George

Gamley see Arbuckle
George* see Agar
Gibson* see Aitchison, J.C. and
    Armstrong, Francis
Gillespie* see Acutt, Robert
Gillmer see Aitchison, J.M.
Glenn see Allan, Thomas
Godden* see Addison, Thomas
Good* see Allan, John
Goodwin see Andrews, John
    (1820–1900)
Gordon* see Andrews, George
Gorrie see Allan, John
Gower* see Acutt, W.H.
Graham* see Acutt, W.H. and
    Alborough
Graumann see Anderson, W.P.
Gray* see Adams, William
    (c. 1824–1894) and Allison,
    John
Green* see Adams, William
    (c. 1820–1916)
Gregory* see Allanson
Gretton see Allen, Philip
Grundy* see Acutt, Julianna

Haigh see Archbell
Hall* see Agar and Allison, J.T.
Hallowes see Addison, W.H.
Handley* see Andrews, George
Hanson see Ashmore, J.G.
Harrison see Addison, W.H. and
    Adams, John
Harwin see Akerman
Hatch see Arbuckle
Hawksworth see Arbuthnot,
    James
Hayes see Anderson, John
    (1812–1898)
Henderson* see Adams, George
    and Arnold, Thomas
Herbert see Allen, Philip
Higham* see Anderson, William
    (c. 1818–1898)
Hirst see Addison, W.H.
Hiscock* see Archbell
Hogg* see Adams, William
    (c. 1820–1916)
Holgate* see Archbell
Holliday* see Ashmore, J.G.
Holmes see Allison, J.T.
Horton* see Andrews, John
    (1820–1900)

Hoyle see Adams, William
    (c. 1824–1894)
Huber see Allison, J.T.
Hurst see Adlam
Hutton see Archibald

Inman see Arbuckle
Innes see Acutt, W.H.
Ireland* see Allerston, William
Irwin* see Arnold, Thomas and
    Austen, M.O.

Jackson* see Addison, W.H.
Jacques* see Allan, John and
    Attwood, Charles
Johnson* see Alder, Charles and
    Armstrong, John
Johnstone* see Anderson, William
    (1790–1873)
Jones* see Adams, William
    (c. 1824–1894)
Jordaan see Allen, James
Joyner* see Anderson, W.P.

Kean see Ashmore, J.G.
Kerr see Allen, Philip
King see Adcock and Anderson,
    John (1812–1893)
Kingdon see Anstie, Paul
Kinsman* see Armstrong,
    Dr William
Kirk* see Anderson, John
    (1812–1898) and Andrews,
    John (1820–1900)
Kitchen see Arnold, Thomas
Knapp* see Allerston, William
Knight* see Acutt, W.H.
    Anderson, Robert
    (c. 1818–1878) and Anderson,
    William (1790–1873)
Knipe see Anderson, James
Koekemoer see Adams, William
    (c. 1820–1916)

Langley see Allison, James
Language* see Arnold, Henery
Laurens see Allan, Thomas
Lavender* see Allerston, William
Lawton see Archbell
Leadley* see Arnold, Henery
Leigh* see Arbuthnot, James
Le Sueur see Allan, Thomas
Leuchars* see Agar
Lindsay* see Allison, James
Lloyd* see Addison, W.H.
Logan* see Adams, George and
    Alison
Long see Akerman
Lucas* see Allen, Philip
Lutkens see Arnold, Thomas

Maby see Arbuthnot, James
McCulloch see Allan, Thomas
McDonald* see Archbell
McDonnell see Adams, John
McKenzie* see Armstrong, Francis
McLean see Andrews, George
McNicol see Alison
McQueen see Andrews, George
McWilliam see Allison, John
Malcolm see Adams, William
    (c. 1824–1894)
Male see Addison, W.H.
Mallandain* see Anderson, John
    (1812–1898) and Arnold,
    Henery
Mansfield see Adcock
Mare see Alborough
Marshall see Arbuckle, and
    Arbuthnot, James
Martin see Adlam
Matthews see Archibald
Maxwell see Allison, James
Mayne* see Allison, J.T.
Meek* see Andrews, George and
    Archer, George
Millar* see Ayres
Miller* see Anderson, James
Milne see Allison, John
Mitchell see Anderson, Robert
    (c. 1818–1878)
Mitchley* see Andrews, George
Moffitt see Anderson, W.P.
Moodie* see Allison, A.B.
Moore* see Aitken
Muller see Allen, James
Munroe see Ashley
Murray* see Anderson, Robert
    (c. 1818–1878) and Anderson,
    William (1790–1873)

Newton* see Anderson, William
    (1790–1873)
Noble see Alborough

Oates* see Adcock
O'Callaghan see Andrews, John
    (1812–1898)
Oliver* see Alder, Charles
Oosthuizen see Allison, John

Patrick* see Alison
Peacock* see Ashley
Peddie* see Arbuckle
Penton see Andrews, George
Pigg* see Anderson, William
    (c. 1818–1898)
Pitman see Allison, J.T.
Pole see Allen, Philip
Polkinghorne see Akerman
Pollard see Ashley, Thomas

Potter *see* Ablett
Prentice *see* Armstrong, Dr William
Price *see* Allison, James

Quirk* *see* Adams, William
 (*c.* 1820–1916)

Rae *see* Allison, James
Redman *see* Arnold, Henery
Reynolds *see* Adams, George
Richards* *see* Anderson, William
 (1790–1873)
Richardson* *see* Anderson, W.P.
Rimmer *see* Alison
Rix *see* Allison, A.B.
Roberts* *see* Adcock
Robinson* *see* Addison, W.H.
 and Allan, Thomas
Root* *see* Arnold, Henery
Rorke* *see* Adams, Williams
 (*c.* 1820–1916)
Ross* *see* Armstrong, John
Rutherford *see* Ayres

Salmon *see* Andrews, George
Sanderson* *see* Ashton, C.J.
Saunders *see* Archer, George
Saveall* *see* Adlam
Shackleford *see* Alborough
Shackelton* *see* Allan, Thomas
Shire* *see* Arbuckle
Simpson* *see* Allison, James
Singer* *see* Anstee
Sleightholm *see* Alborough
Smallwood *see* Allison, J.T.
Smith* *see* Alborough,
 Anderson, William
 (1790–1873) Anderson, W.P.
 and Ashford
Snell* *see* Acutt, Robert
Snelus *see* Anstee
Southell *see* Armstrong, John
Spring* *see* Allison, John
Stantial *see* Akerman

Stephenson *see* Adlam
Stevens *see* Anderson, James and
 Armstrong, Dr William
Stewart *see* Anderson, Alexander
Stott *see* Akerman
Strickland *see* Archbell
Struben* *see* Anderson, William
 (1790–1873)
Struthers* *see* Allen, Philip
Strydom *see* Adams, William
 (*c.* 1820–1916)
Stuart *see* Allison, A.B.
Stutfield *see* Adcock
Surgeson *see* Adams, John
Symonds *see* Andrews, George

Tarboton* *see* Alborough
Taylor *see* Allison, A.B. and
 Anderson, William
 (1790–1873)
Templeton *see* Allison, John
Tennant *see* Arnold, Henery
Thackwray *see* Allison, James
Thompson *see* Adams, George
 and Allison, J.T.
Tilney/Tinley* *see* Anderson,
 William (1790–1873)
Tinlen *see* Arnold, Thomas
Todman *see* Anderson, W.P.
Tomlinson* *see* Andrews, George
Troy *see* Allison, J.T.
Tucker *see* Akerman
Turner *see* Anderson, John
 (1816–1889) and Andrews,
 John (1820–1900)
Turton* *see* Archbell

Van Berkhout *see* Allison, A.B.
Van der Merwe *see* Alder, Charles
Van Maltitz *see* Anderson, William
 (1790–1873)
Van Musschenbrock *see*
 Allison, A.B.
Van Reenen *see* Akerman

Van Rooyen *see* Adams, William
 (*c.* 1820–1916)
Vear* *see* Allan, Thomas

Walker* *see* Arnold, Thomas
Walsh *see* Ashley
Ward* *see* Archer, George
Wardell/Wardle *see*
 Anderson, W.P.
Warren *see* Allison, James
Waters *see* Armstrong, Francis
Watson* *see* Archer, George and
 Ashley
Wells *see* Adlam
Westley* *see* Armstrong, John
Weyman *see* Allison, A.B.
Wetherill *see* Arbuckle
Whelan *see* Adams, William
 (*c.* 1820–1916)
Whiting *see* Anderson, W.P.
Whitson* *see* Anderson, John
 (1816–1889)
Wilcox* *see* Adams, George
Wilkinson* *see* Adlam
Will *see* Arbuthnot, James
Willday *see* Agar
Willes* *see* Ayres
Williams *see* Acutt, W.H., Adams,
 William (*c.* 1824–1894) and
 Allison, J.T.
Williamson *see* Alder, Charles
Willson* *see* Arnold, Thomas
Wilson *see* Andrews, George
Winn *see* Ablett and Alison
Wirsing* *see* Ayres
Woodall *see* Acutt, W.H.
Woodcock *see* Allerston, William
Worst *see* Adcock
Wright* *see* Anderson, William
 (1790–1873) and Arbuckle

Youle *see* Ashton, C.J.
Young* *see* Armstrong, Francis

British Settlers in Natal, 1824 - 1857

This list was complete at the time of going to press, but as research is continuing it may be amended in the future.

Abbott, George
Abbott, John Henry
Abbott, Thomas
Ablett, William Henry
Acutt, Julianna
Acutt, Robert
Acutt, William Hayes
Adams, Charles
Adams, George
Adams, Henry
Adams, Isaac
Adams, John
Adams, John Corbett
Adams, William (born c. 1820)
Adams, William (born c. 1823)
Adams, William (born c. 1824)
Adcock, Joseph
Addison, Thomas
Addison, Dr William Henry
Adlam, Joseph
Agar, Charles Artemus
Aitchison, James Carmichael
Aitchison, John Murray
Aitken, Robert
Akerman, Sir John William
Alborough, William
Alder, Charles
Alder, John Williams
Aldrich, George
Aldridge, Dr Charles Miller
Alison, Frederic William
Allan, John
Allan, Thomas
Allanson, George
Allen, James
Allen, Philip
Allen, William Hill
Allerston, Alfred
Allerston, William
Allerston, William Francis

Allison, Capt. Albert Bidden
Allison, Rev. James
Allison, John
Allison, John Thurlow
Alston, Edmund
Anderson, A. T. (*alias*), *see*
  Thomson, Andrew
Anderson, Alexander
Anderson, James
Anderson, John (born 1812)
Anderson, John (born 1816)
Anderson, Robert (labourer)
Anderson, Robert (born
  c. 1818)
Anderson, William (born 1790)
Anderson, William (born
  c. 1818)
Anderson, William (born
  c. 1818, Glasgow)
Anderson, William (born
  c. 1823)
Anderson, William Henry
Anderson, William Pringle
Andrade, A.F.
Andrews, George
Andrews, John of *Valsch
  River*
Andrews, John (born c. 1820)
Andrews, John E.
Ansell, Henry
Anstee, Alfred
Anstie, John
Anstie, Paul
Arbuckle, William
Arbuthnot, David Carnegy
Arbuthnot, George
Arbuthnot, James
Archbell, Rev. James
Archer, George
Archer, James William

Archibald, Walter James
Armstrong, Francis
Armstrong, John
Armstrong, Dr William
Armstrong, William
Arnold, Henery
Arnold, Thomas
Ashford, Frederick
Ashley, Thomas
Ashmore, Felix George
Ashmore, Joseph George
Ashton, Charles
Ashton, Charles John
Ashton, Henry Prior
Ashton, Richard Bury (or
  Berry)
Ashton, James
Ashton, Sarah Hannah
Atherton, John (or Atherton-
  Howse)
Athrelpho, William
Atkinson, John (ex *Herald*)
Atkinson, John (born c. 1802)
Attwood, Charles
Attwood, George
Austen, George William
Austen, Mary Orpah
Austin, John Bird Sumner
Austin, William (or Austen)
Avison, John
Ayres, John

Babbs, Robert
Badger, Jonathan
Baguley, Edward
Bailey, Thomas
Bailie, John
Baker, Ann
Baker, Helen
Baker, Henry

Baker, Hughbert
Baker, Richard
Baker, Thomas (born *c*. 1818)
Baker, Thomas (born *c*. 1827)
Baker, Thomas Brenchley
Bakewell, George
Balcomb, Benjamin
Balderston, George
Balderston, Richardson
Bale, William Ebrington
Balland, Robert
Balloch, Archibald Smith
Banger, Henry John
Baragwanath, John
Barber, Frederick George
Barber, William
Barclay *see* O'Hara
Barker, H. L.
Barker, Rev. Joseph
Barker, Thomas
Barker, William
Barkeway, Hannah and Mary
Barnett, John Brown
Barns, Robert John
Barr, Matthew
Barrett, Eliza Mary
Barrett, Henry Joseph
Barrett, William
Barrington, William Sutton
Barrow, Edward William
Barter, Catherine (Charlotte)
Barter, Charles
Bartholomew, William
Bartlett, Robert H.
Barton, David
Bascombe, Henry
Baseley, John
Basingwhite, John Stone
Batchelor, William Batt
Batho, William Fothergill
Batt, Charles
Baugh, Rev. Walter
Baxter, John
Bayly, Harry Darke
Baynes, Richard
Bazley *see* Baseley
Beachcroft, Henry George
Beale, James
Beard, Joseph James
Beater, Mrs Mary Jane (born Acutt)
Beaumont, George
Beaumont, Samuel
Beckham, Robert
Beckwith, William
Bedham, R.
Beech, Archibald
Bell, (ex *Elizabeth Jane*)
Bell, Alexander Dalrymple
Bell, Alfred
Bell, Charles Tebbut

Bell, Francis
Bell, James
Bell, Rev. James Glendinning
Bell, William
Bell, Capt. William Douglas
Bellars, E.
Benge, John
Beningfield, Alfred
Beningfield, Samuel
Beningfield, Thomas Ratcliff
Bennee, Edward D.
Bennett, Henry
Bennett, Jemima/Jane
Bennett, Dr Joseph Henry
Bennett, Randle Fölsch
Bennitt, William
Benson, Robert
Bentley, George
Berrington, George
Berry, John
Berry, Peter
Berry, Thomas Robert William
Bertram, Dixon
Bevan, Emma
Bevan, Rev. James William
Bevan, John
Bevan, William
Beveridge, Thomas
Biddle, Thomas
Biggar, Alexander Harvey
Bilborough, George
Bilham, James Joseph
Bingham, Richard Francis
Bingham, Thomas
Bird, Henry
Bird, John (born 1815)
Bird, John (born *c*. 1818)
Birkett, George
Bishop, Frederick William
Bishop, George
Bishop, John
Bishop, Samuel Webb
Blackborough, Mrs Mary Alice
(born Royston)
Blacker, John
Blackwood, James
Blade, Lawrence
Blaine, Dr Benjamin
Blake, George
Blake, William
Blakey, Henry
Blamey, John Cardell
Blandy, Samuel
Blood, Neptune
Bloy, Francis Richard
Blundell, Thomas
Boag, John
Boast, Dr Charles Bird
Boast, David
Boast, Henry (born 1816)

Boast, Henry (born 1823)
Boast, William
Boddy, Thomas
Bodien, Richard G.
Bolt, Charles
Bolt, Elizabeth (Mrs E. M. Dupont)
Bolt, Henry
Bolton, James
Bond, Thomas (born *c*. 1822)
Bond, *or* Bone, Thomas (born *c*. 1811)
Boocock, William
Booklass, Robert
Booth, William
Borain, Valentine
Botterill, Edwin
Botterill, Thomas
Botterill, William Dawson
Bottomley, George (born 1826)
Bottomley, George Frederick (born *c*. 1811)
Boultbee, Richard Joseph
Boulton, Charles
Boulty, Denham Denny
Bound, Charles
Bourke, John
Bousfield, (ex *John Line*)
Bowen, John Webb
Bowen, Mrs Milesina (born Clay)
Bower, Walter
Bowes, Alfred John Cecil
Bowes, Thomas Jennings
Bowness, Henry
Bowser, George
Boyd, John
Boyes, John
Boylen *or* Brady, Sarah (Mrs Andrew Johnstone)
Boyles, George
Boyne, Robert
Bradley, James
Bradley, Rachel (Mrs John William Harris)
Bradshaw, Thomas
Brady, Bernard (*alias*), *see* Jones, Thomas
Brady, Sarah, *see* Boylen, Sarah
Brailsford, Edward L.
Braithwaite, Charles J.
Braithwaite, John
Brambles, George
Bramwell, W. H.
Brander, Alexander
Brandon *see also* Brennan
Brandon, (ex *Borneo*)
Branigan, John
Branwhite, Henry B.
Brayhirst, Thomas Vicar
Brearey, Thomas
Brede, *or* Breede, William

Breede, Xavier Robert
Brennan *or* Brandon, Thomas
Brenton, Henry
Brewer, Jonah William
Brickhill, James
Brickhill, Joseph Chatterley
Bricklebanks, John
Brickwell, John D.
Bridge, Alfred
Bright, Alfred
Bright, Jane (Mrs George Chapman)
Bristow, Charles
Brittain, James
Britton *or* Britten, William
Broad, James
Brocklehurst, James Shelton
Brockman, Henry
Brockman, Joseph
Brockman, William
Brodie, Alexander
Brodie, Francis
Brodie, James
Brodie, Robert
Bromwich, Dr Bryan I'Anson
Brooke, Richard Sarly
Brooker, James
Brooking, Dr Benjamin
Brooks, Emily (Mrs Henry James Meller)
Brooks, John Harold
Brough, Richard
Broughall, Ann (Mrs Charles Wakelin)
Broughton, Richard
Brown, (ex *Bellona*)
Brown, Eliza (ex *Minerva*)
Brown, Mrs Elizabeth
Brown, George Beale
Brown, James
Brown, John (born *c.* 1818), *alias* Nero, Giovanni
Brown, John (born 1824) merchant, Durban
Brown, John (born *c.* 1830)
Brown, John, beershop keeper, Pietermaritzburg
Brown, John, sailor on the *Pilot*
Brown, Mary (ex *Minerva*)
Brown, William
Browne, Hugh Junot
Browne, Robert
Brownfield, Ann *see* Inkson, John
Browning, Edwin
Bruce, George
Brundell, Richard S.
Brunton, Walter
Brunyee, John
Bryan, Annette *see* Cheesebrough
Bryan, Dr Humphry Aram
Bryan, James

Bryan, Patrick *see* Burn, Patrick
Bryant, John Reynolds
Bryant, William Reynolds
Buchanan, David Dale
Buchanan, Ebenezer
Buck, Charles Samuel
Buckley, (ex *Bellona*)
Buerdsell, *see* Clough
Buist, David Aytoun Lindsay
Bull, James Allen Ralph
Bull, John
Bull, Samuel Storer
Bullock, Heselton
Burchmore, Thomas
Burge, Mrs Margaret (later Mrs Andrew Muirhead)
Burgess, William (born *c.* 1810)
Burgess, William (born *c.* 1833)
Burgess, William Henry
Burman, Thomas Abraham
Burn *or* Bryan, Patrick
Burne, John
Burns, James
Burrell, Joseph
Burrell, William
Burridge, William
Burrow, Daniel
Burrows, William
Burrup, Joseph
Burt, Henry E.
Burton, Charles Percival
Burwash, Alfred
Bush, Thomas
Bushby, *see also* Cheesebrough
Bushby, Robert
Bussell, William Torry
Butcher, Samuel
Butler, Ellen
Butler, Emma Henrietta Arabella (Mrs Charles Barter)
Butler, John Patrick
Butler, Samuel
Buttery, Thomas
Button, James Clark
Byrne, John
Byrne, Thomas

Cadle, George Ellis
Caile, James
Cain, Mrs Harriett
Caldecott, Alphonso Torkington
Calder, John
Calder, Robert
Caldwell, Christopher
Caldwell, Henry
Callaway, Rev. Henry
Calverley, James
Calvert, Ralph
Cameron, Charles Duncan
Cameron, John McKenzie

Campbell, Edward (ex *Lalla Rookh*)
Campbell, Edward (born *c.* 1819)
Campbell, John (*alias*), *see* Inkson, John
Campbell, Joseph
Campbell, Mary Ann (Mrs William Newlands)
Campbell, Robert
Campbell, Roderick
Campbell, Rev. William
Campbell, William John
Cane, John
Canham, Benjamin
Canning, Isaac
Cannon, Eliza Ann
Cannon, John
Carbutt, Thomas Munro
Carden, Thomas
Carman, Charles W.
Carnegy, Patrick Adrian
Carpenter, Eliza
Carr, Benjamin
Carruthers, Joseph Swan
Carruthers, Robert
Carter, James Owen
Carter, Jane (Mrs David Nolan)
Carter, Robert
Carter, William
Cartwright, Sampson Edward
Cass, Thomas
Cato, Christopher Joseph
Cato, George Christopher
Cato, John Pearson
Cato, Orlando William
Cato, Thomas Pearson
Catterall, James
Cavill, Henry
Cessford, (ex *Wanderer*)
Chadwick, John Moore Knighton
Challinor, Edwin James
Challinor, George
Chambers, George
Chambers, Henry
Champion, Thomas James
Chandler, John
Channell, George
Chaplin, William
Chapman, John Jex
Chapman, Richard
Chapman, Thomas
Chappe, Paul Laffitte
Charteris, John Charles
Chatterton, Henry
Cheesebrough, John
Chessor, James H.
Chessor, William
Chester, John
Chester, Robert
Chew, Hannah (Mrs James Miller)

Chick, John
Chilcott, C.
Chisholm, Andrew D.
Chisholm, John
Chivers, James
Christie, James
Christopher, Joseph Steer
Christopher, Dr William
Churchill, Frank
Churchill, Joseph Fleetwood
Chuter, William
Clarence, Arthur Frederick
Clarence, Ralph
Clark, Andrew
Clark, Charles
Clark, John (born 1808) of *Mount Pleasant*, York
Clark, John (born 1828)
Clark, W. (ex *Haidee*)
Clark, William J. (ex *Devonian*)
Clarke, Josiah
Clarkson, Francis
Clarkson, Robert
Clarkson, Sarah (Mrs George Jarvis)
Clayborne, Charles
Clayton, Frederick
Cleghorn, James
Clift, Thomas B.
Clough, Mrs Priscilla Buerdsell
Clouston, Thomas
Clowes, Stanfell
Coakes, Charles John
Coakes, Henry
Coats, John
Cock, Charles
Cockburn, John Montagu
Cockerell, Alfred Sydney
Cogan, William
Colborne, Joseph Samuel
Colborne, Richard Lemon
Colburn *or* Colborn, Charles
Cole, Jacob
Cole, James
Coleman, Robert
Colenso, John William, Bishop of Natal
Coles, William Frederick
Colley, James
Colley, William Edwards
Collier, Charles
Collier, Edward
Collins, Daniel James
Collins, William Millward
Collis, James
Comins, Mrs Jane
Compston, Robert C.
Compton, George
Compton, Joseph
Comrie, James
Connelley, John

Connolly, Thomas
Cook, Nicholas Thomas John
Cook, William (a wheelwright)
Cook, William (born 1833)
Cooke, Cuthbert
Cooke, Henry William
Cooke, Joseph
Cookson, Edward
Coombs, Daniel
Coombs, Thomas
Cooper, John
Cooper, Thomas
Cooper, William
Cope, George Augustus
Cope, Henry
Cope, Thomas Spencer
Corbett, Francis
Corbitt, Edward
Cordeaux, *see* Cordukes
Cordukes, Samuel
Corish, Richard
Corlett, George
Corlett, William James
Cornwall, William
Cosons *or* Crowsen, Jabez
Cossar, George W.
Costar, Richard
Cottam, William John
Cottier, John
Coulson, Brian
Coventry, Dr John
Coward, Edward
Coward, Joseph
Cowey, Henry
Cowey, Mary
Cowey, William
Cowie, Mary *see* Cowey, Mary
Cowie, William
Cox, George John
Cox, Moses Savery
Coyle, John
Craig, Francis
Craig, John
Craig, William
Crampton, James Leech
Crane, John
Craw, James
Crawley, Henry Charles
Cresswell, Thomas
Crew, Joseph A.
Cridge, Ellen Maria (Mrs William Lovatt)
Crocker, John
Crocker, William
Crompton, Rev. John Lake
Crossley, William
Crouch, John
Crouch, William
Crowder, Samuel
Crowly, Eugenè Isidore Bernard

Crowly, Theodore George Wagner
Crown, John
Crowsen, *see* Cosons
Cruickshank, James
Cruikshank, (ex *Bellona*)
Cubitt, John
Cullen, Ann (Mrs Lawrence Blade)
Cullingworth, Jeremiah
Cumberland, William
Cunningham, William
Curle, Andrew
Curran, Patrick
Currie, Henry William
Curry, George
Cuthbert, John

Dacomb, Charles
Dacomb, Joseph
Dacomb, William
Daddy, John
Daggett, Thomas
Dales, William
Dallas, John
D'Almaine, William Hewson
Dalton, Edmund
Dalton, Henry
Dand, Thomas
D'Anneley, John Blois
Darby, William Henry
Dare, Edward George Money
Dare, John
Dare, William Charles
Darling, Joseph
Darter, George Blackford Silver
Dathan, John N.
Davenport, Thomas
Davidson, Duncan
Davidson, John
Davidson, Peter Patrick Johnston
Davies, George
Davies, Henry
Davies, John
Davies, Richard
Davies, William (born *c*. 1819)
Davies, William (born *c*. 1830)
Davis, Frederick William
Davis, George
Davis, John Henry
Davis, Peter
Davis, Thomas
Davis, Rev. William Jefford
Dawney, Robert
Dawson, Alfred Francis, *alias* Francis, Alfred
Dawson, Frederick
Day, John
Day, William
Deane, James
Deane, William
Deane, William R.

Dearlove, Joseph
Deer, Thomas William
Deighton, Seymour
Delmore, William
Dench, Charlotte
Denize, John
Denning, Henry Wilford
Dennis, Charles Clay
Devereux, Lewis Edward
Devereux, Lionel
Devey, Edward
Devey, George
Devlin, Henry
Devonshire, Alfred
Dicken, William
Dickens, Woolstan
Dickinson, Beverley
Dickinson, Charles Hammond
Dickinson, Robert William
Dicks, Joseph W.
Dickson, Rev. Robert
Dilks, Robert
Dimock, Frederick
Dimock, Dr George
Dineley, Henry
Dingley, James George
Distin, John
Dixon, Edward Ross
Dixon, Henry
Dixon, William Boddy
Dobson, Thomas
Dobson, William Grayson
Doggatt, Edward B.
Doig, John Duff
Dolphin, Thomas
Donaldson, James
Donaldson, John Malcolm
Donoghue, Richard
Dore, William
Dormer, Joseph
Douglas, Capt. John
Dove, John
Dow, William
Dowbiggin, John
Dowling, George Roach
Down, Thomas
Downey, Francis
Downs, George
Downs, Wilham Parker
Doyle, Denis
Drake, Capt. Spencer French
Draper, George J.
Drew, George
Dreyer, Arnd C.
Dring, William
Drummond, Alexander
Dryden, James
Dubois, James
Duff, John
Duff, Thomas

Duff, William
Duffy, George *or* John *or* Richard
Duigan, Michael
Duncan, George William
Duncum, Joseph
Dunken, John
Dunlop, John
Dunn, Robert Newton
Dunning, Henry
Dunscombe, Robert
Dunstan, Eliza (Mrs William
    Cooper)
Dupont, Edward Mitchell
Duprey, Peter
Durham, Edward James
Dyer, James Greening
Dykes, Alexander
Dykes, John
Dykes, Philip

Eagle, James
Eagle, Dr John Nunn
Eagleston, Thomas
Eaglestone, Gabriel
Eary, George
Easterbrook, William Penrose
Eastwood, Arthur William
Eastwood, Francis Edmund
Eastwood, George Frederick
Eastwood, Henry Charles
Eaton, John George
Eaynor, Stephen
Eccles, William
Eckersley, John
Eckroyd, James
Eckroyd, John
Edgar, John
Edge, John
Edlin, William Brampton
Edmonstone, Charles Waterton
Edmunds, William Conway
Edser, David
Edwards, Frederick John
Edwards, Frederick Lewis
Edwards, Frederick Nelson
Edwards, John
Edwards, John Wheatland
Edwards, Robert H.
Edwards, William
Ellerker, Joseph
Ellerker, Thomas
Elliott, James
Elliott, John Wilkinson
Elliott, Robert
Elliott, William
Ellis, Edmund
Ellis, Henry
Ellis, James
Ellis, Thomas
Ellis, William Frank

Elston, James
Elston, William
Ely, James
Emerson, William Arthur Harrison
Emmanuel, Mark
Emmett, Dr William Dickinson
Emmott, Joseph
Ennals, James
Erwood, Thomas Snelson
Etty, Charles W.
Evans, Alfred Winter
Evans, James
Evans, Joseph
Evans, Thomas
Evans, William Henry
Exall, Henry

Falcon, John C.
Fannin, Thomas
Fanning, James
Farewell, Lt. Francis George
Farley, James
Farmer, F.
Farre, Henry William Richard
Favell, Benjamin
Fayers, James
Fayle, Thomas
Fea, Thomas
Fearne, Rev. Thomas Gleadow
Fearnsides, David
Feilden, John Leyland
Fell, Arden
Felton, George
Fenaby, William
Fender, Andrew
Fenton, William Henry
Ferguson, Archibald
Ferguson, Joseph
Ferguson, Robert
Ferrier, Andrew
Fettyplace, John
Few, Edward
Few, Joseph
Field, Edwin Mackley
Field, John
Field, John Coote
Field, John Hall
Field, William
Field, William Swan
Field, William Wheeler
Fielder, Thomas
Fincent, Fanny
Finer, Joseph
Finnemore, Isaac Powell
Finnis, William
Fisher, Edward
Fisher, Henry
Flatt, Edward
Flay, Ephraim
Fleming, Horace

Fleming, John
Fletcher, Edward
Flood, Hugh Henry †
Flooks, John George
Florey, Charles
Floyd, George
Foden, Alfred
Foggitt, Mark
Foley, John Melville, *alias* Melville, John
Foley, Martin
Foord, James
Foot, Joseph
Forbes, Alexander
Forbes, Alexander Rhind
Forbes, David
Forbes, John
Ford, James
Ford, William Huntington
Forde, Jeremiah
Fordham, John
Fordham, Octavius
Forman, James
Forrest, John
Forsyth, John
Forsyth, Robert
Fosbrooke, Thomas
Foss, Ambrose
Foster, John (ex *John Line*)
Foster, John (ex *Nile*)
Foster, Peter
Foster, Capt. Thomas
Foster, William George
Fowler, James
Fowler, Robert
Fowler, Thomas J.
Fox, James
Fox, William
Foxley, James
Foxon, Edwin Augustus King Cock
Frances, Henry Vernon
Francis, Alfred (*alias*), *see* Dawson, Alfred Francis
Francis, Henry
Francis, James Osborne
Frankish, Mark
Franklin, George
Franklin, John
Fraser, Charles
Fraser, George
Fraser, John
Fraser, John Moir
Fraser, William Archibald
Freeman, George

----

† Born Stafford but never used this surname in Natal. *See also* Talbot.

French, Dr Edwin
French, William
Freshwater, George
Friday, Samuel John
Fuller, Frederick Augustus
Fuller, Henry
Fuller, James
Fulton, Henry
Furnival, John G.
Fynn, Francis
Fynn, Henry Francis
Fynn, William McDowell
Fynney, Augustus
Fynney, Fielding Best
Fysh, Charles
Fyvie, Charles D.
Fyvie, James R.
Fyvie, John Bell

Gadney, William
Gain, George
Galbraith, Dr John Murray
Gale, Henry John
Galley, Thomas
Galliers, William
Galloway, John
Galloway, Thomas William
Gallwey, Sir Michael Henry
Gamble, John
Garbutt, David
Garbutt, Robert
Gardiner, Capt. Allen Francis
Gardiner, Charles
Gardiner, William Henry
Garland, Thomas William
Garner, Richard Crozier
Garnett, Robert
Garrod, William
Gaskell, Thomas
Gaskell, William M.
Gaskin, Rev. Joseph
Gassiott, Henry S.
Gavin, David
Gavin, George
Gavin, John
Gavis, John
Geddes, Walter George
Gee, James
Gee, Stephen
Geldart, James R.
George, Adam, *alias* George, Alfred
George, William
Ghee, William Henry Spencer
Gibbons, Thomas
Gibbons, William
Gibson, (ex *Elizabeth Jane*)
Gibson, (ex *Wilhelmina*)
Gibson, Archibald
Gibson, Frederick W.

Gibson, George W.
Gibson, Robert Thompson
Gifford, Alexander
Gifford, George
Giles, John
Gilfillan, John
Gill, David
Gill, Thomas Bliss
Gillespie, Catharine
Gillespie, Hugh
Gillett, John
Gillitt, William
Gillmore, William
Gilmore, Henry Charles Cameron
Ginger, Alfred Baker
Girault, Peter
Glendinning, Edwin
Glover, Joseph
Glover, William
Gobbett, James
Godden, Isaac
Godden, John
Godden, Richard
Gold, Thomas
Goldstone, Samuel
Good, Denis
Good, James
Goodburn, Benjamin
Gooden, David
Goodricke, John Richardson
Goodwill, James
Goodwill, Thomas
Goodwin, Charles
Goodwin, Edward
Goodwin, Henry
Gordge, William
Gordon, Capt. Alexander
Gordon, Arthur
Gordon, John Anderson
Gordon, Margaret (Mrs. David Barton)
Gordon, William James
Gould, Thomas
Goulden, Alfred Methley
Govan, James
Gower, Dr Samuel
Grafton, Richard William
Graham, Joseph
Graham, Rowland
Graham, Simon
Graham, William
Grainger, William
Grange, Josiah G.
Granger, John
Grant, John (born *c.* 1791)
Grant, John (born 1837)
Grant, John Hannibal
Grant, Nelson
Grant, Samuel
Grant, Walter

Grantham, Major James
Gray, David
Gray, Frederick
Gray, John
Gray, William
Greathead, Samuel
Greathead, Thomas
Greave, Henry L.
Greaves, Francis Mills
Greaves, George Duly
Greaves, George William
Greaves, John W.
Green, Caroline
Green, Charles Edward Andrew
Green, Rev. James
Green, John
Green, Joseph
Green, Sam W.
Green, Thomas
Green, William (a surveyor)
Green, William (ex *Sovereign*)
Greenacre, Sir Benjamin Wesley
Greenaway, George
Greenaway, James
Greene, Laurence Henry St John
Greening, Elisha Smith
Greening, Richard
Greenwood, Mary (Mrs Jane
   Hardman)
Gregory, Charles (ex *Lady Bruce*)
Gregory, Charles (ex *Minerva*)
Gregory, Jacob Davis
Gregory, Thomas George
Greig, Andrew Fletcher
Gresham, Thomas
Grice, John
Grieve, William John
Griffin, Charles Carter
Griffin, Patrick
Griffin, Stephen William Bill
Griffith, Edward
Griffiths, Edwin Philip Jones
Griffiths, John
Griffiths, John Roger
Griffiths, Thomas Powis
Groom, Edward
Groom, Richard
Groom, Thomas
Groombridge, (ex *John Line*)
Grosvenor, Rev. James
Grosvenor, Robert
Grubb, Sergt. J.
Grundy, James
Gudgeon, John
Gurley, Peter
Gutridge, Thomas
Guy, John

Haigh, George
Hair, John

Hale, Edwin
Haley or Healey, Michael
Hall, George (born *c*. 1812)
Hall, George (born *c*. 1825)
Hall, John Alexander
Hall, John Jervis
Hall, Thomas Wykes
Hall, William
Hallett, James
Halloway, John
Halstead, Thomas
Hambridge, William
Hamilton, David
Hamilton, William
Hammond, Charles
Hammond, Fred H.
Hammond, Thomas
Hamp, Edward Alexander
Hampshire, Eli
Hampson, Joseph
Hancock, James
Hancock, Joseph Ebenezer
Hancock, Thomas
Handley, Charles George Hepburn
Handley, James
Handley, Thomas
Hankey, Thomas
Hannah, William T.
Hannon, Daniel
Hanscombe, Alfred
Hanser, James William
Hantot, James
Harben, John
Harcourt, Joseph
Harcourt, William Frederick
Harding, Sir Walter
Hardisty, Jane (Mrs Thomas
   Buttery)
Hardman, James
Hardwick, Henry
Hardwick, Robert
Hare, George
Hargreaves, James
Hargreaves, Thomas
Hargreaves, William
Harley, John
Harman, William James
Harper, Henry
Harper, Isaac
Harper, Thomas
Harper, William
Harrington, Benjamin
Harris, George
Harris, John Robert
Harris, John William
Harris, Jonathan G.
Harris, Joseph (born *c*. 1813)
Harris, Joseph (born *c*. 1830)
Harris, Samuel
Harrison, Charles

Harrison, Charles Samuel
Harrison, Cuthbert J.
Harrison, Harriett
Harrison, Henry
Harrison, James
Harrison, John
Harrison, William
Harrisson, Timotheus
Hart, George
Hart, Henry
Hart, William
Hart, William West
Hartley, Joseph
Hartley, William
Harvey, Francis
Harvey, Josiah
Harvey, Richard
Harvey, William Frederick
Harvey, William Gaskell
Harwin, Mary
Hastie, Michael
Hatfield, Alexander
Hathorn, John Piper
Hawding, Edward
Hawken, Matthew
Hawkins, Arthur Caesar
Hawkins, Sophia (Mrs William
   Vear)
Hay, Edmund J.
Hayes, George Bevan
Hayes, John
Hayes, Michael
Hayes, Patrick
Haygarth, Joseph Williamson
Haynes, Edmund
Hayward, John Sebright
Hazelhurst, Edward
Healey, John George
Healey, Michael *see* Haley,
   Michael
Heap, Charles Rogers
Heap, Walter
Heathcote, George Gage
Hellett, Peter Jurgen Ellis
Henderson, John
Henderson, Joseph
Henderson, Robert
Henderson, Samuel
Henderson, William
Hendley, John
Hendry, James
Henning, Edwin
Henry, Lyster (*alias*), *see* Shire,
   Henry
Henwood, John
Henwood, Paul
Heppenstall, George R.
Herbert, Ewald Benedictus
Hern, George
Herrington/Hewington, Alfred

Herries, Jonathan
Herron, Hugh
Heslop, John
Hesom, George Thomas
Hesom, Robert
Hesslewood, George
Hewitson, David
Hewitt, James
Heys, Thomas
Heywood *see* Hayward, John
    Sebright
Hibberd, Benjamin William
Hicks, George
Higginson, William Leinster
Higham, John Henry
Highfield, George Bellwood
Hilder, Charles Henry
Hill, Clement John
Hill, John
Hill, John Barnby
Hill, Samuel
Hill, Thomas (born *c.* 1820)
Hill, Thomas (born *c.* 1826)
Hill, William
Hillary, George
Hillary, John
Hillary, William
Hilliard, Charles Henry
Hillier, Edward
Hillman, Alfred C.
Hilton, Henry
Hind, Thomas
Hinman, Thomas
Hinton, Thomas
Hirst, Abram
Hiscock, John
Hobday, Richard
Hobson, William Henry
Hodge, William
Hodges, (ex *Nile*)
Hodgson, Charles
Hodgson, Henry
Hodgson, James
Hodgson, Robert
Hodgson, Thomas
Hodgson, William Ashbourne
Hodnett, John Henry
Hodson, James
Hoey, *or* Honey, *or* Huoy, Isidore
    Henry
Hogarth, John
Hogarth, Thomas
Hogg, John
Hoggarth, John
Hogshaw, William
Holden, Joseph
Holden, Rev. William Clifford
Holding, William
Holgate, George Roland
Holgate, Joseph

Holl, Samuel
Holland, Dr Edward William
    Holwell
Holliday, John David
Hollington, Daniel
Holman, Mrs Matilda
Holmans, Daniel
Holmes, James
Holmes, John
Holmes, William
Holton, Henry Richard
Homewood, Alfred
Honey *see* Hoey
Hoodford, Eliza (Mrs George
    Hicks)
Hopkins, John
Hopley, Thomas Starr
Horn, Thomas
Horne, Benjamin
Horne, William
Horning, James Ripley
Horning, William Penney
Horsley, Richard
Horsley, Thomas
Horton, Edward
Hosking, Margaret (Mrs J. L.
    Paull)
Hoskins, Ann
House, Charles
Houston, John
Hovenden, Charles
Howard, Edward
Howard, John Hassall
Howden, Francis W.
Howden, Montague
Howell, James Michiel
Howells, Thomas
Howes, George
Howes, William
Howroyd, Robert
Howse, Thomas
Hubbard, Alfred
Hubbard, Daniel
Hubbard, Jesse
Hudson, John Thomas
Hudson, Thomas
Hughes, Mrs Mary Ann (born
    Willson)
Hughes, William
Hugman, John Henry
Hulett, Sir James Liege
Hull, Daniel
Hulley, Richard Brangan
Hulme, Hugh
Hulme, Dr John Rhodes Davenport
Humble, Peter
Hume, Rev. Charles
Hume, Edmund E.
Humphrey, Robert
Humprheys, William Clayton

Hunt, Adelaide
Hunt, Edward Henry
Hunt, Eliza
Hunt, George
Hunt, George Peyton
Hunt, John
Hunter, Caroline
Hunter, Moses
Hunton, Robert William Sanderson
    Raper
Huoy *see* Hoey
Hurst, Henry
Hurst, John E.
Hursthouse, William
Husher, Richard
Hussey, Henry
Hutchinson, William
Hutton, Adam
Hutton, Henry James Cooper
Hyslop, Sarah

Iliffe, William Gregory
Ingall, Richard
Inglis, James
Inkson, John, *alias* Campbell, John
Inman, Mrs Emma
Ireland, Mrs Ann
Ireland, James
Ireland, Robert
Irons, Theophilus
Irons, William Josiah
Irvine, Augustus
Irwin, John
Isaacs, Nathaniel
Isham, Capt. Edmund

Jackson, Francis Edwin
Jackson, George
Jackson, John Davis
Jackson, John James
Jackson, Rev. Joseph
Jackson, Joseph Allcock
Jackson, William Patrick
Jacobs, Frederick
Jacobs, James
Jacques, Alexander
Jacques, Edmund
Jacques, Henry
Jacques, Thomas Barclay
Jaffray, Peter
James, Henry F.
James, Joseph
James, Robert William
James, Thomas Payne
James, William (born *c.* 1823)
James, William (born *c.* 1828)
Jamieson, Alexander
Jardine, John
Jarman, William
Jarvis, George

Jee, Joseph Lawrence
Jeffels, Michael
Jefferd, John Harris
Jefferies, William
Jeffrey, Miss, (ex *Borneo*)
Jeffreys, Rev. George Y.
Jenkins, Rev. John David
Jenkins, William Hopkins
Jennings, William
Jevons, James E.
Johnason, John James
Johnson, Henry
Johnson, Richard
Johnson, William
Johnston, Catherine
Johnston, Charles
Johnston, Dr Charles
Johnston, Henry
Johnston, James Philip
Johnston, John
Johnston, Robert Francis
Johnstone, Andrew
Johnstone, Augustus James
Johnstone, Bunting
Jolly, Robert Stratford
Jones, Charles
Jones, Dorothy
Jones, Edward
Jones, Henry
Jones, James Jordan
Jones, John
Jones, John Thomas
Jones, Robert
Jones, Samuel
Jones, Thomas
Jones, Thomas, *alias* Brady,
    Bernard
Jones, William (born *c.* 1820)
Jones, William (born *c.* 1826)
Jordon, James
Jordan, Zachariah, *alias* Pittman *or*
    Pettman, Zachariah
Joscelin, William, *alias* Perkins,
    William, *alias* Newton, William
Joslin, John
Josling, George
Joyce, Robert
Joyner, William
Judge, Mary

Kaley, (ex *Wilhelmina*)
Kavanagh, Matthew
Kaye, Frederick B.
Keal, Stamforth
Keane, Anne
Keating, Richard
Keeley, Mary (Mrs W. J. Pole, later
    Mrs John Palframan)
Kelly, Benjamin Swete
Kelly, Patrick (born *c.* 1817)

Kelly, Patrick (born *c.* 1827)
Kelly, Thomas
Kelly, Dr Thomas Tear
Kemp, Thomas
Kemp, William
Kendall, Martha (Mrs William
    Mileman)
Kennedy, Andrew Brown
Kent, James
Kenyon, William
Kermode, Edward
Kershaw, William Thompson
Kerslake, William
Kestell, Charles
Kilgour, John
Killoch, John T.
Kincade, Robert
King, Charles
King, George
King, Lt James Saunders
King, John (born *c.* 1810)
King, John (born *c.* 1819)
King, John (died 1852)
King, Michael Thomas
King, Richard Philip (Dick)
Kingham, R.
Kinghurst, James
Kingston, William
Kinloch, Frederick
Kinsman, George Whitfield
Kippen, George Adam Crooks
Kirby, George
Kirby, John
Kirk, Joseph
Kirk, Thomas
Kirkham, William Cable
Kirkman, Joseph
Knapp, David
Knight, Arthur
Knight, Edgar
Knight, Humphrey Evans
Knowles, John
Knowles, William
Knox, Henry
Koch, John Daniel
Kruse, John B.
Kyle, Patrick

Labron, Charles
Lacey, John
Laing, William
Lake, Chamberlane Hickman
Lally, Michael
Lamb, (ex *Ceres*)
Lambert, Mrs Eliza Elizabeth
Lambert, Rebecca (Mrs William
    Vionnee)
Lamond, George Belwood
Lamont, Alexander Philip
Lamport, Edward Parke

Landers, Joseph
Langford, Robert Samuel
Language, William
Lansdell, George
Lansdell, James
Latchford, John J.
Laurie, Robert N.
Lavender, George
Lawrance, Frederick
Lawrie, George Lancaster
Lawson, Lawson
Lawton, Richard
Lawton, Thomas
Leadbitter, John Graham
Leadley, Frederick Joseph
Leake, John
Lean, Joel
Leathern, William
Leathers, Edward John
Ledson, Thomas Moody
Lee, Edwin
Lee, George James
Lee, German
Lee, Henry
Leech, James Crampton (*alias*), *see*
    Crampton, James Leech
Leeming, Robert
Leigh, James
Lello, Edward
Lello, William
Lennox, Peter
Leslie, Mrs Elizabeth (born Forbes)
Leslie, William
Lester, John
Lester, Robert
Leuchars, Henry
Lewellin, Dr John Henry Hill
Lewis, Thomas
Lewis, William (ex *British Tar*)
Lewis, William (ex *Globe*)
Lindsay, James
Lindsay, Robert
Ling, William
Lister, William
Little, David
Littlewort, Charles T.
Liversage, Samuel
Livingstone, Hugh
Livingston, James
Lloyd, James (born *c.* 1791)
Lloyd, James (born *c.* 1827)
Lloyd, Jane
Lloyd, Capt. Walter
Lloyd, Rev. William Henry Cynric
Loader, John
Loades, Edward
Lockwell, Sarah (Mrs William John
    Sheils)
Lodge, William
Lofthouse, Benjamin

Lofthouse, John
Logan, George Ainsley
Logan, James Fullerton
Logan, Robert
Logue, Charles
London, Edward
Long, Charles
Long, Henry Warren
Longcast, William
Lord, James
Lord, John Poyntz
Lovatt, William
Loveday, George
Low, Andrew
Low, Francis
Lowe, Peter
Loxton, Henry
Lucas, Anne
Lucas, Capt. Gould Arthur
Lucas, Jane
Lucas, Laurence John
Lucas, William
Ludlow, Dr William Henry
Luke, Charles
Luke, Henry Joseph
Lumb, Samuel
Lumsden, John
Lund, Benjamin (born c. 1822)
Lund, Benjamin (born c. 1827)
Lund, William
Lundie, Jonathan
Lundy, John
Luscombe, Henry
Lutman, William
Lyall, James
Lyle, Alexander
Lynn, Joseph

McAdam, James
McAlister, Robert
McArthur, Alexander
McArthur, Donald
McBride, Adam
McCabe, Hugh
McCalman, John
MacCawley, Thomas
McClelland, William
McCombie, Joseph Heyes
McCooey, Edward
McCorkindale, Alexander
McCormick, Martin
McCovey, Edward see McCooey
McCrystal, Patrick
McDonald, Alexander
McDonald, Charles
McDonald, Donald
McDonald, Hugh
McDonald, James
McDonald, Thomas
McDonald, William

McDonell, Robert Taylor
McEvoy, Elizabeth (Mrs J. N. Wheeler)
McEvoy, Margaret (Mrs G. O. Matterson)
Macfarlane, George
Macfarlane, John
Macfarlane, Mary
Macfarlane, Thomas W.
Macfarlane, Walter
Macfarlane, William Stenhouse
McGaydy or McGeady or McGiddy, Edward
McGill, Edward Francis
McGregor, Daniel
Macguire, Charles
McHardie, Joseph
Machell, John
McIntosh, Hector
McIntosh, James
McIntyre, Euphemia (Mrs Edwin Patrick)
McIntyre, John
Mack, Dr James
Mack, Robert Gazley
Mackay, James
McKay, Peter
McKeaney, John
McKechnie, John
McKechnie, Neil Johnston
McKellar, John
McKellar, Neil
McKen, Mark Johnston
Mackenzie, Anne
McKenzie, Charles
Mackenzie, Rev. Charles Frederick
McKenzie, Duncan
McKenzie, John (born c. 1818)
McKenzie, John (born c. 1822)
McKenzie, John Thomas
Mackenzie, William (born 1816)
McKenzie, William (born c. 1818)
McKeown, William
Mackinnon, Lachlan
McKnea, James
McKnight, James
McLachlan, John
McLachlan, Peter
McLachlan, Robert M.
McLachlan, Thomas
McLaren, John
McLaren, Peter
MacLean, Alexander (born c. 1816)
McLean, Alexander (born c. 1827)
Maclean, Alexander (born c. 1828)
McLean, Alexander (born 1834)
McLean, John (born c. 1825)
McLean, John (born 1840)
McLean, William Hay
Maclean, William Hector (Moses)

McLeod, Edward
McLeod, George More
McLeod, Roderick
McLeod, William
Macleroy, George
Macleroy, Thomas
McLindon, William
McMillan, Neil T.
McMillan, William
McMinn, William Hutchinson Calderwood
Macnab, Alexander
McNicol, Archibald
McPhail, Donald
Macpherson, Daniel
McPherson, John
Macrae, Kenneth
MacSorley, William
McWilliam, Thomas
Maddock, Peter
Madigan, Richard
Magee, John
Maguire, John Rhind
Maguire, Robert
Major, Stephen John
Mallandain, Robert
Mallet, Charles
Maltby, Matthew
Mann, Alexander John Augustus
Mann, Dr Robert James
Mannington, James
Marchant, George
Marcus, George
Marillier, Henry Philip Augustus
Markham, Rev. Benjamin
Markham, James Frederick
Marriott, George
Marriott, Thomas O.P.
Marshall, Atherstone Corbet
Marshall, Cuthbert N.
Marshall, John
Marshall, William (born 1814)
Marshall, William (born c. 1830)
Martin, (ex Jane Morice July, 1851)
Martin, John
Martin, John W.
Martin, Thomas James
Martin, William
Mason, Rev. Frederick
Mason, Rev. George Holditch
Mason, James
Mason, Joseph
Mason, Richard
Mason, Robert
Mason, Robert Charles
Masterman, Isabella (Mrs Frederick Jacobs)
Masterman, Prudence (Mrs James Philip Johnston)

Matterson, George Octavius
Matterson, John Kitching
Matthews, Frederick
Matthison, Angus
Maughan, James
Maurice, Mrs Elizabeth (born King)
    (later Mrs William Lutman,
    later Mrs Thomas Green)
Maxwell, Francis Severn
Maxwell, Patrick Joseph
May, John Meredith
Mayne, Charles Washington
Mayo, George
Mayoss, Henry George
Maytom, Alfred
Mead, John Laurence
Meadows, James *see* Metters,
    James
Meara, Martin
Medley, John
Meek, John
Meller, Henry James
Mellerd, (ex *Ceres*)
Mellersh, Gawen
Mellersh, Robert
Mellish, Thomas Robert
Melville, James
Melville, John (*alias*), *see* Foley,
    John Melville
Merryweather, James
Mesham, Arthur
Mesham, Lloyd Evans
Metcalfe, George
Methley, James Erasmus
Methley, Rev. John
Methley, Thomas
Methuen, Rev. H.H.
Metters, James
Meyer, John
Middleborough, Elijah James
Middlebrook, Matthew
Middleton, William Henry
Mileham, John
Mileman, William, (ex *Hebrides*)
Mileman, William, (ex *Sovereign*)
Miles, John
Miles, William Perkins
Millan, James
Millar, John
Millar, Mary
Miller, David
Miller, George
Miller, James
Miller, James Black
Millett, Alfred
Milloy, Neil
Milne, George
Milne, John
Milne, Thomas
Milner, Henry

Milner, Philip Splidt
Milner, Thomas Cross
Mitchell, James
Mitchell, William Ferrier
Mitchley, Thomas J.
Molloy, Dr, (ex *Jane Morice*,
    July 1851)
Molton, William
Monies, John Hugh
Monro, James Wright
Moodie, Donald
Moor, Frederick William
Moore, Alfred
Moore, Arthur Godfrey
Moore, David
Moore, Jane, (Mrs Richard
    Thomas?)
Moore, Robert
Moore, William
Morehead, Thomas David Wilson
Moreland, John Swales
Morewood, Edmund
Morgan, Edward Lewis
Morgan, Hugh Thomas
Morgan, Richard Elliott
Morley, Mary (Mrs Richard
    Smithers)
Morris, George William
Morrison, Alexander
Morrison, Andrew
Morrison, Robert
Morton, George
Morton, Thomas
Morton, William Frederic
Moss, Charles Gabriel
Moss, John
Moss, Robert Arnold
Moss, Samuel
Moss, Thomas
Mossop, James
Mould, William
Moyles, Henry James
Muirhead, Andrew
Mulhall, Martin
Mullenger, William
Mullett, James
Mullins, John
Munday, John
Munro, Byron
Munro, Roderick
Munro, William
Munroe, Alexander
Murdoch, Alexander Cruikshanks
    Jolly Shand
Murdoch, John James
Mure, Alexander
Murphy, Joseph Edward
Murray, Archibald Keir
Murray, Fergus
Murray, Patrick

Murray, William
Myers, Thompson

Nadauld, Elizabeth (Mrs Robert
    Stevens)
Nash, John
Neil, John H.
Nelson, James Edward
Nero, Giovanni (*alias*), *see* Brown,
    John (born *c*. 1818)
Nevins, Eliza (Mrs William Cooper,
    later Mrs Andrew Johnstone)
Newberry, Luke
Newbold, George
Newell, Joseph
Newlands, Henry
Newlands, William
Newling, William
Newman, Noah
Newman, Thomas R.G.
Newman, William
Newmarch, George William
Newmarch, Henry Keyworth
Newmarch, John
Newmarch, Thomas Brown
Newnham, Rev. William Orde
Newson, Sarah
Newton, David
Newton, John
Newton, Lancelot
Newton, Louisa (Mrs Joseph
    Kirkman)
Newton, William (*alias*), *see*
    Joscelin, William
Nicholson, John Duggleby
Nicholson, Thomas
Nicholson, William
Nickson, Abraham
Nimmo, Robert
Nisbett, Rev. William
Noël, John
Nolan, David
Noon, Clara Jane (Mrs R.P. King)
Norgate, George
North, James Price
Nowell, Frederick
Nowlan, John
Noxon, William M.
Nurse, Thomas
Nuske, (ex *Bellona*)
Nuttley, Jesse

Oates, William Edward
O'Brien, James
Ockerby, Mrs Josephine (later
    Mrs George Bishop)
Odell, Livins William
Odell, Thomas Gilbert
Ogle, Henry
O'Hara, William

Okes, Thomas Holt Edward
Oliver, Isaac
O'Meara, Martin
O'Neil, John
O'Neill, Patrick
Orchard, Benjamin
Orchard, Joseph
Ordish, Thomas
Ordish, William
Orgill, Matthew
Orgill, Robert
Ormiston, James
Ormston, (ex *Bellona*)
Osborn, (ex *Tuscan*)
Osborn, Aling
Osborn, John
Osborn, Sir Melmoth
Osborne, Ormonde
Osborne, William
Otterbourne, Richard
Owen, Charles
Owens, Owen
Oxenham, Samuel

Pacey, Robert
Page, Alfred Harrison
Paice, Albert
Palframan, William
Palmer, Eliza (Mrs John Jervis Hall)
Palmer, Francis
Palmer, Job
Palmer, John
Palmer, John C.
Palmer, Thomas
Parish, Samuel
Parker, Charles
Parker, George
Parker, Joshua
Parker, Martha Elizabeth
Parker, Richard
Parker, Thomas
Parkin, William
Parkinson, Edwin
Parnaby, Matthew
Parnaby, William
Parry, John Gascoigne
Parsons, Charles Henry
Parsons, David
Parsons, Edgar
Parsons, James
Parsonson, Rev. George
Pateman, Richard
Paterson, David
Paterson, John
Patience, Francis
Patrick, Edwin
Patterson, Alexander
Patterson, Mary
Patterson, Matthew

Patullo, Francis
Patullo, James
Paull, James Louis
Paverd, William
Pavey, Edward
Paxton, Henry Frederick
Pay, George
Payn, Philip Jourdain
Payn, William
Payne, George
Payne, Thos. Ashbourn
Peachey, Thomas
Peacock, Joseph
Pearce, John
Pearce, William
Pearse, Rev. Horatio
Pearse, William
Pearson, Thomas
Pearson, William Tarleton
Peddie, John Crofton Grant
Peddie, William Henry
Peel, Augustus
Peel, Sidney
Peel, Thomas
Peel, William Accrington
Pellow, John
Penfold, Marchant
Penn, Henry
Penney, Robert
Pennington, Richard
Penny, William
Penrose, Charles
Pepler, J.
Peppercorne, George Ryder
Pepworth, Henry
Perfect, Mrs Mary Eliza (born Boast)
Perkins, Griffith Williams
Perkins, Henry
Perkins, William (*alias*), *see* Joscelin, William
Perrin, James
Perry, William Cranley
Petchell, William
Peters, Frederick Augustus
Peters, John
Peters, William Adolphus
Peterson, Frederick William
Petrie, Archibald
Pettigrew, Gavin
Pettman, Zachariah (*alias*), *see* Jordan, Zachariah
Petty, William Thomas
Philipps, Edward
Phillips, Frederick
Phillips, Samuel Vincent Price
Philpott, Thomas
Phipson, John Bond
Phipson, Thomas
Pickering, Robert

Pickering, Stephen
Pickman, Charles J.
Pierce, David Towers
Pierce, Grenville Hugh
Pierce, Richard
Pigg, Anthony
Pigot, Catherine Mary
Pike, William
Pindlebury, John
Pink, William
Pinckney, Thomas
Pinsent, Savery
Pitcher, James
Pittam, John
Pittman, Zachariah (*alias*), *see* Jordan, Zachariah
Plant, Henry
Plant, Robert William
Platt, Ellen
Platt, Laurence
Platt, Richard William Robert
Platt, Sidney
Platts, William
Player, James
Plowes, George
Plummer, George
Plunkett, William Tomyns
Pole, William James
Polkinghorne, John Trevenen
Pollard, W.
Polleyblank, Robert
Ponsford, Philip B.
Pontin, Henry
Porrill, Matthew
Porteous, Alexander
Potter, George
Potterill, John
Pottle, B.
Povall, Charles
Povall, John
Powell, Henry
Poynton, William
Pratt, Henry
Preist, Thomas
Prender, Rosanna
Preston, Robert
Prestwich, George
Prettyman, Edward
Price, (ex *Lalla Rookh*)
Price, Daniel John
Price, Edward Ralph or Relph
Price, Francis
Price, Joseph
Priddle, Edward
Pridgeon, George
Pridham, William F.
Pridham, Lawrence S.
Prince, John
Pritchard, Charles
Proudfoot, James

Proudfoot, Richard
Proudfoot, William
Prouting, James William
Pryce, Edward
Puckering, Thomas
Puckle, William
Pulford, William
Pulleyn, James
Pullock, William Ricketts
Purcocks, David
Purse, Stephen
Putterill, James
Pybus, Mrs Hannah M. (later
    Mrs Jacob Cole)

Quested, Mrs Harriet Susannah
Quick, William Robert
Quirk, Patrick

Raddon, Alfred Samuel
Radford, John
Rafter, George Augustus
Ralfe, James F.
Ralfe, Robert
Ramsbottom, James A.
Randall, John
Randall, William Ellis
Randelhoff, John Edward Lloyd
Randle, James
Rapson, Josiah
Ratcliff, John
Rathbone, Ephraim Frederick
Ratsey, Capt. Edward
Ratsey, Capt. Robert Henry
Raw, James
Raw, Robert
Rawden, William M.
Rawlinson, Robert C.
Read, Isabella (Mrs William
    Newman)
Read, James
Read, John
Read, William
Reay, Richard
Reddish, Mrs Eliza Ann
Redman, Henry
Redshaw, Jonathan
Reed, John
Reed, Robert
Reed, William
Reid, Edward
Reid, Frederick William
Reid, James
Reid, Moses Newman
Reinhard, Alfred
Relph, Joseph
Reynolds, Charles Henry
Reynolds, Esther (Mrs John
    Burne)
Reynolds, James

Reynolds, John
Reynolds, Lewis
Reynolds, T. Edward
Reynolds, Thomas (born 1820)
Reynolds, Thomas (born c. 1830)
Rhodes, Isaac Field
Rich, John Augustus Carey
Richards, Charles
Richards, Edward
Richards, Francis
Richards, Henry John
Richards, Rev. John
Richardson, Alfred
Richardson, Dr James
Richardson, James Arbuckle
Richardson, James Birch
Richardson, John Alfred
Richardson, Richard
Rider, William Robert Rowlett
Ridgway, James
Rigby, Joseph
Rigby, Robert
Riley, Charles
Riley, John
Rishton, Peter
Risley, Joseph
Rivett, Rev. Alfred William Lovely
Rivett, Mary (Mrs R.W. Grafton)
Robarts, Emery
Robbins, James
Roberts, Alfred Brooksbank
Roberts, Charles
Roberts, David Davies
Roberts, Edward
Roberts, James
Roberts, James Baker
Roberts, William
Roberts, William Henry
Robertson, David
Robertson, James
Robertson, Rev. Robert
Robertson, Robert Thomas
Robertston, Thomas (solicitor,
    Pmb.)
Robertson, Thomas (born c. 1831)
Robertston, William
Robinson, Charles (born c. 1815)
Robinson, Charles (born c. 1823)
Robinson, Frederick
Robinson, George (ex Justina)
Robinson, George (baker, Pmb.)
Robinson, George Edgecumbe
Robinson, George Eyre
Robinson, William Samuel
Robinson, William
Robson, John Sutcliffe
Robson, Oman
Robson, Ralph H.
Rock, Henry
Rockley, John

Rogers, George
Rogers, John
Rogers, Richard
Rogers, William
Rolfe, James
Roome, Frederick John
Root, John Samuel
Rorke, James Alfred
Rose, George
Rose, James
Rose, John Broadbank
Rose, Samuel
Rosier, Charles
Ross, David
Ross, Edward
Ross, George (born c. 1818)
Ross, George (born c. 1822)
Ross, James Augustus
Rothwell, James Paley
Row, Alice
Rowe, John
Rowse, Samuel Walter
Roy, John
Royston, Joseph
Royston, William Robinson
Rudder, Sarah
Russell, Archie
Russell, George
Russell, Henry
Russell, Robert
Russell, William
Russom, John
Rutherford, George
Ryan, Caroline (Mrs Richard
    Smart)
Ryan, John
Ryan, Margaret (Mrs H. A. Bryan)
Ryan, Thomas
Ryder, George
Ryder, Robert
Ryley, Robert Ralph

St. George, Sir Theophilus John
St. Paul, George
Saker, George William
Salmon, Farquhard Campbell
Salter, Easton
Salter, Richard
Sampson, Mrs Susan
Sanderson, John
Sanderson, Septimus
Sanderson, William
Sanderson, William Terrot
Sarles, Henry
Saunders, James Renault
Saunders, William H.
Saveall, Jesse
Saville, Rose
Savory, John
Savory, William Henry

Schofield, James
Scholes, Jabez
Schrieber, Emil Augustus Bernard
    Talansier
Schwikkard, Ludwig Bernard
Scorgie, Alexander
Scotson, Samuel
Scott, Rev. Charles
Scott, Daniel Burton
Scott, Edward
Scott, George
Scott, John Richard
Scott, Thomas
Scrutton, Joseph
Seager, George
Seager, Robert
Seal, William
Searle, Arthur
Searle, Henry
Selby, Dr Prideaux
Selwood, Dr Josiah Henry
Shackelton, Ann (Mrs John
    Fleming)
Shackelton, Mary (Mrs William
    James)
Shackelton, Samuel Edward
Shadwell, Richard William
Shafto, Jane (Mrs William Hopkins
    Jenkins)
Shanklin, Fred
Sharp, Andrew
Sharp, Arthur
Sharp, George
Sharpe, C. W.
Sharphouse, John
Shaw, (ex *Bellona*)
Shaw, Alexander
Shaw, Mrs Ann
Shaw, Charles (ex *Sovereign*)
Shaw, Charles (ex *Trent*)
Shaw, Margaret (Mrs John Nicholas
    Stone)
Shaw, Susannah (Mrs Richard
    Mason)
Shearer, John
Sheers, Thomas
Sheldon, John
Shepherd, William Gregg
Shepstone, John Wesley
Shepstone, Sir Theophilus
Sherrin, Charles
Shields, Thomas
Shiels, John
Shiels, William John
Shipley, John
Shire, Henry, *alias* Henry, Lyster
Shires, Joseph Brooke
Shooter, Rev Joseph
Short, Robert
Shorthouse, James

Shortt, James William
Shortt, Portland Bentinck
Shuter, John David
Shuttleworth, Mrs Catherine
Shuttleworth, Henry
Sidway, George
Silvester, Adolphus
Simon, John
Simons, Alfred
Simpson, Elizabeth Allison
    (Mrs T. W. Fannin)
Simpson, Henry George
Simpson, John (born *c.* 1820)
Simpson, John (born *c.* 1826)
Simpson, John (born *c.* 1828)
Simpson, John Rhind
Simpson, Margaret (Mrs E. F.
    McGill)
Simpson, William Henry (born
    c. 1820)
Simpson, William Henry (born
    c. 1827)
Sims, James
Sinclair, Charles Ross
Sinfell, Charles
Singer, William
Sink, Thomas
Sissison, Joseph
Skinner, William (born *c.* 1826)
Skinner, William (born 1828)
Skipper, A. J.
Slack, William
Slatter, Alfred Joseph Payne
Slatter, David
Slatter, John Clarke
Slatter, William
Small, Henry Alexander
Smarfit, James
Smart, Mary
Smart, Master Benjamin
Smerdon, Capt. William
Smith, (ex *Nile*)
Smith, Alexander (born 1818)
Smith, Alexander (born 1834)
Smith, Archibald (*alias*), *see*
    Balloch, Archibald Smith
Smith, Charles
Smith, Edward Alfred
Smith, Ellen
Smith, George Brown
Smith, George Frederick
Smith, Hans G. L.
Smith, Henry (born *c.* 1813)
Smith, Henry (*c.* 1813–1853)
Smith, Hugh
Smith, J. F.
Smith, Jack
Smith, James
Smith, Jane
Smith, Jesse

Smith, John (ex *Jane Morice*,
    July 1851)
Smith, John (born 1816)
Smith, John (born *c.* 1826)
Smith, John (born 1829)
Smith, John (born 1830)
Smith, Joseph
Smith, Joseph Crampton
Smith, Joshua
Smith, Mary
Smith, Robert (born *c.* 1804)
Smith, Robert (born *c.* 1825)
Smith, Robert (born *c.* 1826)
Smith, Robert Anderson
Smith, Thomas
Smith, Thomas Paterson
Smith, W.
Smith, William (born *c.* 1790)
Smith, William (born *c.* 1797)
Smith, William (born *c.* 1819)
Smith, William (born *c.* 1825)
Smith, William Ashmore
Smith, William Hart
Smith, William M.
Smithers, Richard
Smithes, Francis
Smithwick, Richard
Snell, Edward
Soane, Fred
Solomon, Isaiah Saul
Solomon, John (Jacob Saul)
Sorrell, William *see* Sowell, Capt.
    William
South, Jabez
Southam, Alfred
Southam, James
Sowell, Capt. William
Sparks, David
Spearman, George
Speck, Arthur Aitcheson
Speirs, Robert
Spencer, Charles
Spencer, Robert
Spencer, William
Spensely, Rev. Calvert
Spillane, Michael
Spilsbury, Henry
Spradbrow, Charles
Spratt, Holden
Spring, Arthur
Spring, Francis
Spruce, John
Stabler, John
Stacey, Charles T.
Stacpoole, Frank Alexander
Stafford, Berkeley Buckingham
    see Talbot, Berkeley Buckingham
Stafford, Edward Sparrow
Stafford, Frederick
Stafford, Hugh Henry *see* Flood,
    Hugh Henry

Stafford, William Alexander *see*
 Talbot, William Alexander
Stageman, Samuel
Stainbank, Dering Lee Warner
Stainbank, Henry Ellerton
Stanbridge, Herbert E.
Standish, Edwin
Stanford, Martha
Stanger, Dr William
Stanley, John
Stansfield, George
Stanton, James
Starey, Charles Richard
Starkey, Zechariah
Starr, Stephen
Starr, William
Stead, Matthew
Steel, John Stollery
Steel, Peter
Steele, John
Steele, John Polodore
Stenhouse, James
Stephenson, Capt. David
Stephenson, George
Stephenson, Josias
Stevens, Andrew
Stevens, Francis Powell
Stevens, Henry William
Stevens, John
Stevens, Robert
Stewart, Alexander
Stewart, John G.
Stewart, Margaret
Stewart, Mary (Mrs John Brown)
Stirton, John Andrew
Stockill, Christopher
Stockill, William
Stoddard, James
Stokes, William Wakeling
Stone, John Nicholas
Stonell, William Henry
Stote, James
Stott, Frederick Sarley
Strachan, Adam
Strachan, Andrew
Strachan, Robert (died 1852)
Strachan, Capt. Robert (died
 c. 1856)
Strapp, Samuel
Strapp, William
Stratford, John
Stredder, Robert
Stretch, Charles St. Leger
Struben, Capt. Johannes Hermanus
 Marinus
Struthers, Dr Robert Briggs
Stuart, John Sidey
Stubbs, James
Styles, Robert
Suddaby, Charles James

Sudlow, Charlotte (Mrs F. S. Stott)
Summers, Robert
Summerville, I. T.
Surtees, Robert
Sutherland, Dr Peter Cormac
Suttie, David
Suttie, Laurence
Swift, William
Swindon, William
Swithenbank, Ellen (Mrs Thomas
 Foster)
Sykes, George
Sykes, Robert
Symes, Frederick
Symons, John Philip

Tait, (tailor, Durban)
Talbot, Berkeley Buckingham †
Talbot, William Alexander †
Tallack, Francis
Tanner, Thomas
Tapper, John
Tarboton, David Hainsworth
Tarboton, Henry
Tarn, Edwin Horatio
Tate, William
Tatham, Edmund
Tatham, Robert Bristow
Tattersall, Christopher
Taubman, Thomas
Taylor, Daniel
Taylor, David
Taylor, Edward (ex *Bellona*)
Taylor, Edward (ex *Justina*)
Taylor, Henry
Taylor, James
Taylor, James Alfred
Taylor, John (died 1855)
Taylor, John (born *c.* 1807)
Taylor, John (born *c.* 1824)
Taylor, John (born *c.* 1828)
Taylor, John Horrocks
Taylor, Capt. Maxwell Hannay
Taylor, Moses David
Taylor, T.
Taylor, William
Taylor, William Allen
Taylor, Dr William Garbutt
Tedder, Charles
Tedder, James
Teeson, David
Terney, Francis
Tetley, John
Thomas, Edward Medlicott
Thomas, J.
Thomas, Rev. John S.

† Born Stafford but never used this
 surname in Natal. Brothers of
 H. H. Flood.

Thomas, Mary Ann
Thomas, Richard Jenkyns
Thomas, Samuel James
Thomas, T.
Thompson, (ex *Tuscan*)
Thompson, Charles
Thompson, Edward
Thompson, Francis
Thompson, George
Thompson, John George
Thompson, John Luke
Thompson, Jonah
Thompson, Jonathan
Thompson, Margaret (Mrs Harry
 Darke Bayley)
Thompson, Reuben
Thompson, Robert
Thompson, Thomas (ex *Narcissus*,
 August 1852)
Thompson, Thomas (ex *Sovereign*)
Thompson, William Rowland jnr.
Thomson, Andrew, *alias*
 Anderson, A. T.
Thomson, George
Thomson, James
Thomson, John D.
Thomson, John George Ringler
Thomson, William
Thring, Samuel
Throssell, Charles
Thurston, Henry Leggatt
Tierney, Michael
Tight, B. A.
Tilly, Walter
Tilney/Tinley, Edward William
Timaeus, George William Plevy
Tindal, William
Tinley *see* Tilney
Tipper, Loton
Tissiman, Joseph
Titmarsh, David
Todd, Edwin
Todd, John
Todd, William
Tomlinson, Edward
Tomlinson, George
Tomlinson, John Robert
Toohey, Daniel Charles
Toohey, Patrick *see* Tuohey,
 Patrick
Torry, Dr John Cooper
Tosen, William Frederick
Tovey, William
Towning, Frederick Thomas
Townsend, Henrietta
Townsend, John William
Travers, Miss, (ex *Bellona*)
Trenowth, George
Trood, Edward Thomas
Trotter, David

111

Trotter, George (born *c*. 1827)
Trow, George
Troy, John Butler
Tuck, William
Tucker, Alfred Octavius
Tucker, William
Tulley, George
Tunmer, William
Tuohey, Patrick
Turnbull, Adam
Turnbull, James Maitland
Turner, Betsy
Turner, George Thomas
Turner, John
Turner, Margaret S.
Turpin, Philip Alexander
Turton, Josiah
Tutin, James
Twyford, Thomas
Twyman, James Edwin
Tye, Elizabeth (Mrs Edward Tomlinson)
Tyson, William
Tyzack, Richard Webber

Umbers, William
Upton, Robert Sellers
Urquhart, Mrs, (ex *Bellona*)
Urquhart, Hector

Vale, Edwin
Vanderplank, John
Varty, Arthur Clarke
Varty, Thomas Boyd
Varty, William Boyd
Vause, Richard
Vear, George
Vear, William (born 1819)
Vear, William (born *c*. 1823)
Vernon, Joseph
Vertue, Arthur Leopold
Vertue, Horatio
Vertue, Philip Algernon
Vialls, John
Vickery, Samuel
Vincent, Charles
Vincent, James
Vine, William Sutherland
Vinnicombe, George
Vinnicombe, John
Vinnicombe, Valentine S.
Vinson, Alexander
Vinson, Henry
Vionnee, L. William
Vivian, Charles George
Vivian, Mrs Mary
Vowles, Thomas
Voysey, John Payne

Waddelove, George

Wade, Mrs Alice
Wade, John (born *c*. 1805)
Wade, John (born *c*. 1820)
Wagner, Abraham
Wainwright, Edward
Wainwright, Richard
Wakefield, John
Wakelin, Charles
Walcott, John Charles
Walkden, Thomas
Walker, Arthur
Walker, Dennis
Walker, E. S.
Walker, Edward Henry
Walker, Edward William
Walker, Mrs Elizabeth (Mrs George Sharp)
Walker, George (born *c*. 1827)
Walker, George (born *c*. 1829)
Walker, George Edwards
Walker, Henry Percival
Walker, John
Wall, Eliza (Mrs Denis Good)
Wall, Julia (Mrs Sidney Smith)
Wall, Nicholas
Wallace, John
Wallace, William
Waller, John
Walmsley, Capt. Joshua
Walsh, Albert Eugene
Walsh, Garret
Walsh, Thomas
Walsh, William
Walters, John Charles
Walton, Rev. James
Walton, Joseph
Ward, Francis
Ward, Mrs Harriet (born Griffin)
Ward, John
Ward, Josiah
Ward, Robert
Ward, Sarah (Mrs Leonard Clark)
Wardell, John
Wardell, William
Warn, John
Warner, William
Warren, Elizabeth *see* Allison, Rev. James
Warren, Henry Albert
Warrington, Thomas
Warwick, Edward
Warwick, Francis
Warwick, Thomas
Washbourne, Daniel
Waters, William
Waterson, Christopher
Wathen, George Henry
Watkins, Edmund
Watkins, John
Watkins, Thomas (born 1810)

Watkins, Thomas (born *c*. 1812)
Watling, John Walter
Watson, (ex *Bellona*)
Watson, Charles
Watson, James
Watson, John
Watson, Dr John Benton
Watson, John Ross Malcolm
Watson, Joseph Bradley
Watson, Richard
Watson, Thomas
Watson, William (born *c*. 1787)
Watson, William (born *c*. 1809)
Watson, William (born *c*. 1814)
Watson, William Tottie
Watton, Samuel
Watts, Stephen
Waugh, James
Webb, Francis G.
Webb, Henry (ex *Jane Morice*, July 1851)
Webb, Henry (ex *Minerva*)
Webb, James
Webb, Sarah
Webb, Thomas
Webber, Frederick
Webber, Joseph
Webster, David
Webster, George Kemp
Webster, Joseph
Weeks, William
Weir, James
Weir, William
Welburn, Mrs Mary (later Mrs Robert Whitaker)
Welch, Andrew
Welch, James
Welch, John William
Welden, Hannah
Welford, Joseph
West, James Baugham
West, John
West, Joseph Ellis
West, W.
Westbrook, Henry Fletcher
Westbrook, James Alexander
Westell, John
Westly or Westley, Edward
Weston, George Kemp
Weston, James
Wetherdon, William F.
Wetherell, John Dent
Wheeler, James Napoleon
Wheeler, Joseph
Wheelwright, Charles Thomas
Whenstone, James
Whipp, John
Whitaker, Robert
White, Alfred Samuel
White, Andrew

White, Henry
White, Henry Jeffreys
White, John A. (Elephant)
White, William Marshall
Whitehead, George James
Whitehorn, William Robert
Whitehurst, Joseph Cross
Whiteways, William
Whiting, William
Whitridge, Matthew
Whittaker, Daniel Faber
Whittaker, Edward Leyland
Whittaker, Thomas
Whitworth, Edward Clayton
Whyte, Andrew
Wickes, John
Wigg, James
Wiggett, Joseph
Wiggett, Joshua
Wilcox, John
Wildman, W.F.
Wiles, James
Wiles, William
Wilford, Henry
Wilkin, James
Wilkinson, Anthony
Wilkinson, Emma (Mrs John Jardine)
Wilkinson, Richard
Wilkinson, Sydney Lee
Wilkinson, William
Wilkinson, William George
Wilkinson, William John
Willan, Ann
Willan, Emily
Willan, Rhoda M.
Williams, (ex *Tuscan*)
Williams, Abraham
Williams, Capel Hanbury
Williams, Charles
Williams, Francis
Williams, James (born c. 1808)
Williams, James (born c. 1826)
Williams, James (born c. 1830)
Williams, James Kings
Williams, John Owen
Williams, Michael Edward
Williams, Samuel
Williams, William
Williamson, David Bond

Williamson, David Hollowell
Williamson, George (born 1800)
Williamson, George (born c. 1820)
Williamson, John
Williamson, Mary
Willis, James
Willis, Samuel
Willis, Sarah (Mrs T. Ayres)
Willis, William
Willson, Alfred
Willson, Mrs Elizabeth (born Holness)
Willson, George
Willson, George William Church
Willson, William Thomas
Willy, Robert Beck
Wilson, Cyrus
Wilson, Eliza (ex *Ina*)
Wilson, Eliza (ex *Minerva*)
Wilson, George
Wilson, Henry
Wilson, Isabella (Mrs Charles Collier)
Wilson, James
Wilson, Jeremiah
Wilson, John (born c. 1824)
Wilson, John (born c. 1825)
Wilson, John (born c. 1831)
Wilson, John Alexander
Wilson, Capt. Lewis
Wilson, Thomas
Wilson, William (born c. 1813)
Wilson, William (born c. 1818)
Wilson, William (ex *Haidee*)
Wilson, William Donald
Wilson, William Robert Shaw
Winder, George
Windham, Ashe Smyth
Winn, William
Winter, James William
Winter, John Joseph
Wirsing, George Henry
Wirsing, John Otto
Wishart, Capt. John
Withers, William Bramwell
Witherspoon, John Davis
Wolley, George
Wood, Charlotte
Wood, Mrs Harriett

Wood, James Riddall
Wood, John
Wood, Richard
Wood, William
Wood, William, *alias* Heslop, William
Wood, William Medley
Wood, Willson
Woodcock, Alexander Francis
Woodcock, John
Woodhead, Henry
Woodhead, Joseph Robert
Woodhouse, William
Woods, Hugh
Woodward, Charles J.S.
Woodward, Fred
Woodward, Marcus
Woodward, Oswald
Woolley, Mary
Wootton, William
Worsley, Richard
Wray, James
Wray, Leonard Hume
Wright, Humphrey J.
Wright, John (born c. 1817)
Wright, John (ex 45th Regiment)
Wright, Leonard
Wright, Robert
Wright, Thomas Dickinson
Wright, William
Wymark, Daniel

Yardley, A. Joseph
Yates, Thomas
Yeo, Frederick Richard
York, William
Young, Adelaide (Mrs Henry Harper)
Young, Edwin
Young, George (born c. 1812)
Young, George (born c. 1822)
Young, Henry
Young, James
Young, Margaret (Mrs Thomas Pearson)
Young, Margaret Ann
Young, Sidney Smith

Zohrab, Peter T.H.

Source List

A. MANUSCRIPT SOURCES

Private source material

   Archives and libraries
   Church registers
   Church plaques
   Cemeteries
   Miscellaneous

Unpublished official papers

   Natal Archives, Pietermaritzburg
   Registers of births, marriages and deaths
   Master of the Supreme Court's Office, Pmb.
   Public Record Office, London
   Registrar of Deeds Office, Pietermaritzburg
   Cape Archives, Cape Town
   Durban Corporation
   Ladysmith Corporation
   Pietermaritzburg Corporation

B. OFFICIAL PRINTED SOURCES

   Great Britain. *Ordnance survey*
   Natal. *Colony*
   Pietermaritzburg. *Corporation*
   South African archival records

C. UNOFFICIAL CONTEMPORARY PRINTED SOURCES

   Printed documents
   Periodical publications
      Newspapers
      Journals
      Yearbooks

   Periodical articles
   Journals, biographies, autobiographies, letters
   Miscellaneous

D. LATER SOURCES

   Memoirs
   General secondary works
   Periodical articles
   Unpublished theses, essays, etc.

E. PERSONAL COMMUNICATION

F. PORTRAITS, PHOTOGRAPHS, etc.

G. ADDITIONAL SOURCES

Source List for Biographies in Volume 1

A. MANUSCRIPT SOURCES

PRIVATE SOURCE MATERIAL

Archives and libraries

Durban

Killie Campbell Africana Library

1 Ablett papers
2 Acutt papers
3 Adlam papers
4 Akerman papers
5 A. B. Allison papers
6 Behrens papers
7 James Bell papers
8 Blamey, John Cardell: Diary, 1 July 1851 – 6 Oct. 1854. (Typescript)
9 Churchill papers (copies consulted – originals in Local History Museum)
10 Essery papers
11 Lamport/Gillespie papers
12 McLeod, Ellen and George: Letters, 1850, 1851, 1858, 1859, 1868.
13 Methley, J. E.: Letters, 1854, 1855, 1858.
14 Millar papers

Local History Museum

15 Acutt papers
16 Addison papers
17 Akerman papers
18 A. M. Anderson papers
19 W. P. Anderson papers
20 Arbuckle papers
21 Arbuthnot papers
22 Archibald papers
23 Armstrong papers
24 Ayres papers
25 Essery papers
26 Royston, Mary: Diary, 1851
27 Sanderson, John: Diary, 1851

Pietermaritzburg

Natal Archives

28 Archives of the Natal Wesleyan Mission
29 Bird, Christopher (Kit): Papers
30 Crompton papers
31 Fleming, John: Diary 1856, 1862
32 Garden, Capt. R. J. (45th Regiment): Papers
33 Knight, H. E.: Diary, 1857–1862
34 Moreland papers
35 Shepstone, Theophilus: Diaries, 1865, 1872, 1874, 1876, 1879, 1880, 1881, 1891

Natal Society Library

36 Irons papers

London

London University. School of Oriental and African Studies.

Methodist Mission Society papers (references supplied by Ms Sheila Meintjies, Cape Town)

37 South African correspondence
    Box 302: File – Cape 1825, letter 59, dated 25 Oct. 1825, and
             File – Cape 1827, letter 1, dated 9 Jan. 1827

38 South African synod minutes
    Box 334: 1823–1840
             Report of the Coranna Station 1835
    Box 335: 1841–1848
             5th annual meeting of the Bechuana District, 21 Dec. 1841
    Box 336: 1848–1856
             Albany and Kaffraria special committee 14 June 1848. Natal District minutes and reports, 15 Oct. 1851.

Church registers

(The general rule here has been that the cut-off dates for the copying of these has been 1880 in the case of baptisms and 1920 in the case of marriages. A number of churches do not have burial registers or only incomplete ones. Where possible these records have been copied well into the middle of this century.)

39 Clydesdale mission station (Anglican), 1867–1950
   Durban Anglican
40   Christ Church, Addington, 1861–1898 (1861–1874 in St Paul's register).
41   St Cyprian's, 1863–1946
42   St James's, 1889–1934
43   St Matthew's, 1868–1908
44   St Paul's, 1849–1915
45   St Thomas's, 1864–1915
46 Durban Baptist, 1866–1919
47 Durban Roman Catholic
48 Durban Congregational, 1852–1891 (fire-damaged)
   Durban Presbyterian
49   Baptisms and marriages, 1862–1920
50   Communion rolls, 1862–1880
51   Minutes of Session, and Board minutes
52   Newscuttings
53 Durban Wesleyan (Methodist), 1842–1931
54 Edendale mission station (Methodist), 1852–1885 (Natal Archives)
55 Greytown Dutch Reformed, 1859–1923 (D.R.C. Archives, Pmb.)
56 Greytown Anglican: St. James's, 1864–1920
57 Himeville Anglican: Parish of the Drakensberg, 1885–1950
58 Howick Anglican: Parish of the Karkloof, 1866–1950
59 Howick Presbyterian, 1877–1920 (fire damaged)
60 Indaleni mission station (Methodist), 1846–1851 (Natal Archives); 1856–1896 (at Ndaleni)
61 Isipingo Anglican: St James's, 1856–1918 (housed in C.P.S.A. Diocesan Office, Durban)
62 Ixopo Anglican: Parish of Ixopo, 1900–1950
63 Ixopo Wesleyan (Methodist), 1903–1950
64 Ladysmith Anglican: All Saints', 1857–1950
65 Ladysmith Dutch Reformed, 1854–1878
66 Ladysmith Wesleyan (Methodist), 1864–1950
   Mount Moreland, *see* Verulam
67 Newcastle Anglican: Holy Trinity, 1877–1950
68 New Hanover Anglican: Parish of York-cum-Ravensworth, 1912–1950

Pietermaritzburg Anglican
69 St Andrew's, 1855–1867
70 St George's, Fort Napier, 1870–1907. (The only register not housed in the Cathedral Office, Pmb.)
71 St Peter's, 1849–1920
72 St Saviour's, 1866–1941
73 Pietermaritzburg Roman Catholic, 1850–1923
74 Pietermaritzburg Congregational, 1860–1923
75 Pietermaritzburg Dutch Reformed, 1837–1926
Pietermaritzburg Presbyterian
76 First Presbyterian Church, 1850–1920 (also St John's, 1865–1942)
77 Pietermaritzburg Wesleyan (Methodist), 1846–1945
Pinetown Anglican
78 St John's, 1852–1939 (including St Andrew's, 1868–1883)
79 Pinetown Presbyterian, 1852–1889. (Original in possession of Mr Peter Brown, *Easingwold*, Nottingham Road.)
80 Richmond Anglican: St Mary's, 1853–1964
81 Stanger Anglican: Parish of Nonoti, 1866–1947
Tongaat *see* Verulam
82 Umhlali Anglican: St James's, 1851–1873 (copied into registers of St Paul's, Durban)
Umhlanga *see* Verulam
83 Umzinto Anglican: St Patrick's, 1860–1930
84 Verulam Anglican: St Thomas's, 1850–1961. (Includes Mount Moreland, Umhlanga and Tongaat.)
85 Verulam Wesleyan (Methodist), 1859–1966. (Includes Mount Moreland, Nonoti, Kearsney, Smerdon's Flat, Sinkwazi, Umhlanga, Umhlali, Inanda and Tongaat. Prior to 1859 Verulam was part of the Durban circuit.)

Church plaques
Greytown
86 St James's (Anglican)

Cemeteries
87 Boston
88 Bulwer
Durban
89 Camp cemetery
90 St Thomas's, Berea
91 Stamford Hill
92 West Street
93 Equeefa
94 Greytown
95 Harding
96 Highlands (near Mooi River, St Mary's churchyard)
97 Ladysmith
98 Malton (on Pmb./Greytown road)
99 Mid-Illovo
100 Milkwood Kraal, Little Umhlanga
101 New Guelderland
Pietermaritzburg
102 Commercial Road
103 Mountain Rise
Pinetown
104 St Andrew's
105 St John's
Richmond
106 General cemetery
107 Presbyterian churchyard
108 Stanger
109 Umhlali, St James's churchyard
110 Umzinto, St Patrick's churchyard

Miscellaneous
111 Allison family Bible (Mrs D. T. Allison, 3 Miller St., Pmb.)
112 Button, Fred: Notes (Mr Denis Button, *Ebuta*, Umzimkulu)
113 Dove, & Co.: List of burials in Durban, 1875–1922
114 Grundy, James: Memoranda. (Mrs J. M. Muller, Sunningdale, Burger Street, Pmb.)
115 Hathorn, Cameron & Co.: Legal files
116 History of the Pmb. Congregational Church (housed with the church registers)
117 Mackenzie, William: Diary, 1873 (Mrs Dorothy Gibson, *Brock Lodge,* Richmond)
118 Middleton, Kate: Birthday book (Mrs M. Relph, 62 College Road, Pmb.)
119 Sinclair/Boddy scrapbooks (2) (Miss A. Sinclair, *Holme Lodge,* Impolweni – deceased)
120 Singer family Bible (Miss Shirley E. Singer, 9 Westminster, Povall Road, Dbn)
121 Smith, W. H.: A sketch of my life in Natal. Type-script, n.d. (Mrs Kay Dales, P.O. Box 87, Pinetown)
122 Stainbank, D. L. W.: Diary (Transcript supplied by Mrs K. L. Stainbank, *Coedmore,* Bellair)
123 Struben family Bible (Ladysmith Museum)
124 Windham, Juliet (nee Maclean): Diary, 1858, 1860. Typescript. (Miss Maeve Windham, Wawne Cottage, Offton, Suffolk – photocopy in University of Natal library, Pmb.)

UNPUBLISHED OFFICIAL PAPERS
Natal Archives, Pietermaritzburg
125 Colonial Secretary's Office vols. 3, 7, 13, 15, 16, 21, 27, 37, 38, 41, 51, 55, 56, 103, 126, 129, 135, 136, 147, 2238–2250, 2252–2254, 2257, 2263, 2265, 2282–2288 (special licences), 2295, 2297.
126 European Immigration department vols. 64, 65, 73, 74
127 Government House vols. 22, 28, 30, 33–36, 38–40, 48, 52, 783, 1209, 1211, 1213, 1299, 1324, 1584
Master of the Supreme Court
128 Assigned estates
129 Deceased estates
130 Insolvent estates
131 Supreme Court Illiquid cases. I/5/41 Notarial protocols. (Protocols of all notaries who started practising in the 1840s and 1850s have been consulted.)
132 Surveyor General's office vols. III/5/3, 12, 13, 18, 19, 24–27, 31 and 32 III/12/1, III/11/11
133 Secretary for Native Affairs vols. I/1/9, 10, 11, 15, 17 and 32 II/1/3

Official registers of births, marriages and deaths. (Compulsory registration of births and deaths began only in 1868. These registers were originally housed in the offices of the various magistrates, but have since been sent to the Department of the Interior, Pretoria.)

134   Bergville – deaths, 1894–1950
135   Dundee – marriages, 1890–1917
136   Durban – births, 1868–1880
137   Durban – deaths, 1868–1931
138   Greytown – births, 1868–1880
139   Greytown – deaths, 1868–1950
140   Harding – deaths, 1868–1950
141   Howick – deaths, 1883–1955
142   Ladysmith – births, 1868–1880
143   Ladysmith – deaths, 1868–1939
144   Newcastle – marriages, 1864–1919
145   New Hanover – deaths, 1935–1950
146   Pietermaritzburg – births, 1868–1903
147   Pietermaritzburg – deaths, 1868–1941
148   Pinetown – deaths, 1913–1950
149   Richmond – births, 1868–1900
150   Richmond – deaths, 1868–1967
151   Stanger – deaths, 1868–1946
152   Umzinto – deaths, 1868–1947
153   Utrecht – marriages, 1870–1919
154   Verulam – deaths, 1868–1949
155   Vryheid – marriages, 1889–1905

Master of the Supreme Court's office, Pmb.

156   Deeds/Wills, 1852–1910

Public Record Office, London

157   i)   Lists of emigrants ex *Ballengeich, Dreadnought, Haidee, Hebrides, Henry Tanner* and *Washington*. (References supplied by the late Professor A. F. Hattersley.)
      ii)   War Office
158   Muster rolls of the 45th Regiment (W.O. 12/5751, 5755–5756)

Registrar of Deeds office, Pmb.

159   Deeds of transfer, 1851, nos. 1–71

Cape Archives, Cape Town

160   GH 9/3 (Lists of unapproved Byrne emigrants – reference supplied by the late Professor A. F. Hattersley.)

Durban Corporation

161   Mayor's Minute, 1862, 1867, 1877, 1878, 1881, 1882.

Ladysmith Corporation

162   Town Guard Roll, 1899
163   Ration list, 1899–1900
      (Both housed in Ladysmith Museum)

Pietermaritzburg Corporation

164   Minutes of the Town Council, 1864. (Housed in the Natal Archives)

B.   OFFICIAL PRINTED SOURCES

165   **Great Britain**. Ordnance survey. *Gazetteer of Great Britain* . . . Chessington, Director of Ordnance Survey, 1953. (Used for verifying spelling of place names.)
166   **Natal**. Colony. *Blue book*. Pmb. 1850–1892/3. (Consulted mainly for lists of public service officers.)
167   **Natal**. Colony. *The Natal civil service list . . . to which is added the Civil service calendar.* Pmb., 1895–1910.
168   **Natal**. Colony. *Government Gazette*. Pmb., 1849–1876. (Consulted mainly for jury lists and voters' rolls. It is realised that these lists are not always accurate, but in the absence of other sources they have had to be used.)
169   **Natal**. Colony. *Further papers relating to the case of Mr A. B. Allison (late Resident Magistrate, Upper Tugela division)*. Pmb., 1890.
170   **Natal**. Colony. *Papers relating to the case of Mr A. B. Allison (late Resident Magistrate, Upper Tugela division)*. Pmb., 1889.
171   **Pietermaritzburg**. City council. *Corporation yearbook*, 1966. Pmb., the Council. (This was consulted for the list of mayors.)
172   *South African archival records, Natal, no. 2: Records of the Natal executive council, 1846–1848.* Cape Town, Government printer, 1960.
173   *South African archival records, Natal, no. 4: Records of the Natal executive council, 1853–1856.* Cape Town, Government printer, 1963.
174   *South African archival records, Natal, no. 5: Records of the Natal executive council, 1856–1859.* Cape Town, Government printer, 1964.

C.   UNOFFICIAL CONTEMPORARY PRINTED SOURCES

PRINTED DOCUMENTS

175   Bird, John: *The annals of Natal*. 2 v. Cape Town, Struik, 1965. (Originally published in 1888)
176   Chase, J. C.: *The Natal papers: a reprint of all notices and public documents connected with that territory*. Cape Town, Struik, 1968. (Originally published in 1843)

PERIODICAL PUBLICATIONS

Newspapers

177   *D'Urban Advocate*, 1852–1854
178   *D'Urban Observer*, 1851–1852
179   *Natal Chronicle*, 1855–1856
180   *Natal Commercial Advertiser* (later *Natal Advertiser*), 1854–1855
181   *Natal Courier and Pietermaritzburg Advertiser*, 1859–1865
182   *Natal en Zuid-Oost Afrikaan*, 1853
183   *Natal Guardian*, 1856
184   *Natal Independent*, 1850–1855
185   **Natal Mercury*, 1852–
186   *Natal Patriot*, 1846–1848
187   *Natal Star*, 1855–1863
188   *Natal Times and Durban Mercantile and Agricultural Gazette*, 1851–1853
189   **Natal Witness*, 1846–

190 *De Natalier and Pietermaritzburg True Recorder,*
     1844–1846
191 *Times; Natal and South-East Africa, 1855–1857*

*These two were thoroughly researched to the end
of 1857. Thereafter, except in isolated instances,
only domestic notices and obituaries have been
used, in the case of the *Mercury* to 1885, and the
Witness to 1920.

Journals

192 *Byrne's Emigrants' Journal and Natal News,* no.1,
     Feb. 1850–no.6, July 1850
193 *Hart's Army List, and Militia List,* Apr. and Oct.
     1854
194 *Natal Journal,* 1858
195 *Vineyard,* 1884, 1885

Yearbooks

196 *Cape Town Directory,* 1865. Cape Town. Martin.
197 *Natal Almanac and Yearly Register,* 1863–1905.
     Pmb., P. Davis. (Entitled *Natal Almanac,
     Directory and Yearly Register* from 1871.
     The main sections consulted were postal direc-
     tories, lists of officers in government departments
     and various bodies and organizations, and advertise-
     ments. The issues for 1882, 1884, 1888 and 1895
     are most often quoted for postal addresses and
     occupations, as these are the numbers of this now
     rare publication to which constant access has been
     possible. Addresses and occupations as given in
     directories have to be treated with caution for
     they sometimes tend to be out of date. As far as
     possible these have been checked against other
     sources.)
198 *Port Natal Almanac,* 1851, 1852. Durban,
     Cullingworth. (Consulted mainly for its
     advertisements.)
199 *South African Who's Who, 1908, 1910.* Johannes-
     burg. Donaldson. (Useful mainly for the second
     generation.)

PERIODICAL ARTICLES

200 Sir J. W. Akerman (obituary), *South Africa,* 1 July
     1905).

JOURNALS, BIOGRAPHIES, AUTOBIOGRAPHIES,
LETTERS

201 BACKHOUSE, JAMES
     A narrative of a visit to Mauritius and South Africa.
     London, Hamilton, Adams & Co., 1844.
202 BALDWIN, W. C.
     *African hunting and adventure from Natal to the
     Zambesi.* 3rd ed. London, Bentley, 1894. (first ed.
     1863)
203 BLEEK, W. H. I.
     Natal diaries, 1855–1856; translated by O. H. Spohr.
     Cape Town, Balkema, 1865.
204 COLENSO, J. W.
     *Ten weeks in Natal: a journal of a visitation among
     the colonists and Zulu Kafirs of Natal.* Cambridge,
     Macmillan, 1855.
205 CRAW, ISABELLA
     A diary of the siege of Ladysmith . . . Ladysmith,
     Ladysmith historical society, 1972.

206 CURREY, R. N., *ed.*
     *Letters and other writings of a Natal sheriff: Thomas
     Phipson, 1815–1876.* Cape Town, Oxford univ.
     press, 1968.
207 DOBIE, J. S.
     South African journal, 1862–6; ed. by Alan F.
     Hattersley. Cape Town, van Riebeeck society, 1945.
208 FEILDEN, E. W.
     *My African home; or, Bush life in Natal when a
     young colony, (1852–1857).* London, Sampson
     Low, 1887.
209 FYNN, H. F.
     The diary of Henry Francis Fynn; compiled from
     original sources and edited by James Stuart and
     D. McK. Malcolm. Pmb., Shuter, 1950.
210 GOODWIN, HARVEY
     Memoir of Bishop Mackenzie. 2nd ed. Cambridge,
     Deighton Bell, 1865. (first ed. 1864)
211 MATTHEWS, J. W.
     *Incwadi yami; or, Twenty years' personal experience
     in South Africa.* New York, Rogers & Sherwood,
     1887.
212 *The Natal Who's Who: an illustrated biographical
     sketch book of Natalians.* Durban, Who's who publ.
     co., 1906. (Useful mainly for the second generation.)
213 O'BYRNE, W.
     Naval biographical dictionary . . . London, Murray,
     1849.
214 RIVETT, A. W. L.
     Ten years' church work in South Africa. London,
     Jarrold, 1890.
215 SMITH, THORNLEY
     Memoir of Rev. J. W. Appleyard. London, Wesleyan
     missionary society, 1881.
216 WOLSELEY, Sir G.
     South African diaries . . . 1875. Ed. by Adrian
     Preston. Cape Town, Balkema, 1971.
217 *Women of South Africa: a historical, educational
     and industrial encyclopaedia and social directory of
     the women of the sub-continent;* ed. and comp. by
     Thomas H. Lewis. Cape Town, Le Quesne and
     Hooton-Smith, 1913. (Useful mainly for the second
     generation.)

MISCELLANEOUS

218 BURKE, B.
     *Genealogical and heraldic history of the colonial
     gentry.* 2v. London, Harrison, 1891–5.
219 DICK, W. M.
     *The four books of the prophet Ignoramus; being the
     chronicles of the reign of Er Keet in Ophir.* Pmb.,
     Keith & Co., 1872.
220 *Directory of Durban and Pietermaritzburg, district
     of Natal . . .* Pmb., Lumb, 1852.
221 FOSTER, JOSEPH
     *Peerage, baronetage and knightage of the British
     empire* for 1880. Westminster, the Author, 1880.
222 HOLDEN, W. C.
     History of the colony of Natal, South Africa. London,
     Heylin, 1855.
223 MANN, R. J.
     The colony of Natal: an account of the character-

istics and capabilities of this British dependency.
London, Jarrold, 1859.

224 ROBINSON, JOHN
Notes on Natal: an old colonist's book for new settlers. Pretoria, State Library, 1967. (Reprint of 1872 ed.)

225 RUSSELL, GEORGE
The first twenty-five years of Freemasonry in Natal. Durban, Davis, (1883).

226 STALKER, JOHN
The Natal Carbineers ... Pmb. and Durban, Davis, 1912.

D. LATER SOURCES

MEMOIRS

227 ACUTT, A
The simple chronicle of a South African family. Durban, Priv. print, 1926. (pamphlet)

228 ANDERSON, ALEXANDER
Windjammer yarns ... London, Witherby, 1923

229 ANDERSON, C. J.
Reminiscences and memories of early Durban and its pioneers. [Durban, 1946]. (pamphlet)

230 ARBUTHNOT, JANE
Autobiographical sketch, by J. A. Pmb., City printing works, 1919.

231 BUCHANAN, BARBARA
Natal memories. Pmb., Shuter, 1941.

232 HOLLIDAY, J. D.
Dottings on Natal as published in 1865, and, Sundry tit-bits of colonial experience. Pmb., Davis, 1890.

233 MARX, BEATRICE
She shall have music: the memoirs of Beatrice Marx. Cape Town, Flesch, 1961.

234 RUSSELL, GEORGE
The history of old Durban, and reminiscences of an emigrant of 1850. London, Simpkin Marshall, 1899.

235 WILLIAM, A. E. BEATRICE
My life and two South African pioneers. Cape Town, Unie-Volkspers, 1946.

GENERAL SECONDARY WORKS

236 ADDISON, F.
The family of Dr W. H. Addison. Priv. print, 1961.

237 BATTS, H. J.
History of the Baptist church in South Africa. Cape Town, Maskew Miller, [1920].

238 BERNING, J. M.
Index to obituary notices of Methodist ministers, 1815–1920. Johannesburg, Public library, 1969. (pamphlet)

239 BRABY, A. C.
Natal directory ... 1937. Durban, Braby.

240 BROOKES, E. H. and WEBB, C. deB.
A history of Natal. Pmb., Natal univ. press, 1965.

241 BURNETT, B. B.
Anglicans in Natal. Durban, Churchwardens of St Paul's, 1953.

242 BURROWS, E. H.
A history of medicine in South Africa. Cape Town, Balkema, 1958.

243 BURROWS, E. H.
Overberg outspan: a chronicle of people and places in the southwestern districts of the Cape. Cape Town, Maskew Miller, 1952.

244 CAMPBELL, E. D.
The birth and development of the Natal railways. Pmb., Shuter, 1951.

245 CAMPBELL, ETHEL
In the brave days of old. Durban, Robinson, 1926. (pamphlet)

246 CLARK, JOHN
Natal settler-agent: the career of John Moreland, agent for the Byrne emigration-scheme of 1849–51. Cape Town, Balkema, 1972.

247 *Dictionary of national biography: the concise dictionary from the beginnings to 1930* ... London, Oxford univ. press, 1939.

Dictionary of South African biography. v.1. Cape Town, Nasionale boekhandel for National council for social research, 1968.

248 *James Allison,* by D. C. Visagie, pp.11–12.
249 *John Whittle Appleyard,* by J. D. v.d. Poll, pp. 18–20.
250 *Joseph Barry,* by D. J. van Zyl, pp.56–57.

Dictionary of South African biography. v.2. Cape Town, Tafelberg for Human sciences research council, 1972.

251 *W. H. Addison,* by A. F. Hattersley, pp.1–2.
252 *John William Akerman,* by B. J. T. Leverton, pp.4–5.
253 *James Archbell,* pp.12–15.

Dictionary of South African biography. v.3. Cape Town, Tafelberg for Human sciences research council, 1977.

254 *Friend Addison,* by B. J. T. Leverton, p.2.
255 *James Swithin Franklin Allen,* by B. J. T. Leverton, p.19.
256 *Joseph Allison,* by J. C. Moll, pp.19–20.
257 *William Arbuckle,* by B. J. T. Leverton, p.29.
258 *Thomas Ayres,* by V. F. M. Fitzsimons, pp.36–37.
259 *Edward Arthur Robert Innes,* by B. J. T. Leverton, pp.433–34.

Encyclopaedia Britannica. 11th ed. Cambridge, Univ. press, 1910–11.

260 *Madagascar,* v.17 pp.270–79.
261 *Pharmacy,* v.21, pp.355–358.

262 ETHERINGTON, NORMAN
Preachers, peasants and politics in Southeast Africa, 1835–1880: African Christian communities in Natal, Pondoland and Zululand. London, Royal historical society, 1978.

263 FITZROY, V. M.
Dark bright land. Cape Town, Maskew Miller, 1955.

264 GOETZSCHE, E.
Rough but ready: an official history of the Natal Mounted Rifles ... Durban, the Regiment, [1972].

265 HATHORN, P. L. H.
Henderson heritage, by Peter Hathorn and Amy Young. Pmb., the Authors, 1972.

266 HATHORN, P. L. H.
Joseph Henderson: being a record of some episodes in the life of the founder of a family in Natal. Pmb., the Author, 1973.

267 HATTERSLEY, A. F.
The British settlement of Natal: a study in imperial migration. Cambridge, univ. press, 1950.

268 HATTERSLEY, A. F.
Carbineer: the history of the Royal Natal Carbineers. Aldershot, Gale & Polden, 1950.

269 HATTERSLEY, A. F.
The first South African detectives. Cape Town, Timmins, 1960.

270 HATTERSLEY, A. F.
Hilton portrait: South African public school, 1872–1945. Pmb., Shuter, 1945.

271 HATTERSLEY, A. F.
Hospital century: Grey's Hospital, Pietermaritzburg, 1855–1955. Cape Town, Balkema, 1955.

272 HATTERSLEY, A. F.
More annals of Natal. Pmb., Shuter, 1936.

273 HATTERSLEY, A. F.
The Natal settlers, 1849–1851. Pmb., Shuter, 1949. (pamphlet)

274 HATTERSLEY, A. F.
The Natalians. Pmb., Shuter, 1940.

275 HATTERSLEY, A. F.
Pietermaritzburg panorama. Pmb., Shuter, 1938.

276 HATTERSLEY, A. F.
Portrait of a colony: the story of Natal. Cambridge, univ. press, 1940.

277 HATTERSLEY, A. F.
The Victoria club, Pietermaritzburg, 1859–1959. Cape Town, Balkema, 1959.

278 HENDERSON, W. P. M.
Durban: fifty years' municipal history. Durban, Robinson, 1904.

279 HERD, N.
The bent Pine: the trial of Chief Langalibalele. Johannesburg, Ravan, 1976.

280 HINCHLIFF, P.
John William Colenso, bishop of Natal. London, Nelson, 1964.

281 HOCKLY, H. E.
The story of the British settlers of 1820. Cape Town, Juta, 1957.

282 HURST, G. T.
Short history of the volunteer regiments of Natal and East Griqualand. Durban, Knox, 1945.

283 JACKSON, G. S.
Music in Durban: an account of musical activities in Durban from 1850 to the early years of the present century. Johannesburg, Witwatersrand univ. press, 1970.

284 JONES, E. MORSE
Roll of the British settlers in South Africa, part one, up to 1826. Cape Town, Balkema, 1969.

285 KEARNEY, B. T.
Architecture in Natal from 1824–1893. Cape Town, Balkema, 1973.

286 LADYSMITH HISTORICAL SOCIETY
Langalibalele and the Natal Carbineers: the story of the Langalibalele rebellion, 1873. Ladysmith, the Society, 1973.

287 LOWVELD 1820 SETTLERS' SOCIETY
Some Lowveld pioneers. Pretoria, Minerva, (printer), n.d.

288 LUGG, H. C.
Historic Natal and Zululand. Pmb., Shuter, 1949.

289 McCRYSTAL, A. M.
The dawn of Durban. Springs, Priv. print, 194?.

290 MACKEURTAN, GRAHAM
The cradle days of Natal (1497–1845). 2nd ed. Pmb., Shuter, 1948.

291 MEARS, W. J. G.
The Rev. James Allison, missionary: biographical outline. Priv. print, n.d. (pamphlet)

292 MENDELSSOHN, SIDNEY
South African bibliography. 2v. 3rd ed. London, Holland, 1968.

293 MILLER, A. YVONNE
Acutts in Africa. Durban, Priv. print, 1978.

294 NATAL UNIVERSITY. Department of Economics.
Experiment at Edendale: a study of a non-European settlement with special reference to food expenditure and nutrition. Pmb., Natal univ. press, 1951.

295 NUTTALL, N.
Lift up your hearts: the story of Hilton College, 1872–1972. Durban, Hiltonian Society, 1971.

296 NATAL WITNESS
A century of progress in Natal, 1824–1924; being the centenary number of the Natal Witness. Pmb., Natal Witness, 1924.

297 OSBORN, R. F.
Valiant harvest: the founding of the South African sugar industry, 1848–1926. Durban, South African Sugar Assoc., 1964.

298 ROSENTHAL, ERIC
On 'Change through the years: a history of share dealing in South Africa. Cape Town, Flesch, 1968.

299 RUVIGNY and RAINEVAL, Marquis of
The Moodie book; being an account of the families of Melsetter, Muir, Cocklaw, Blairhill, Bryanton, Gilchorn, Pitmuies, Arbekie, Masterton, etc. Priv. print, 1906.

300 *South African Women's Who's Who, 1938.* Johannesburg, Biographies, [1938?].

301 STRUTT, D. H.
The story of the Durban Club. Cape Town, Timmins, 1963.

302 STUART, JAMES
The James Stuart archive of recorded oral evidence relating to the history of the Zulu and neighbouring peoples; ed. and translated by C. de B. Webb and J. B. Wright. v.1. Pmb., Natal univ. press, 1976.

303 TABLER, E. C.
Pioneers of Natal and South-eastern Africa. Cape Town, Balkema, 1977.

304 TABLER, E. C.
Pioneers of Rhodesia. Cape Town, Struik, 1966.

305 *Twentieth century impressions of Natal; its people, commerce, industries and resources.* [Durban], Lloyds, 1906.

306 VERBEEK, J. A.
Natal art before Union: extracts from a catalogue at the Library, University of Natal, Pietermaritzburg. Pmb., Natal univ. library, 1974.

307 VIETZEN, S.
A history of education for European girls in Natal with particular reference to the establishment of some leading schools, 1837–1902. Pmb., Natal univ. press, 1973.

308 WALKER, E. A.
A history of Southern Africa. 3rd ed. London, Longmans, 1972.

309 WEBB, C. de B.
A guide to the official records of the colony of Natal. 2nd rev. ed. Pmb., Natal univ. press, 1968.

310 *Who's Who in Natal, with which is incorporated Women of Natal.* Durban, Knox, 1933.

311 WRIGHT, J. B.
Bushmen raiders of the Drakensberg, 1840–1870: a study of their conflict with stock-keeping peoples in Natal. Pmb., Natal univ. press, 1971.

312 YOUNG, L. M.
A history of the Royal Agricultural Society of Natal, 1851–1953. Pmb., the Society, 1953.

PERIODICAL ARTICLES

313 BAYER, A. W.
Aspects of Natal's botanical history, *Libri Natales*, v.4, 1974, pp.7–23.

314 CLANCEY, P. A.
A one-time Mecca for ornithologists, *Natalia*, v.5, 1975, pp.29–35.

315 HEWSON, L. A.
The Watkins papers, *Journal of the Methodist Historical Society of South Africa*, v.2, no.7, 1957, pp.162–179.

316 GOETZSCHE, ERIC
James Archbell, *Sunday Tribune*, 10 Mar. 1963.

317 JUDD, U. E. M.
Origins of the Natal Society, Chapter 6, *Natalia*, v.6, 1976, pp.24–27.

318 LEVERTON, B. J. T.
Weenen school, *Natal Witness*, 19 Oct. 1977.

319 MARAIS, EUGENE
[Article on the Ayres brothers], *Die Volkstem*, 28 and 29 Nov. 1935.

320 PLOEGER, JAN
Besonderhede uit die kerklike registers van 'Nieuw Guelderland', *Tydskrif vir Wetenskap en Kuns*, v.18, no.2, Okt. 1958, pp.182–191.

UNPUBLISHED THESES, ESSAYS, ETC.

321 AKITT, H.
Government assisted immigration to Natal, 1857–1862. Thesis, M.A. (Natal), 1953, pp.126–164.

322 *Blamey family history.* Typescript, ?1967. (Killie Campbell Africana Library)

323 DAVIES, J. H.
Sailing vessels engaged in trading on the South African coast, 1806–1849. Typescript, n. d. (photocopy in Natal Archives).

324 ENGLISH, G. D.
The story of the Royal Durban Rangers. 3 v. Typescript, 1954. (Loaned by Dr D. M. Scotney, 35 Ridge Road, Howick.)

325 FRANGENHEIM, E. H.
A short history of the Natal Railway Company, 1859–1877, and early railway schemes in Natal. Essay, B.A.Hons. (Natal), 1973.

326 HALL, J.
Government policy and public attitudes during the administration of Natal of Lt. Governor Pine, 1850–1855. Thesis, M.A. (Natal), 1969.

327 HENNESSY, E. F.
Early Natal settlers: the Franklin family. Typescript, 1968.

328 KEMP, B. H.
Johan William Colenbrander, 1879–1896. Thesis, Ph.D. (Natal), 1962.

329 MILLER, A. Y.
Family album. Typescript, 1967.

330 MUDIE, M. N.
The Grays of Loskop, Natal, South Africa: an adaptation of The History of the Gray Family, by Andrew Sclanders. Typescript, 1956. (Loaned by Miss Peggy Gray, University of Natal, Pmb.)

331 NAIDOO, B.
David Dale Buchanan as editor of the Natal Witness, 1846–1856. Thesis, (Durban/Westville), 1972.

332 SCHOLTZ, P. L.
Die geskiedenis van die Wesleyaanse sending in Natal met spesiale verwysing na Indaleni, 1840–1960. M.A. Heidelberg–South Africa, 1946.

333 VIETZEN, S.
The Rev. James Archbell: a study in missionary activity. Essay, B.A. Hons (Natal), 1962.

E. PERSONAL COMMUNICATION

334 Dr Conrad Akerman (deceased).
335 Mrs D. T. Allison, 3 Miller Street, Pmb.
336 Mrs Barbara Anderson of Donnybrook (deceased).
337 R. W. Anderson, 5 Lewis Suttie Place, Blackridge, Pmb.
338 G. H. F. Archer (deceased). (Grandson of George Archer)
339 Miss Myrtle Andrews. (Grand-daughter of John Andrews)
340 G. Buntting, 67 Bulwer Street, Dundee.
341 Q. E. Carter, 25 Harry Miller Road, Estcourt.
342 Prof. A. F. Hattersley (deceased).
343 Mrs Anne Hemmings and Mr Adrian Koopman, Department of Zulu Language and Literature, University of Natal, Pmb.
344 Ms Sheila Meintjies, c/o Department of Comparative African Government and Law, University of Cape Town.
345 Mrs Anna Holliday (deceased).
346 C. O. Holness, 60 Taunton Road, Pmb.
347 A. S. B. Humphreys, 13 Stuart Park, Granton Place, Pmb.
348 Dr D. J. B. Killick (reference supplied by Mrs Sheila Henderson, *Evenlode*, Waschbank, Natal).

349 R. J. H. King, 167 Highridge Road, Durban North.
350 R. A. Laing, P. O. Box 61791, Marshalltown, Tvl.
351 J. G. Lindsay, 505 Beacon Hill, Roberts Road, Pmb.
352 Mrs A. Y. Miller, Villa Assumpta, 55 Tanner Road, Pmb.
353 R. Naylor, Midmar, Sanchen, Inverurie, Aberdeenshire.
354 Rev. Father Howard St George, Catholic Cathedral, Cathedral Road, Durban.
355 Mrs Pearl Scotney, Curator, Howick Museum.
356 Rev. C. Scott Shaw, 23 Harwin Road, Pmb.
357 Dr S. Vietzen, Edgewood College of Education, Pinetown.

F. PORTRAITS, PHOTOGRAPHS, etc.

(Where possible photographs, etc. in published works have been cited in the individual source lists.)

358 Natal pioneers: composite photograph prepared by James Brickhill, 1872. Copy in Natal Museum.
359 *Neon* no.14, May 1974.
360 Hilton College (Campbell Hall).
361 Killie Campbell Africana Library, Durban
362 Local History Museum, Durban.
363 Macrorie House Museum, Pmb.
364 Natal Archives, Pmb.

G. ADDITIONAL SOURCES

(These came to light when this book was already at an advanced stage. The originals are in the possession of Mr Neil Lofthouse, Met. Office, HQ 9 Regt. AAC, Detmold, Germany.)

365 Boast, William: Letter to his brother John. Durban, 5 Jan. 1851.
366 Lofthouse, Martha: Diary written aboard the *Haidee*, 1850.

Index

Settlers who are the subjects of biographies are only entered in this index when they are referred to in another biography. Settler children are listed with their fathers' biographies and are entered here when they figure in another biography. Where there are several settlers with the same surname their wives have been indexed to aid identification.

INDEX

126